'*Environing Media* offers a conceptually rich and theoretically sophisticated exploration of media forms' role in shaping environments. Moving beyond the separation of nature and culture, the authors chart an array of new, mediated epistemologies for the planet. This text will be an essential contribution to the discourse on media and environment.'

Nicole Starosielski, New York University, USA

'*Environing Media* explores the history of relations between humanity and the Earth through a series of fascinating and far-reaching case studies. Environing technologies produce both environmental knowledge and environments themselves. In this novel and important book, the concept of environing media becomes a key that unlocks the interplay of ideas, technologies and physical transformations. Environing is the process of human shaping of the Earth, and it is environing media that has pushed the planet into the new geological epoch of the Anthropocene. From the record keeping of Spanish imperialism to debates about planetary boundaries and biosphere, from floating ocean robots to expedition to collect deep sea cores, from the diagrams of climate modelers to the air around us, *Environing Media* shows the critical importance of historical understandings of the interplay among technology, history and society.'

Bill Adams, University of Cambridge, UK, and the Geneva Graduate Institute, Switzerland

'Through rich case studies, this book offers new and important insights into the field of the environmental humanities and a broader understanding of the evolving human-Earth relationship. By drawing on examples such as climate scenarios, air pollution, oceanography, planetary vision, Human-earth histories, technospheres and media infrastructures, the chapters in the volume provide fresh perspectives and, in a witty way, reveal how media ties into the environment by rethinking the relationship between humans and nature. This is a book that deserves a wide readership in the field of environmental humanities and beyond.'

Birgit Schneider, Professor for knowledge cultures and media environments, Potsdam University, Germany

ENVIRONING MEDIA

This edited volume interrogates the role of media technologies in the formation of environments, understood both as physical spaces and as epistemological constructs about them. Using the concept of 'environing media', the book advances a deeper understanding of how media processes – defined here as the storage, process, and transmission of data – influence human-Earth relations.

Virtually all aspects of the interconnected global ecological crisis can be related to the intensification and acceleration of scaling up the human imprint on the planet by technological means. Combining ideas from the humanities, arts, and humanistic social sciences, *Environing Media* offers a perspective on how we entered the current geological epoch – the Anthropocene. The ten chapters explore colonial, planetary, and elemental environing media, with cases including indigenous history, ocean monitoring, computational history, climate modeling, environmental history, the air as medium, the biosphere, and the Earth system.

Drawing upon a breadth of examples and expertise in history, anthropology, geography, cultural history, science and technology studies, and media studies, the book discovers a novel approach to human-Earth histories that demonstrates how technologies have mediated between humans and environments and in the process contributed to a societal feedback loop between knowing and doing environment, each impacting the other. *Environing Media* is a timely addition for scholars and upper-level students in environmental humanities and media studies.

Adam Wickberg is a researcher in the history of media and environment at KTH Stockholm, Sweden, and a visiting research fellow at the Max Planck Institute for History of Science in Berlin (MPWIG I), Germany.

Johan Gärdebo is a researcher in the history of climate transition policies and environmental expertise at Uppsala University, Sweden, and a visiting research fellow at the University of Cambridge, UK.

Routledge Environmental Humanities

Series editors: Scott Slovic *(University of Idaho, USA)*, Joni Adamson *(Arizona State University, USA) and* Yuki Masami *(Aoyama Gakuin University, Japan)*
Dipesh Chakrabarty, University of Chicago, USA

The *Routledge Environmental Humanities* series is an original and inspiring venture recognising that today's world agricultural and water crises, ocean pollution and resource depletion, global warming from greenhouse gases, urban sprawl, over-population, food insecurity and environmental justice are all *crises of culture*.

The reality of understanding and finding adaptive solutions to our present and future environmental challenges has shifted the epicenter of environmental studies away from an exclusively scientific and technological framework to one that depends on the human-focused disciplines and ideas of the humanities and allied social sciences.

We thus welcome book proposals from all humanities and social sciences disciplines for an inclusive and interdisciplinary series. We favour manuscripts aimed at an international readership and written in a lively and accessible style. The readership comprises scholars and students from the humanities and social sciences and thoughtful readers concerned about the human dimensions of environmental change.

International Advisory Board

William Beinart, University of Oxford, UK
Jane Carruthers, University of South Africa, Pretoria, South Africa
Dipesh Chakrabarty, University of Chicago, USA
Paul Holm, Trinity College, Dublin, Republic of Ireland
Shen Hou, Renmin University of China, Beijing, China
Rob Nixon, Princeton University, Princeton NJ, USA
Pauline Phemister, Institute of Advanced Studies in the Humanities, University of Edinburgh, UK
Sverker Sorlin, KTH Environmental Humanities Laboratory, Royal Institute of Technology, Stockholm, Sweden
Helmuth Trischler, Deutsches Museum, Munich and Co-Director, Rachel Carson Centre, Ludwig-Maximilians-Universität, Germany
Mary Evelyn Tucker, Yale University, USA
Kirsten Wehner, University of London, UK

For more information about this series, please visit: www.routledge.com/Routledge-Environmental-Humanities/book-series/REH

ENVIRONING MEDIA

Edited by
Adam Wickberg and Johan Gärdebo

Cover image: Studio Folder, Uncharted—Footnotes to the Atlas, 2016–2018. Photo by Mattia Balsamini.

First published 2023
by Routledge
4 Park Square, Milton Park, Abingdon, Oxon OX14 4RN

and by Routledge
605 Third Avenue, New York, NY 10158

Routledge is an imprint of the Taylor & Francis Group, an informa business

© 2023 selection and editorial matter, Adam Wickberg and
Johan Gärdebo; individual chapters, the contributors

The right of Adam Wickberg and Johan Gärdebo to be identified as the
authors of the editorial material, and of the authors for their individual
chapters, has been asserted in accordance with sections 77 and 78 of the
Copyright, Designs and Patents Act 1988.

With the exception of Chapters 1, 2 and 7, no part of this book may be
reprinted or reproduced or utilised in any form or by any electronic,
mechanical, or other means, now known or hereafter invented,
including photocopying and recording, or in any information storage or
retrieval system, without permission in writing from the publishers.

Chapters 1, 2 and 7 of this book are available for free in PDF format as
Open Access from the individual product page at www.routledge.com.
They have been made available under a Creative Commons Attribution-
Non Commercial-No Derivatives 4.0 license.

Trademark notice: Product or corporate names may be trademarks
or registered trademarks, and are used only for identification and
explanation without intent to infringe.

British Library Cataloguing-in-Publication Data
A catalogue record for this book is available from the British Library

ISBN: 978-1-032-25385-5 (hbk)
ISBN: 978-1-032-25382-4 (pbk)
ISBN: 978-1-003-28289-1 (ebk)

DOI: 10.4324/9781003282891

Typeset in Bembo
by codeMantra

The OA version of chapters 1, 2 and 7 are funded by KTH Royal Institute of Technology.

CONTENTS

List of figures	*ix*
Contributors	*xi*

1 Editors' introduction: what are environing media?   1
  Adam Wickberg and Johan Gärdebo

PART 1
Colonial environing media   **13**

2 Environing empires and colonial media   15
  John Durham Peters and Adam Wickberg

PART 2
Planetary environing media   **33**

3 Environing and the human–earth relationship:
  synchronizing geo–anthropology   35
  Sverker Sörlin

4 Planetary environing: the biosphere and the Earth system   54
  Giulia Rispoli

5 1948   75
  Christoph Rosol

viii Contents

PART 3
Elemental environing media 93

6 Winds, miasma, pollution: pathologies of the air as an
   environing medium 95
   Eva Horn

7 Ocean environing media: datafication of the deep sea 114
   Susanna Lidström, Adam Wickberg and Johan Gärdebo

8 Environing time: mediating climate modeling 134
   Nina Wormbs

9 Timing the ocean floor: environing media and the Swedish
   deep-sea expedition (1947–1948) 150
   Erik Isberg

10 Afterword: catch the vapors: getting steamrolled by
   environing media 167
   Bernard Dionysius Geoghegan

Index 177

FIGURES

2.1	The Relaciones Geograficas Map of Teozacoalco, 1580	25
4.1	The Bretherton diagram	65
7.1	Map of Argo Floats in operation 2022	124
7.2	Assembling cross braces to protect the float antenna on the RV Melville	126
8.1	FAR, Policymaker summary, page 74	138
9.1	A sketch of the piston corer as it was presented in 1944	153
9.2	Deep-sea cores recovered during the Swedish Deep-Sea Expedition 1947–1948	157
10.1	To clear all barriers for the human voice	169
10.2	Flirt with her again. Call the U.K	170
10.3	Ökolopoly: Ein kybernetisches Umweltspiel von Frederic Vester	171

CONTRIBUTORS

Bernard Dionysius Geoghegan is a media theorist and historian of technology. His work appears in journals including *Critical Inquiry*, *Representations*, and *Grey Room*. His work in environmental studies includes serving as co-curator for the Technosphere Project and Anthropocene Curriculum at the Haus der Kulturen der Welt. He may be reached online at www.bernardg.com.

Johan Gärdebo is a postdoctoral fellow in environmental politics at Linköping University, studying how Swedish industrial towns transition from fossil fuel dependence. His monograph dissertation *Environing Technology* (2019) analyzed the role of 20th-century Swedish satellite remote sensing for environmental imperatives of technoscientific expertise, diplomacy, and corporatism. Gärdebo is also starting the project *The Mediated Planet* where he researches the history of automation and computation of environmental data.

Eva Horn is professor of modern German literature and cultural theory at the Department of German at the University of Vienna. She recently published *The Anthropocene. Key Issues for the Humanities* (Routledge, 2020), co-authored with Hannes Bergthaller. Her essay *Air as Medium* was published in *Grey Room* 73 (Fall 2018). She is currently working on a cultural theory of climate.

Erik Isberg is a PhD student at the Division of History of Science, Technology and Environment at KTH, Stockholm. His work concerns the scientific construction of a global environment and, particularly, how planetary timescales were increasingly incorporated into human history and global environmental governance between 1950 and 1980.

xii Contributors

Susanna Lidström is a researcher in environmental humanities at KTH and has been a visiting scholar at Scripps Institution of Oceanography since 2015. She specializes in the form and function of environmental narratives about the oceans. Ongoing work concerns the scientific construction of a global environment and, particularly, how planetary timescales were increasingly incorporated into human history and global environmental governance between 1950 and 1980. She has a PhD in English literature from King College, London.

John Durham Peters is María Rosa Menocal of English and professor of film and media studies at Yale. He is the author of *Speaking into the Air: A History of the Idea of Communication* (1999), *Courting the Abyss: Free Speech and Liberal Tradition* (2005), *The Marvelous Clouds: Toward a Philosophy of Elemental Media* (2015), and, most recently, *Promiscuous Knowledge: Information, Image, and Other Truth Games in History* (2020), co-authored with the late Kenneth Cmiel, all from the University of Chicago Press.

Giulia Rispoli is an assistant professor at Ca' Foscari, University of Venice where she teaches Environment, Science and Global Politics, and a visiting scholar at the Max Planck Institute for the History of Science (MPIWG). Her research focuses on the conceptual history of the Anthropocene and Earth system thinking, Russian biosphere theories, and global environmental knowledge during the Cold War. Rispoli has recently co-edited the multimedia publication Anthropogenic Markers: Stratigraphy and Context which was part of a long term cooperation between the MPIWG, the Anthropocene Working Group (AWG), and the Haus der Kulturen der Welt (HKW). She also co-edited the special issue Science Diplomacy (HSNS, 50/4, 2020) and is currently working on a project entitled *Planetary genealogies: Historicising the Anthropocene*.

Christoph Rosol leads the Anthropocene umbrella project at the Max Planck Institute for the History of Science (MPIWG) and is curator and researcher at Haus der Kulturen der Welt (HKW). As such he currently co-leads large-scale international projects such as the *Anthropocene Curriculum, Anthropogenic Markers*, and the new *Geoanthropology* initiative which seeks new research avenues to study the coevolution of the geosphere and the technosphere. His own research deals with the deep-rooted history and the technical as well as epistemic foundations of the climate and Earth system sciences.

Sverker Sörlin is professor of environmental history in the Division of History of Science, Technology and Environment at KTH, Stockholm, where he was also a co-founder of the KTH Environmental Humanities Laboratory in 2011. His current work focuses on the history and science politics of climate change, the cryosphere, and the Anthropocene and on the formation of global environmental governance.

Contributors **xiii**

Adam Wickberg is a researcher in the history of media and environment at KTH Stockholm and the Max Planck Institute for History of Science in Berlin (MP-WIG I). He is the author of *Pellucid Paper: Poetry and Bureaucratic Media* (London: Open Humanities Press, 2018) and his work appears in journals including *Critical Inquiry, Necsus, Resillience*, and *Media Theory*. He is currently finishing a project on media and environment in the Spanish colonial empire and working as researcher in the collaborative project *The Mediated Planet*, which focuses on global environmental data and the SDGs.

Nina Wormbs is professor of history of technology at the KTH Royal Institute of Technology. She has written on media and broadcasting history and the electromagnetic spectrum as a technology-dependent commons. During the last decade she has taken greater interest in environmental history and humanities and the mediation and understanding of climate change. Examples include the sublime of satellite imagery and how individuals legitimize non-action.

1
EDITORS' INTRODUCTION

What are environing media?

Adam Wickberg and Johan Gärdebo

Editors' introduction

Over the past decades, we have come to see the divide between nature and culture as an illusory construction. Consequently, there is at present more need than ever for detailed analysis of how the human-Earth relationship is shaped.[1] Media, often associated with society and humans, can and should be understood in a broader sense as the technical enabler of knowledge *about*, and interventions *into*, the environment. Environing was first suggested as a theoretical concept in environmental history a decade and half ago as a way to overcome the problem of the separation between a natural environment – nature *out there* – and a human-induced environment, like farmlands. By showing how these borders were in fact continuously produced rather than given, thinking in terms of environing as a historical process was conceived of as way to integrate the natural environment into the social.[2]

With the concept "environing media" we want to zero in on the role played by various media forms – from early modern rutters registering global wind patterns to remote sensing satellites and artificial intelligence – in shaping the human-Earth relationship. The chapters of this book are divided into three analytical categories – colonial, planetary and elemental – that each helps explain how our world came to be environed through media at different historical phases. Starting in the early modern colonial environing and continuing into the 20th century, we get an idea of how the environing media of the first globalization changed conceptions of nature and society. The 20th century also saw the steady rise of the planetary perspective as new ecological concepts and material realities emerged which we now recognize as biosphere, Earth system, global environment and technosphere. A different view of environing media is afforded by focusing on the elemental, which in this volume are represented by air, climate and ocean in the final section of the book.

DOI: 10.4324/9781003282891-1

2 Adam Wickberg and Johan Gärdebo

The etymological meanings of media and environment are in fact not dissimilar. Environment, from the word *environ*, historically meant "in the middle of" or "surroundings," while the strong nature connotation of this word is largely a modernist conception.[3] Media is derived from the Latin word *medius* meaning "middle" or "in between." It shares etymology with "milieu" that stems from *medius locus* – a place in the middle.[4]

Both the natural connotation of environment and the cultural connotation of media are thus modernist conceptions of the 20th century that we may benefit in overcoming today at the onset of the Anthropocene. This new geological epoch names humanity as a species with the word *Anthropos*, although a particular form of Western human culture associated with colonialism, capitalism and extractivism are the primary drivers of this global environmental change.[5] However, the material conditions of possibility for the Anthropocene are environing media, without which the shifting scale and Great Acceleration, which is its hallmark, could not have happened. In this way, the analytical juxtaposition of media and environment can become an impasse to study the varying expressions of an ever-changing environment at a given moment in history.[6] Environmental epistemologies are contingent upon – but not determined by – the media technologies at hand. The concept offers insight into the conditions of possibility for knowing the Earth as well as the complex feedback loop that is generated continuously by new knowledge that enables new interventions and alterations of the environment. In the Anthropocene, being on and knowing the Earth have become so tightly intertwined that they are now inseparable.

Simply put, knowing and doing environment since the early modern era have presupposed a technologically complex interface. It allowed for changing scales from direct human observation and intervention *in situ* to instead interact at a mediated level, separated in both space and time. The aim of this volume on environing media is to propose new perspectives on how that separation took place. In brief, the volume raises and addresses new questions about how we entered into the Anthropocene, as modern environmental epistemologies grew out of ever more efficient forms of exploitation and extraction built on new markets of labor and consumption over the last five centuries.[7]

Environing and media

Starting with environing, the term connotes *the environment* to be less of a fixed space and more of a process where humans play the role of intervenor. We could add here that non-humans too intervene in and shape their environments – think of beavers building dams, for instance – as captured by niche construction theory, which recently has been put to use to explain similar processes in human culture.[8] What we want to articulate with environing media is the scale and intensity of human interventions over roughly the past five centuries that have produced new kinds of environments. Importantly, it is through environing media that we have pushed the planet into a new geological epoch.

Editors' introduction: What are environing media? **3**

Over time, a range of everyday practices – such as forest clearing, grazing, farming or iron production – established historical relationships between land and people that were at once social and environmental. These uses of the environment also shaped historical knowledge of, and ideas about, environments, resulting in demarcations of and norms about who had access to a place or how a resource should be used.[9] Practices of environing also produced environmental knowledge. For example, natural resource inventories or cadastral mapping often corresponded with shifts in which groups of people could translate knowledge about the environment and over time transform it further, to environ it differently.[10] By analyzing the middle ground of environing as media – for instance how data are collected, acted upon and give rise to new epistemologies – we can gain a better understanding of the past, present and future of the human-Earth relation.

The meaning of "environment" changed during mid-20th century from a local to a global phenomenon. This shift corresponded with new practices of computerizing measurements and monitoring systems, such as orbiting satellites, which made it possible to systemize and combine many different forms of environmental data.[11] The postwar era saw the rapid rise of such technologies that were put to use for both military and environmental purposes, giving rise to what has been called "cultures of prediction."[12] Illustrating how these monitoring systems emerged historically is also part of explaining why they became important for environmental management and thus central to the formulation of present-day's human-Earth relationship.[13] In his contribution, Sverker Sörlin details a genealogy of how the humanities – and the field of history in particular – began working with the concept of environment. He sees the conceptual shift toward environing as indicative of a larger processual understanding for the importance played by media in making and making known the Earth. In analyzing the new conditions of the human-Earth relation in the Anthropocene, Sörlin also emphasizes the necessary co-existing of multiple timescales in what he terms the Great Synchronization, as a deliberate parallel to the Great Acceleration. In this new episteme, Earth system scientists, historians and environmental humanists are co-exploring new ways of understanding planetary times, a matter that becomes all the more urgent as the eco-crisis proceeds.

Turning to the concept of media, we draw on the tradition of German media theory that during the last decade has gained analytical traction well beyond media studies as part of explaining how media operations generate new world views. In this context, "media" have been conceived of as a transdisciplinary endeavor to overcome certain humanist technophobia and to emphasize the techno-epistemic effects in the production and processing of power and knowledge. Instead of the more common conceptualization of media as being synonymous with the content they transmit, as in "news media" or "mass media," we rely on a more material understanding of media as cultural techniques.[14] The concept of environing media draws on this turn in German media theory toward cultural techniques, which attempts to subvert the dualism between media and culture by

4 Adam Wickberg and Johan Gärdebo

focusing on the "operative sequences that historically and logically precede the media concepts generated by them."[15] In brief, the theoretical thrust of environing media is to reorient focus from ontological concepts – that are often taken for granted – to the ontic operations that exist before they are conceptualized. Writing, reading, painting or counting are practices – or cultural techniques – that predate the concepts generated from them.[16] Drawing on this philosophical insight to bear on the ontology of the environment, environing media designate the manifold technical processes that are involved in the recursion between environmental epistemology and environmental change.

It is worth emphasizing that both environing and cultural techniques are theoretical concepts that draw on agricultural history in their reinvention of an older material practice. Bernard Dionysius Geoghegan points out that in the pre-humanistic conception of the Latin word *colere*, on which Agri cultura is based, "culture" was already associated with nature and understood as a way of technically bringing forth the potential of the natural.[17] In the 19th and 20th centuries, however, "culture" attained a metaphorical meaning as the culturing of the human spirit, which is the basis of the commonplace understanding of the word today. Thus, the German word *Kulturtechnik* came to be redefined as a media theoretical concept to draw culture back to its material and technical operations in analyzing a broad range of practices in a new way. Instead of starting with the ontological level as a given, the study of cultural techniques insisted on the historical priority of techniques and practices – ontic operations – that would subsequently be understood as given concepts. During the same period, environmental historians proposed environing to zero in on the continuous production of the environmental through historical techniques and practices. Environing here similarly became a way of upending a dualistic understanding of the environment as something historically stable to gain a process-oriented understanding of the rise of the environmental in our age. Geoghegan contributes to this volume with an afterword which spells out the affordances of the concept of environing media today, by casting it through the vapor and steam of the 19th century nonmodernism of Wagnerian opera and Marx's proposition that "all that is solid melts into air." As Geoghegan puts it, "to consider how media environ is, also, to acknowledge their unsettled grounds today."

Over the last two decades, another related area of study under the label of "ecomedia" has rapidly grown into its own field, particularly in the US. Meanwhile, the European tradition of media theory has been more hesitant and cautious toward embracing the environmental challenge of our time. While ecomedia studies have overlaps with the concept of environing media that this collection is focused on, there are important differences. Ecomedia studies is defined as a field concerned with cultural *representations* of the environment in media as well as the environmental *impact* of media forms. Environing media is less interested in representations as it builds on the German media theoretical tradition discussed above and ties it closer to emergent theories of the environmental humanities that focus on environmental epistemology and its conditions of possibility. Instead of representations, it is oriented toward the ontic operations of environmental sciences as these produce new ontologies and epistemologies.

The theoretical combination of environing and media turns the concept toward environmental sciences, like Earth system science and climatology, and makes it well suited to take on macro-analysis of epistemic objects, like the global environment. A theoretical point of departure is that the data-driven natural sciences will benefit from an integrative humanities approach, and that the environmental and planetary epistemologies they produce should be understood genealogically as part of a longer history of human attempts at knowing and shaping the Earth on a global scale.[18]

Research within the rapidly growing field of media and environment has different theoretical conceptualizations, usually depending on what aspect of human-Earth relations is to be analyzed. Environing media builds on the German media tradition mentioned above but ties it closer it to emergent theories of the environmental humanities that focus on environmental epistemology and its conditions of possibility. Where the theory of environing contends that environment is the product of human technological intervention, German media theory has long maintained on a parallel theoretical point that human culture is materially constructed and technically mediated to a much larger degree than has generally been understood. Thus, a key phrase in that tradition from its founder Friedrich Kittler is that media are devices that process, store and transmit data.[19]

John Durham Peters' *The Marvelous Clouds* (2015) builds on German media theory and its roots in Martin Heidegger's philosophy to demonstrate how we may think of environments in terms of "elemental media."[20] In this volume, Peters and Adam Wickberg contribute with an exploration of environing media in Mexico's complex history over the past five centuries. To do this, they draw on a theoretical development consisting in a shift in understanding from media as content-delivery systems to data processors. Message dissemination is a critically important role for media, but it is only one part of what they do. Media are as much in the business of organizing people and data as in transmitting messages via sound, image or word. As processors of data, media are also instrumental in our understanding and management of the environment. Calendars, clocks, towers, names, addresses, maps, registers and money are examples of media that help handling matters related to space and time, which has been of central concern for civilizations in general and for empire building in particular. An aspect of media highlighted by Peters and Wickberg is the understudied scholarly area of indigenous media. The Aztec empire was as dependent on media forms as the Spanish colonizers that replaced it, and there are numerous cases of knowledges and practices surviving in hybrid forms, for example as part of maps.

Returning to Peters' work on elemental media, these are more often than not in the business of *environing*, but environing media are not necessarily *elemental*. For example, we can think of air and water as elemental media in the case of Earth system science, but the epistemic effect of environing comes from understanding their function as "atmosphere" and "hydrosphere," and subsequently to process them as data to know their function in the global environment. One anecdote about how our understanding of air on planet Earth changed radically is from the 1960s when NASA (US) recruited James Lovelock to the Jet Propulsion Laboratories. Lovelock was to help build instruments that investigated the probability of life on Mars, whereupon he proposed that one need only look at the composition of the planet's atmosphere, which could be seen from Earth. In order to stay alive, any organism must consume materials, transform them chemically and release waste products into their surroundings.[21] If the atmosphere of Mars contained only carbon dioxide, it was a clear sign that the planet lacked life.

The atmosphere of Earth, by contrast, contained a mix of highly reactive gases such as ozone, methane, carbon monoxide, nitrogen and sulfur actively maintained and regulated by life on the surface (the biosphere) and held in a state of constant chemical disequilibrium through biogeochemical cycling and feedback loops – creating a habitable planet for humans and other lifeforms – which subsequently also formed the basis for Lovelock's Gaia hypothesis.[22]

By looking at the atmosphere of another planet, scientists began to think differently of Earth's atmosphere in turn. From this combination of ideas (the atmosphere as an extension of the biosphere) and media technologies (infrared telescopes and satellites) came atmospheric analysis and biogeochemistry, which are absolutely crucial for environmental epistemology about the Anthropocene. The link between ideas and media is further underlined by new phenomena being explored through, and depending on, a growing computerization of science from 1960s onward. The dialectics of feedback – between knowing and doing the environment through media – continues to present time, where we may speak about a fully mediated planet of data. Data are now gathered on a global scale using media technologies like the Argo floats program consisting in 4,000 buoys in the world oceans that continuously senses the water in real time, or NASA's various satellite missions that envelop the planet to remotely sense it, producing vast amounts of environmental data. This data is then processed using supercomputers that model and analyze oceans, climate or biodiversity, to take only a few examples, that in turn are transmitted via environmental sciences into the public perception of global environmental change.

In their chapter, Susanna Lidström, Adam Wickberg and Johan Gärdebo explore the emergence of the Argo program against the background of ocean media history, beginning in the 1500s and then tracing the environing of the oceans until present time. They analyze the technological mediation of the marine realm and how specific media technologies condition our understanding of what the ocean is, how it changes and what is considered essential and "actionable" ocean knowledge. Different historical phases of knowing the ocean can be characterized with reference to developments in and application of sensing technologies. Drawing on a longer history of increasing exploration and innovation, the arguably most influential contemporary infrastructure for how the ocean is known and mediated is the Argo program, which has been in operation since the early 2000s. Argo consists of a fleet of around 4,000 autonomous instruments, floating with ocean currents in the upper 2,000 meters of the water column, recording key variables such as temperature and salinity, and providing fundamental input for oceanographic research as well as for broader Earth system sciences, including, importantly, climate change models.[23] As such, the Argo floats act as datagatherers and are the first-level interface in the mediation process of knowledge about the Earth system from the oceanic part of the hydrosphere.

Another essential history of how the deep ocean came to be known is offered by Erik Isberg in his chapter on Swedish Deep-Sea Expedition, 1947–1948. Isberg demonstrates how the new technology of piston cores enabled new data extraction from ocean sediments. The extraction of these *deep-sea cores* effectively paved the way for the subsequent establishment of paleoceanography as a scientific discipline that today allow us to asses current climate and ocean states against the deep history of the Earth. Time, and not only space, appears in Isberg's account as a crucial category for producing planetary-scale environmental knowledge in the early postwar era. By approaching deep-sea cores as environing media, he argues that they have been realizing different temporal and geographical conceptualizations of the ocean floor at different points in time. Contrary to the popular description of deep-sea cores as "natural archives," Isberg argues, they can instead be understood as historical in themselves, deeply interwoven with data gathering practices, scientific infrastructures and computational capabilities.

The notion of a mediated planet is also relevant for a neighboring concept to environing media – the *technosphere* – popularized by geologist Peter Haff to describe an emerging planetary layer spread throughout and above the biosphere, lithosphere, hydrosphere, cryosphere and atmosphere. Similar to the biosphere that makes up the Earth's total biomass, the interconnection of 30 trillion tons of human-manufactured objects can be observed as a technosphere – an interconnected parasitical system that draws resources and fuel from all other spheres in order to grow but in the process tampers with the Earth system as a whole. Paradoxically, the observation of the technosphere, for example through sensors spread over land, throughout the seas, and up into or beyond the atmosphere, is crucial for knowing about this planetary phenomenon while also playing a part in its material perpetuation and expansion.[24] Where environing media points out the epistemological in-between of the human-Earth relation, the technosphere offers a planetary macro-perspective of the changes brought about in this process.

Both environing media and technosphere are concepts that describe how we entered into the Anthropocene. To catch a snapshot of this process, Christoph Rosol's chapter uses the year 1948 to pivot his analysis of the fundamental role played by environing media in the co-evolution of both the Earth system science and the technosphere. Introducing the reader to a series of historical-geographical vignettes juxtaposing various events that took place from January to December of 1948, it was a year, Rosol argues, that pointedly marks a decisive moment in which the juggernaut of modernity was greatly accelerated by recombining itself into a highly dynamic, mutually reinforcing technological, scientific, political, economic and medially environed complex. Perambulating the rise of electronic computing, molecular genetics and petro power, the commodification and universalization of global relations under the West's domination, as well as new concepts that reposition humans in nature, Rosol's vignettes chart a strikingly similar origin and mutual unleashing of the digital-, the nuclear- and the environmental age. Moreover, they highlight in how much that shift can be attributed to the increasing control over elementary building blocks such as bits, molecules, atoms and genes. Rosol thereby creates a sense of how many complex and interconnected processes led to the emergence of a new environmental epistemology. New media technologies created new environmental conceptions that in turn informed alterations of the environment itself, which is the complex feedback loop at the heart of the theoretical concept of environing media.

At the same time as digital media technologies have had a tremendous stake in the unleashing of Anthropocene drivers, Rosol argues that these are the very same technologies that are key to detecting, understanding and addressing this transition. This new techno-medial regime is one in which manipulations at the micro-level have massive effects at the macro-level. The regime presents a powerful but largely overlooked signature of humanity's mid-20th century embarkment on an unintended planetary experiment – the very experiment that has now resulted in the socioeconomic and technoscientific gridlock that our societies are stuck with when facing the multiple crises of the Anthropocene.

A crucial dimension of environing media is that different media produce different epistemologies. Depending on if one chooses to look at life on Earth from below or from above, the resulting knowledge will be very different, as argued by Giulia Rispoli who continues the volume's study of a mediated environment in the form of the biosphere and the Earth system. The biosphere concept grew out of a longer history of thinking about life *on* of the Earth whereas Earth system science depicted life from the *outside*, hence ignoring the role played by humans in environing the planet. Hinting at the prehistory of the cosmological crisis that is currently unfolding in the clash of global and planetary perspectives, the two views from inside and outside carry incommensurable values about the Earth itself. It is through the intellectual and material history of epistemological objects like biosphere and Earth system, Rispoli argues, that we can hope to understand the current state of the planet and work toward resolving tensions in the now unfolding human-Earth relation.

Another central aspect of planetary mediation is climate, and our understanding of it is fully dependent on a process that goes from data gathering and processing to transmission in the form of models, which come to guide our view of the possible future. Nina Wormbs' chapter shifts environing media, from space- to timescales, by analyzing where climate modeling's projections end.

As she reminds us, the Anthropocene is not just about the past but also about the future. Studying the UN IPCC's Assessment Reports, Wormbs details the most common target year 2100 and what affordances this timescale has in terms of human timespans, Western civilizational meaning and relevance for addressing the wickedness of continued anthropogenic climate change. How we can understand time in the Anthropocene is a seemingly straightforward question. But as we learn more about the past of this epoch, the future seems to vanish. This chapter focuses on the mediation of the future in the assessment reports and specifically on the target years of the model-based scenarios. This in turn has historical reasons that relate to issues of modeling capacity and the pace of climate change. The result is a tension between scales that do not synchronize the different temporalities of climate change.

The rapid datafication of the planet means that areas like the air itself can be tracked in real time and analyzed in detail. In her chapter, Eva Horn takes the current COVID-19 pandemic as a point of departure for historicizing the air itself as an environing medium. Horn tells a story about how air, for the longest time in Occidental thought, was conceived of as an environing medium, connecting bodies with other bodies, bodies with locations, locations with spaces and all of these to the cosmos. In contrast to the modern view of air as a body of gases, as in the example of Lovelock's discovery of Earth's atmosphere via Mars, Horn analyzes older conceptions of air to grasp the changing mediality of the air. In these understandings, the relationality of air becomes apparent in that it is not only that which surrounds individual bodies, but also something that connects bodies with one another by transporting the "exhalations" of one organism to another, as we have become painfully aware of during the COVID-19 pandemic where the contagiousness of airborne virus was often underestimated. In the pre-modern understanding, then, air was not just a medium of individual bodies but also considered a medium of the social. What differentiates earlier conceptualizations of the air as an environing medium is the fact that the air and its pathologies can be sensed – smelled, felt and seen. While modern concepts of the air and its varying states have tended to emphasize the imperceptibility of the air's pathologies, the pre-modern theories help regain a sense of the air as a palpable medium of life, both biological and social.

Together, the chapters of this book demonstrate how the recent human-Earth history can be fruitfully understood and analyzed through the concept of environing media. The integration of environing and media is a significant step forward in thinking about the environment today in that it brings the theoretical forefront of media studies and environmental humanities into an exploration of the various historical, present and future ways of environing the planet. The combination of these two fields is necessary to spell out the implications of contributions by environmental humanists in the past decades, namely, that life in the Anthropocene is as much a social dilemma as a physical one. One must grasp both positivist disciplines and interpretive ones to make sense of anthropogenic environmental change. It is the argument of this book that we do so by reconsidering and closing the theoretical gap between media and environment as it allows us to produce historically specific understandings of how ideas, humans and machines come together in the production of both environmental knowledge and environments themselves.

Notes

1 Sara Pritchard, "Joining Environmental History with Science and Technology Studies: Promises, Challenges and Contributions," *New Natures: Joining Environmental History with Science and Technology Studies*, eds. Dolly Jørgensen & Finn Arne Jørgensen (Pittsburgh: University of Pittsburgh Press, 2013), 1–17.
2 Sverker Sörlin & Paul Warde, "Making the Environment Historical: An Introduction," *Nature's End: History and the Environment*, eds. Sverker Sörlin & Paul Warde (Palgrave Macmillan 2009), 8.
3 Etienne S. Benson, *Surroundings: A History of Environments and Environmentalism* (Chicago: The University of Chicago Press, 2020); Vin Nardizzi, "Environ," *Veer Ecology. A Companion for Environmental Thinking*, eds. Jeffrey Jermoe Cohen & Lowell Duckert (Minnesota: University of Minnesota Press, 2017), 183–195; Paul Warde, "The Environment," *Local Places, Global Processes*, eds. Peter Coates, David Moon & Paul Warde (Oxford: Windgather Press, 2016), 32–46.
4 John Durham Peters, *Marvelous Clouds: Toward a Philosophy of Elemental Media* (Chicago: University of Chicago Press, 2015), 46.
5 Adam Wickberg, "Reconfiguring Temporality in the Anthropocene: Coloniality and the Political Eco-Crisis," *Resilience: A Journal of the Environmental Humanities* 8 (2020): 1, special issue "Roots of the Future," ed. Anthony Lioi, 37–59; Rolando Vazquez, Precedence, Earth and The Anthropocene: Decolonizing Design, *Design Philosophy Papers Design Philosophy Papers* 15, no. 1 (2017), 77–91, DOI: 10.1080/14487136.2017.1303130; Kathryn Yusoff, *A Billion Black Anthropocenes or None* (Minneapolis: University of Minnesota Press, 2019).
6 Adam Wickberg & Johan Gärdebo, "Where Humans and the Planetary Conflate: An Introduction to Environing Media," *Humanities* 9, no. 3 (2020).
7 Jürgen Renn, *The Evolution of Knowledge: Rethinking Science for the Anthropocene* (Princeton: Princeton University Press, 2020); Thomas Piketty, *Capital and Ideology* (Harvard: The Belknap Press, 2020); Simon Lewis & Mark Maslin, *The Human Planet: How We Created the Anthropocene* (New Haven, CT: Yale University Press, 2018).
8 Kevin Laland & Michael O'Brien, "Cultural Niche Construction: An Introduction," *Biological Theory* 6, no. 3 (2011): 191–202.
9 Tim Ingold, *The Perception of the Environment: Essays on Livelihood, Dwelling and Skill* (London: Routledge, 2000); cf. Karl-Johan Lindholm, "Environing: The Archaeology of 'Real Life' Remains," *The Resilience of Heritage: Cultivating a Future of the Past*, eds. Anneli Ekblom, Christian Isendahl & Karl-Johan Lindholm (Uppsala: Uppsala University, 2018), 253–256.
10 Johan Gärdebo, *Environing Technology: Swedish Satellite Remote Sensing in the Making of Environment 1969–2001* (Stockholm: KTH Royal Institute of Technology, 2019).
11 Paul Warde, Libby Robin, & Sverker Sörlin, *The Environment – A History of the Idea* (Baltimore, MA: Johns Hopkins University Press, 2018).
12 Matthias Heyman, Gabrielle Gramelsberger, & Martin Mahoney, *Cultures of Prediction in Atmospheric and Climate Science: Epistemic and Cultural Shifts in Computer-based Modelling and Simulation* (New York: Routledge, 2017).
13 Sverker Sörlin & Nina Wormbs, "Environing Technologies: A Theory of Making Environment," *History and Technology* 34, no. 2 (2018): 101–125.

14 Eva Horn, "Editor's Introduction: 'There Are No Media,'" *Grey Room* 4, no. 29 (fall 2007): 6.
15 Bernhard Siegert, "Cacography or Communication? Cultural Techniques in German Media Studies," *Grey Room* 29 (2008): 28.
16 T. Macho, "Zeit und Zahl: Kalender- und Zeitrechnung als Kulturtechniken," *Bild – Schrift – Zahl*, eds. Sybille Krämer & Horst Bredekamp (München: Fink), 179.
17 Bernard Dionysus Geoghegan, "After Kittler: On the Cultural Techniques of Recent German Media Theory," *Theory, Culture, Society* 30, no. 6 (2013): 72.
18 Cf. Dipesh Chakrabarty, *The Climate of History in a Planetary Age* (Chicago: Chicago University Press, 2021).
19 Friedrich Kittler, *Draculas Vermächtnis. Technische Schriften* (Leipzig: Reclam Verlag: 1993), 8.
20 Peters, *Marvelous Clouds*.
21 Timothy Lenton, *Earth System Science: A Very Short Introduction* (Oxford: Oxford University Press, 2016), 1.
22 James Lovelock, "Life Detection by Atmospheric Analysis," Originally published in *Icarus: International Journal of the Solar System* 7, no. 2 (September 1967): 149–159.
23 Stephen C. Riser, Howard J. Freeland, Dean Roemmich, et al., "Fifteen Years of Ocean Observations with the Global Argo Array," *Nature Climate Change* 6 (2016): 145–153.
24 Johan Gärdebo, Agata Marzecova, & Scott Knowles, "The Orbital Technosphere: The Provision of Meaning and Matter by Satellites," *Anthropocene Review* 4, no. 1 (2017): 44–52.

References

Benson, Etienne S. *Surroundings: A History of Environments and Environmentalism*. Chicago: The University of Chicago Press, 2020.
Chakrabarty, Dipesh. *The Climate of History in a Planetary Age*. Chicago: Chicago University Press, 2021.
Dionysus Geoghegan, Bernard. "After Kittler: On the Cultural Techniques of Recent German Media Theory." *Theory, Culture, Society* 30, no. 6 (2013): 72.
Durham, John Peters. *Marvelous Clouds: Toward a Philosophy of Elemental Media*. Chicago: University of Chicago Press, 2015.
Gärdebo, Johan. *Environing Technology: Swedish Satellite Remote Sensing in the Making of Environment 1969–2001*. Stockholm: KTH Royal Institute of Technology, 2019.
Gärdebo, Johan, Agata Marzecova, & Scott Knowles. "The Orbital Technosphere: The Provision of Meaning and Matter by Satellites." *Anthropocene Review* 4, no. 1 (2017): 44–52.
Heyman, Matthias, Gabrielle Gramelsberger, & Martin Mahoney. *Cultures of Prediction in Atmospheric and Climate Science: Epistemic and Cultural Shifts in Computer-Based Modelling and Simulation*. New York: Routledge, 2017.
Horn, Eva. "Editor's Introduction: 'There Are No Media'." *Grey Room* 4, no. 29 (fall 2007): 6.
Ingold, Tim. *The Perception of the Environment: Essays on Livelihood, Dwelling and Skill*. London: Routledge, 2000.
Kittler, Friedrich. *Draculas Vermächtnis. Technische Schriften*. Leipzig: Reclam Verlag, 1993.
Laland, Kevin & Michael O'Brien. "Cultural Niche Construction: An Introduction." *Biological Theory* 6, no. 3 (2011): 191–202.
Lenton, Timothy. *Earth System Science: A Very Short Introduction*. Oxford: Oxford University Press, 2016.

Lewis, Simon & Mark Maslin. *The Human Planet: How We Created the Anthropocene*. New Haven, CT: Yale University Press, 2018.

Lindholm, Karl-Johan. "Environing: The Archaeology of 'Real Life' Remains." *The Resilience of Heritage: Cultivating a Future of the Past*, edited by Anneli Ekblom, Christian Isendahl & Karl-Johan Lindholm, 253–256. Uppsala: Uppsala University, 2018.

Lovelock, James. "Life Detection by Atmospheric Analysis." Originally published in Icarus: *International Journal of the Solar System* 7, no. 2 (September 1967): 149–159.

Macho, Thomas. "Zeit und Zahl: Kalender- und Zeitrechnung als Kulturtechniken." *Bild – Schrift – Zahl*, edited by Sybille Krämer & Horst Bredekamp, 179–192. München: Fink, 2003.

Nardizzi, Vin. "Environ." *Veer Ecology. A Companion for Environmental Thinking*, edited by Jeffrey Jermoe Cohen & Lowell Duckert, 183–195. Minnesota: University of Minnesota Press, 2017.

Piketty, Thomas. *Capital and Ideology*. Harvard: The Belknap Press, 2020.

Pritchard, Sara. "Joining Environmental History with Science and Technology Studies: Promises, Challenges and Contributions." *New Natures: Joining Environmental History with Science and Technology Studies*, edited by Dolly Jørgensen & Finn Arne Jørgensen, 1–17. Pittsburgh: University of Pittsburgh Press, 2013.

Renn, Jürgen. *The Evolution of Knowledge: Rethinking Science for the Anthropocene*. Princeton: Princeton University Press, 2020.

Riser, Stephen C., Howard J. Freeland, Dean Roemmich, et al. "Fifteen Years of Ocean Observations with the Global Argo Array." *Nature Climate Change* 6 (2016): 145–153.

Siegert, Bernhard. "Cacography or Communication? Cultural Techniques in German Media Studies." *Grey Room* 29 (2008): 26–47.

Sörlin, Sverker, & Paul Warde. "Making the Environment Historical: An Introduction." *Nature's End: History and the Environment*, edited by Sverker Sörlin & Paul Warde, 1–17. London: Palgrave Macmillan, 2009.

Sörlin, Sverker, & Nina Wormbs. "Environing Technologies: A Theory of Making Environment." *History and Technology* 34, no. 2 (2018): 101–125.

Vazquez, Rolando. "Precedence, Earth and The Anthropocene: Decolonizing Design." *Design Philosophy Papers Design Philosophy Papers* 15, no. 1 (2017): 77–91. DOI: 10.1080/14487136.2017.1303130.

Warde, Paul. "The Environment." *Local Places, Global Processes*, edited by Peter Coates, David Moon & Paul Warde, 32–46. Oxford: Windgather Press, 2016.

Warde, Paul, Libby Robin, & Sverker Sörlin. *The Environment – A History of the Idea*. Baltimore, MD: Johns Hopkins University Press, 2018.

Wickberg, Adam. "Reconfiguring Temporality in the Anthropocene: Coloniality and the Political Eco-Crisis." *Resilience: A Journal of the Environmental Humanities* 8, no. 1 (2020): 37–59, special issue "Roots of the Future," edited by Anthony Lioi.

Wickberg, Adam, & Johan Gärdebo. "Where Humans and the Planetary Conflate: An Introduction to Environing Media." *Humanities* 9, no. 3 (2020).

Yusoff, Kathryn. *A Billion Black Anthropocenes or None*. Minneapolis: University of Minnesota Press, 2019.

PART 1
Colonial environing media

2
ENVIRONING EMPIRES AND COLONIAL MEDIA

John Durham Peters and Adam Wickberg

For much of its history, the field of media studies has been biased toward questions of (1) ideological or attitudinal influence caused by (2) modern or emergent technologies. This chapter goes in another direction by thinking about media as (1) environing and (2) residual. Media are not only bright and shiny electronic gadgets produced by Silicon Valley or the vast information and entertainment empires of broadcasting, press, and film; they are also, more fundamentally, the means of organizing our cultural and natural worlds. They not only work upon hearts and minds but shape societal habits and ecological habitats. Media are agencies of civilizational and environmental order. The rise of digital media in recent decades has reinforced the fundamental logistical role of media as agencies that arrange, catalog, organize, network, and index people, places, and things. Digital media manage people and resources, time, space, and power, but this is also true of a long and diverse history of pre-electronic media. The tools of media theory that we have developed for audiovisual and digital media can be productively applied to the great pyramids of Giza and biblical scrolls, the Persian postal office and Roman roads, Venetian counting houses and medieval cathedrals. All of them process data, connect across space and time, and alter, to one degree or another, their cultural and natural environments.

Our understanding of media as fundamental constituents of organization joins the recent interest in infrastructures, defined as "large, force-amplifying systems that connect people and institutions across large scales of space and time" or "big, durable, well-functioning systems and services." Thus, nature can be viewed as the ultimate infrastructure.[1] Calendars, clocks, towers, names, addresses, maps, registers, arms, and money are all infrastructural media. Such media become second nature, morphing biorhythms and altering ecosystems. Today's planetary digital infrastructure builds upon the long legacy of resource management via databases. The deep sea, the global yield of corn, and planetary public health

DOI: 10.4324/9781003282891-3

depend for their very existence upon the circulation of data. In rural China today, AI affects pig farming as blockchain shapes chicken farming.[2] We argue for a longer genealogy of the nature-shaping logistical role of media that is so evident today. The technosphere had a long prehistory.

In this chapter, we refine and exemplify these claims via a case study of some environing media in Mexico. The country has a deep and rich media history. The past century has many examples. One is the fascinating history of Mexican broadcasting as told by our colleague Joy Hayes in her book *Radio Nation*.[3] Rubén Gallo's splendid book, *Mexican Modernity*, also illuminates the central role played by even more elemental media in both avant-garde artistic and architectural developments in the period immediately following the Mexican revolution.[4] By way of cameras, typewriters, radio, cement, and stadiums in the 1920s, Gallo shows how the energies released by the revolution took up these new media as things to think with and to design a new society with. They not only were topics for art or literature but were material shapers of art-making itself. This chapter follows Gallo's underlying assumption that media are not only channels for transmitting ideologies; they are modes that shape what it means to exist in a given time and place. Media have ontological force: they define what is and who we are. Mexican history has seen diverse media of control, surveillance, and spectacle.

In this chapter, our focus will be mostly on the 16th century, especially on the momentous clash of Spanish paper power and indigenous culture following *la conquista*. First, we turn to relevant work from two scholars who hail from two nations with rich media histories: Canada and Germany.

Innis and Siegert

In speaking of media as central constituents of civilization we draw on the work of the great Canadian historian and media theorist, Harold Adams Innis (1894–1952), who remains one of the most suggestive sources for understanding media in a deep historical and environing way. Like his younger and more famous Canadian colleague Marshall McLuhan, Innis held an expansive definition of media. Trained as an economic historian, he came to media through the study of staples – basic economic goods such as timber, fur, and fish that were so important for the historical development of Canada. The Canadian fur trade, the topic of an important book by Innis, was not just an obscure bit of economic history. Rather, the fur trade was the embryo for much of Canada's later history, and foreshadowed lasting dilemmas: the clash of native peoples and European settlers, ecological relations between fauna such as the beaver and world markets, the rise of a center-periphery system (a few families in Montreal more or less controlling much of Canada's territory via trading networks), and international relations with Europe and the United States (where the furs were typically sold as hats before falling out of fashion). Canadian history for Innis was a story of control of space across mountain, prairie, lakes, rivers, and oceans. But the control of time was also always important for him, both in integrating the country (standardized time and time zones were invented in part by a Canadian, Sir Sandford Fleming) and in remembering the richness of the past (what Innis called the oral tradition).

From the analysis of staples, it was a short step to studies of media. In Innis's last, cancer-shortened years, he worked on a treatise that reinterpreted the history of civilization in terms of various media of communication.[5] He was particularly interested in the long span of history, in particular, in stone, clay, papyrus, paper, and electricity (to a lesser extent) as key media in civilizations such as ancient Egypt, India, China, Greece, Rome, medieval and modern Europe, and modern north America. (With his long-range perspective, Innis never would have dreamed of calling newspapers, cinema, radio, or television "old media" as they sometimes are in comparison to digital media!) He read widely in English and French and his massive, dense, and difficult texts are crammed with facts, events, and interpretations. Though this is not the place to explicate his work, one focus of his media theory was the relative weight that civilizations gave to space and time and the "bias" that media imposed on those two dimensions. Monuments and statuary, as heavy, durable media, are time-biased, and transmit along the time axis. Thus, ancient Egypt, with its pyramids and death cult, was a time-biased society. Documents and newspapers, as light, ephemeral media, are space-biased, and transmit along the space axis. The Roman Empire, with its roads, postal service, and military spread, or the United States, with its love of territorial expansion along various frontiers and disregard for the past, were space-biased societies.[6] So was Canada, to a lesser degree, whose geography was shaped by lightweight and easily transportable beaver pelts. He'd no doubt see the internet as grotesquely space-biased.

In Innis's view, media were fundamentally about power. For him the question was not so much how new media change our sensory perception or proprioception (as it was for McLuhan) but how they give advantages to new classes of experts. Each new medium grants some new occupational group a "monopoly of knowledge," special insider control and leverage that gives them advantage over others. Bill Gates held a kind of monopoly of knowledge on operating systems as Jeff Bezos has for online retail. Such figures who get hold of technical innovations at their most strategic chokepoint are found throughout history. For Innis the large political and ethical task of media theory was to fight monopolies and counter the massive space bias of modern civilization, especially the United States. Canada, a nation formed by various media of space and time, was precariously perched between past and future, between the empires of England, France, and the United States and its indigenous past.

Strangely enough, Innis never paid much attention to Mexico or to Latin America, and he hasn't received much attention there either. This is unfortunate, since he was a scholar of empire and communication, and an outspoken political critic of the way his nation was dependent on the ambitions of empires. He would have appreciated the saying:

Pobre México
Tan lejos de dios

Tan cerca de estados unidos. [Poor Mexico, So far from God, So close to the U.S.]

He felt the same way about Canada. Innis is productively read as a dependency theorist from a northern cold rich country instead of a southern warm poor one.[7] To Innis's way of thinking, Canada and Mexico would be siblings in several ways: their shared borders with the same colossus, their long *mestizaje* of native and European stock, their heritage of being the plaything of battling empires, their internal center-periphery relations that give so much power to one or two urban centers, and the importance of media in their histories. Innis was deeply concerned with the political, ethical, and cognitive imbalances that great power brings, and thought that US-style modernity had a dangerous "space bias." He always insisted on "the creativity of the periphery" or what liberation theologians call the "epistemological privilege of the oppressed," and believed that his marginal, Canadian point of view gave him special insight. Innis's research on the circulation of staples could apply richly to Mexico's economic and cultural history with its gold, silver, feathers, maize, and slaves all the way through the recent tragic and lucrative staple of narcotics, presided over by the cult of *la santa muerte*. An analysis of any one of these staples could reveal much about Mexico's complex and contradictory history.

Unlike Innis, recent German-language work in media history has much to say about Latin America and Mexico. Bernhard Siegert in particular has taken an intense interest in the Spanish empire and the media it used to invent and colonize Latin America.[8] Two of his books, not yet translated from the German, provide an analysis of Spain and New Spain. The first, *Passage des Digitalen* (The Digital Passage, 2003), is a deep history of the digital revolution.[9] The digital computer, in Siegert's argument, trails a long history of data processing that goes back at least to medieval Europe. An "inquisition" was originally a census or inventory of a kingdom, an effort to count people and property. In England, for example, the famous *Domesday Boke* (book of reckoning) in 1086 listed men of standing and their property. The Norman conquerors wanted to know who they could tax! Such practices were widespread in feudal Europe.

Siegert focuses on 16th-century Spain which took such data-gathering enterprises to new extremes. He shows that the spectacular, torture-filled side of "inquisition" in the Spanish empire was just part of its insatiable desire for information about its ever-increasing dominion. This information took three main forms: pictures (especially maps), numbers (especially lists, registers, and accounts), and words (narrative descriptions). Various institutions and actors, especially the Council of the Indies and the Casa de la Contratación [The House of Trade], were charged with the job of representing the Spanish empire. New professions defined by writing proliferated: scribes, accountants, cosmographers, notaries, and chroniclers. Philip II, the most important king of Spain in the 16th century, liked to say something that media theorists such as Siegert are fond of quoting: *Quod non est in actis, non est in mundo*. That is: if it is not on file, it doesn't exist. He was also known as "el rey papelero" – the paper king – thanks to his love of governing through documents.[10]

Siegert's key point of transformation was the 1570s, though there was a longer prelude. The Casa de la Contratación in Seville was first founded in 1503 as a storehouse for managing trade with the new world but soon it became a clearinghouse for managing data about ships, cargo, people, and places. The record and the reality were supposed to match one to one. Under the initial leadership of Amerigo Vespucci, who was appointed to lead the Casa in 1508 and gave his name to the Americas, the Casa housed the "padrón real" (royal register), a constantly updated register of Spanish possessions. Siegert calls the *padrón real* a "metamedium" – the standard against which all other inquiries into the new world were measured. All returning ships' captains were required by oath to supply updates from their logs, something they seem to have done without enthusiasm. The position of royal cosmographer, nautical map- and instrument-maker, was created in 1523 and was occupied by a number of important scholar-bureaucrats in the next few decades. The most important cosmographer for Siegert was Juan de Ovando, who assessed the inefficiency of the Council of the Indies in the 1560s and then introduced sweeping administrative reforms in 1571. Ovando's aim was a total natural history of the Indies, involving, yet again, three kinds of data: graphical, tabular, and textual. Section 3 of his *Ordenanzas* called for nothing less than a complete and certified description and investigation of all things in the state of the Indies.[11] According to Ovando, if the crown's data were incorrect or out of date, the empire itself would be threatened with ruin. He dreamed of a permanent inquisition in the new world. In a sense, the aim was to create a simulation of the Spanish empire as a manageable totality. Of course, the Council of the Indies never achieved anything like this, but the ambition was a paper-machine filtering massive amounts of data. For Siegert, Spanish bureaucracy was a gigantic computer *avant la lettre* that processed documents instead of bits. As he remarks of this early Google, drawing an explicit line between digital and logistical media, "The colonial heterotopia in Latin America achieves for the first time a model of storage that we recognize today in the processing units [Arbeitsspeichern] of our computers."[12]

Siegert's next book *Passagiere und Papiere* (Passengers and Papers, 2006) directly concerns the transatlantic passage between Spain and New Spain. It examines how acts of writing helped to create new kinds of identity in the 16th century.[13] Like Innis, Siegert is interested in bottlenecks. He sees sea and ship as essential media in the history of the world.[14] The House of Trade in Seville had a royal monopoly overseeing all passengers and cargo to and from Spain. Seville was better suited for this task than a seaport such as Cadiz since it was more tightly controlled: everything coming or going had to pass through the Guadalquivir River.

Paper served as a similar kind of chokepoint. Writing, not torture, was the great instrument of *inquisición*: the legalistic inspection of identity, using the tools of documentation and legal hearings, oversaw the borders of the Spanish domain. Inquisition's procedures made it impossible for anyone to pass to the new world without going through an ordeal of testifying, writing, and counting in an "interrogatorio." Each person had to attest to – and in many cases thus create – their identity. As a by-product of all this bureaucracy, new ways of thinking about the self-emerged. A person's identity was legitimate only when their oral account matched the written account on file. One motive for the paperwork was to prevent frauds and impostors – and to discover crypto-Jews and Muslims. The invention of the *pasajero* went together with the invention of the *picaro*, the sneaky, identity-defying rogue that populates Spanish literature and much else. Official records came to define personal identity, just as in our own time. "Spanish America is a special world: a world in which everything is counted – commodities, people, ships, books." To be a passenger was not only to sail across the sea; it was to have your data transferred from one register to another. The Spanish empire, for Siegert, was an empire of documents. Its task was to assemble an "exhaustive view of things." This was reflected even in urban design, as cities such as Santo Domingo, Lima, and Buenos Aires were laid out on grids – every point, in the spirit of Renaissance perspective, lying on an X-Y coordinate system. The spirit of registration bound people to places. The legal culture of inspection and documentation forever saturated Latin American culture with letters, in every sense of that word.[15]

Spanish media in the conquest

Logistical and environing media were central to the conquest of New Spain, and thus to the history of Mexico. Maps and names, calendars and compasses, horses and gunpowder, the biological agents of disease and *mestizaje*, and "cruz y campana" (cross and bell) – many media mixed in the 16th-century cauldron. But above all, the medium *primus inter pares* was writing. As Hernan Cortés lamented: "Oh, if one were only illiterate, so as not to have to sign so many death certificates." He knew all too well the connection between writing and death. Though no man of letters (*letrado*) himself, Cortés was a diligent Spanish bureaucrat, scrupulously following procedures of documentation, sometimes to an almost absurd degree. The chronicler Bernal Diaz del Castillo, who like Cortés was an adventurer rather than man of letters, reports of one encounter with hostile natives: "and as always, Cortés wanted to attend to documentation and made a demand in front of a Royal scribe." The natives were not impressed and responded with "a great shower of arrows." According to Bernal Diaz, Cortés conducted a formal ceremony, making three slashes into a tree to take possession of the land for the king and defend his right with the sword. "And in front of a Royal scribe they did this declaration," duly notes Bernal Diaz.[16] The legalistic scrupulousness with which the conquistadores warned the native peoples and documented everything before notaries and witnesses is almost Quixotic – to mention a later figure in the Spanish culture of documentary simulation in which fact and fiction blended together for both kings and knights errant.

Bernal Diaz's *Historia verdadera* may be profitably read for media history. Its story is logistical in the clearest military sense: the conquistadores sail, seek, map, name, build fortifications, seek food, fight enemies, tend wounds, forge battle plans, and have relationships with native women. The Aztecs soon adopted the Spanish paper fetish even if they didn't understand how it worked.

> And the three first natives understood our language very well and demanded a letter from Cortés, using it not because they could read it, but because they understood well that when we sent messengers or orders, there was a paper called *amal*, a sign as an order.
>
> ["Y los tres principales lo entendieron muy bien por nuestras lenguas y demandaron a Cortés una carta, y ésta no porque la entendían, sino que ya sabían claramente que cuando enviábamos alguna mensajería o cosas que les mandábamos, era un papel de aquellos que llaman *amales*, señal como mandamiento"].

Thus, messengers to Cuauhtémoc ask for the authenticating mark of an official message. (Note how nicely the phrase "sign as order" unites the classic mixtures of communication and command, symbol and military, semiotics and tactics.)[17]

Classificatory and collecting zeal must certainly count as one of the most important of cultural techniques used by the Spanish. The period between 1570 and 1590 saw several projects with the common goal of achieving a description of the territories ("descripción de tierra"). One of the most significant was Ovando and López de Velasco's questionnaires that were sent out to every local governor several times during this period. The questionnaire consisted of 50 key questions, according to the art of geography, with data on provinces, seas, islands, rivers, mountains, and other places in relation to longitude, latitude, and size. This corpus of data survives as the *Relaciones geográficas de indias* and comprises thousands of pages, as well as a large number of maps and illustrations. It came to be the first statistical study performed by any nation and constitutes one of the primary sources of information about the early colonial period and the pre-Columbian era.

Francisco Hernández, a Doctor of Medicine and Philip II's personal physician, shows just how intense this collecting zeal could be. He was named "Chief Medical Officer of the Indies" in 1570 and sent on a five-year expedition to map all the natural resources of New Spain, as part of the ambition to achieve a description of the territories. The position meant that Hernández would do something similar to the cosmographers' work on geography in mapping the biodiversity of the Americas, for the purpose of advancing trade and exports from the region. At the same time, the cosmographer and navigator Andrés de Urdaneta had been the first ever to perform a cross-Pacific return voyage between Mexico and Southeast Asia, where the empire had just colonized the Philippines. Where the cosmographers of the Casa de Contratación like Ovando and Lopez de Velasco scaled up using the environing paper media of censuses, registers, questionnaires, astronomical observations, and maps, Hernández scaled down to the most minute detail of each plant, mineral, and animal that could be found in the American territories. Hernández sent back several shiploads of cargo with large quantities of plants and instructions for their domestication and cultivation in European soil. Philip II impatiently wrote him several letters urging him to complete and send back the natural history of New Spain that he was compiling aided by local knowledge and painters. In the end, Hernández sent back no less than 16 volumes containing around 3,000 plants on 893 pages of text and 2,071 illustrations.[18] In an unpublished letter to Philip II dated 30 August 1577, Hernández writes that he has just returned from New Spain with a fleet a week earlier in very bad physical shape and with a great amount of valuable cargo that he wishes to present to the King.

> I will go [to Madrid] as soon as I can and bring with me the books that had already been sent, as well as translations of them into Mexican language, our commentaries of the things of the Indies and description of New Spain. I have also sent several boxes of medicinal herbs from this land that I have discovered and described, as well as wonderful plants to be planted here in Spain.[19]

Media of documentation thus played a crucial role for the Spanish not only with churches, schools, and offices but also in the environing process of new knowledge about the natural and cultural world. The Franciscan priest and missionary Bernardino de Sahagún spent most of his life in New Spain based at a Franciscan *colegio* at Tlatelolco. He and his native Aztec colleagues spent around 30 years on an encyclopedic project of gathering and showing "the things of New Spain." They described the people, their religion, history, agriculture, political structure, and natural world. In the preface to the book, written in 1576 during an epidemic outbreak, Sahagún compares the Aztecs to the Old Testament prophecy in which Jeremiah cursed Judea and Jerusalem, promising the arrival of a violent and aggressive people who would destroy them and their societies. According to Sahagún, this was exactly what had happened to the Aztecs, and the fear of their extinction and loss of their culture was a motivation for compiling the encyclopedia.[20] Sahagún also notes that "in this land which is now called New Spain, these people have lived for at least two thousand years, and that their knowledge and political structure far exceeds those of many European nations."[21] The book was completed in New Spain around the same time that Hernández was finalizing his work. In 1575 Rodrigo de Sequera arrived in New Spain with orders from Ovando to produce an illustrated bilingual edition of Sahagún's encyclopedia. The result was the incredibly richly illustrated 12 books with 2,468 hand-colored illustrations now known as the Florentine Codex, because of its 1,580 arrival in Florence as a diplomatic gift for Cardinal Ferdinando I de Medici.[22]

Aztec media

Certainly not only the Spaniards had media, as the case of Sahagún makes clear. Clearly the Aztecs had cultural techniques for controlling space, time, and people.

Let us mention just two among many. First, their calendar was clearly a data processor, a logistical organizer of days and years into larger recurring systems. As is well known, the Aztec calendar (derived from the Mayans) featured a nested system of two cycles, a 365-day agricultural-political calendar and a 260-day religious-sacred calendar (perhaps related to the period of human gestation). The two cycles coincided every 52 of the long years or 73 short years. The calendar was the central computer of the Aztec social order, a kind of massive algorithm that directed agriculture, war, reproduction, labor, and religious ritual. It was sort of like the television schedule of the 1950s through 1970s on steroids. It was run by priests who had what Innis would call a "monopoly of knowledge" in how to reckon dates and declare auspicious and inauspicious times. The calendar was a device of abstract calculation (a cognitive tool), but it also took form in concrete works of sculptural art in stone. It was not only a model of cosmic cycles; it was an instrument of power.

Aztec temples were broadcasting towers. The mark of towers as communicative devices is optical and acoustic leverage: they can be seen and heard from great distances, and they can also see and sound at great distances.[23] In their battles with the Spanish, the Aztecs used their temples to great military advantage. The temples afforded vista points and strategic look-outs to survey the Spaniards' movements, and they were command posts that were very hard to capture. In earlier, more peaceful times, Montezuma showed Cortés and his men the amazing sight of Tenochtitlán from the Templo Mayor, a panoramic 360-degree view. The Spanish, in turn, were very eager once the fighting began to occupy the temples and to replace the deities there with their own banners. The Aztec elites used the temples as agents of spectacle and intimidation for their own people and for neighbors as well. Temples amplified the visibility of human sacrifices. As the mutilated bodies were cast down the steps, the elevated position of the altar afforded a cinematic view for many spectators. The priests also used the temples as a center point for broadcasting sound. Bernal Diaz reports that the Aztec drum – an excessively large drum – could be heard for two leagues from the temple. He thought "the sound of it was so horrible that they called it the instrument of hell." It was accompanied by conch shells, horns, and trumpets. (His dislike for the sound may come from hearing it herald the sacrifice of his captured comrades.)[24]

For the Aztecs, temples were not only places of religious sacrifice, but centers of political control and social organization. The Spaniards recognized their importance at once, installing "cruz and campana" as if they were taking over the television network, which has always been the first item of business for any revolutionary.[25] Temples were certainly agencies of social control, just as the cathedrals and churches built later from the same stones would become some of the key media of Mexican history.

Spanish and indigenous media yielded hybrids. Among them are fascinating maps of local municipalities drawn and painted by indigenous artists.[26] The maps were often produced in an indigenous cartographic tradition which defined territory by an enclosed sphere of logographic place-names representing boundaries and referring to common history. The representation of a closed circle, a sphere, establishes the inside of the community for its self-representation on the map. The map of Teozacoalco in Oaxaca from 1580 (Figure 2.1) is a good example of indigenous cartography in colonial New Spain. The animals, plants, mountains, and figures dotted around the circle are such logographic place-names, which mark the border by referring to a feature of each area. As an environing medium, the map has many interesting features spanning centuries of environmental change. Apart from the current border, it also includes the boundary of a previous dynasty from four centuries before the current, when the neighboring Eoltepec was its subject.[27] In the top-right corner of the circle rises an arc like a crescent moon which shows the logographic place-names of the old territory of Eoltepec (the mountain of God). The environment changed as the colonizers introduced new animals like horses and pigs. The painter of this map reflects the Spanish presence in the area by interlacing the traditional footprints of the paths with hoofprints to show that horse transportation was now used there.[28] In the 21st century a team of archaeologists used the same map to unearth the lost sites of this Mixteca kingdom, which now resided under modern building structures but that the map correctly pointed out with the place-names. The spherical shape of the map does not depart from a geometrical projection however, but is rather a pictorial rhetoric of the community's importance and unity as expressed in the closed circle. The environing effect of this map lies in how it constitutes humans and their surroundings, while simultaneously serving the interest of securing overview and orientation over time.

The list of Mixtec couples shows the genealogy of rulership of the town with over 20 generations from the 11th century, ending with Montezuma, before the small kingdom was subdued by the Spanish empire in the 1520s. Presenting the genealogy on the map – one made at the request of the Spanish authorities – was also a way of asserting the elevated history of the Mixtec kingdom of Teozacoalco. This environing medium thus encapsulates both the space and time axis that Innis articulates, becoming simultaneously monumental archive and an instrument for colonial settlement. Perhaps this effect is due to the hybrid nature and results from the clash between the very space-biased Spanish empire and the more time-biased Mixtec kingdom. It is also possible that the inclusion of the old boundaries in 1580 was the result of copying from an original map which had simply been revised on the same manuscript rather than remade.

The map marks an interesting moment in Mexico's media history. It measures 176 × 138 cm and is made on a patchwork of about 23 blank paper folios of European origin that was used by the imperial bureaucracy.[29] While native paper-making techniques were never fully abandoned in New Spain, the use of the Spanish standard medium of the folio is characteristic of the hybrid nature that characterizes the maps made in response to the questionnaires. When the maps came back to Royal Cosmographer López de Velasco in the 1580s, however, they were formatted according to various local indigenous cartographic traditions.

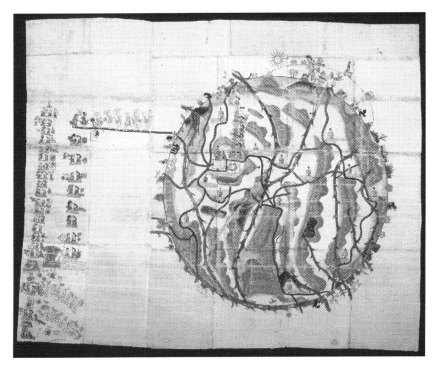

FIGURE 2.1 The Relaciones Geograficas Map of Teozacoalco, 1580. Courtesy of the Benson Latin American Collection, the General Libraries, the University of Texas at Austin.

This mosaic of communities and land went against his wish to standardize all territory under the label of New Spain. The clash of space-representation techniques was never resolved, and the project was subsequently abandoned, but the hybrid form is one of several consequences of the cataclysmic blending of genes, mores, languages, and pathogens after 1519.

Environing media – tragic and global

Such media as paper, maps, temples, bells, and cross clearly marked the political, religious, and lived landscape for people in 16th-century New Spain. In this sense, they were clearly environing. Both Innis and Siegert drop hints about the ecological impacts of their time-space-archiving media, but neither brings them into the foreground. But the clash of Spanish and indigenous media accompanied one of the most catastrophic environmental transformations of the past millennia, the depopulation due to new diseases. In what is known as the Great Dying in the Americas, a hard to calculate number of people, often estimated at 60 million, disappeared over a century.[30] The decrease in population occurred initially through European epidemics but their effects were aggravated by civil wars, ethnocide, slavery, and resource expropriation.[31] The abandoned farmland, which has been estimated at 1 hectare per person, i.e. 60 million hectares of land, quickly began to regrow into dense woodlands with quick CO_2 uptake. This reforestation led to a dip in global CO_2 levels first stratigraphically attested around 1611 from 285 ppm to 272 ppm over the next 50 years, the last low point before the steady rise to our current 417 ppm. The decrease in CO_2 concentration also led to a planetary cooling of about 0.5°C. These data have been used to argue for a starting date of the Anthropocene in 1611 in what is known as the Orbis hypothesis.[32]

In this way, events in the media history of the early years of contact between the Old and New Worlds turn out to be directly connected to changes to the deep history of the Earth system. The Great Dying in the Americas contributed to the Little Ice Age in Europe, driving famine and wars in the 17th century.[33] The "teleconnections" in the atmosphere were parallel by the space- and time-transcending media of ship, document, gun, and map. These not only enabled a global exchange of human, animal, plant, and pathogen populations, but also started a world economic system linking local and global spaces: Seville, Havana, Callao, Manila, Madrid, Mexico City. Pacific and Atlantic joined in the world's first global trade network controlled by the Spanish empire, over which "the sun never set," a phrase probably first used by Carlos V. 1611 witnesses a moment not only when humans have built a genuine world system, but one capable of influencing its nonhuman Earth system of weather and climate. A radical shift in *cultural techniques* – taken in that term's most basic sense as agricultural engineering – altered the global climate. Not all of the environing media we have discussed carry Earth system forcing in this way, but that some of them might is highly suggestive.

Conclusion: toward an environing media history of Mexico

The media history of Mexico is yet to be written. We have emphasized similarities between old and new media more than their differences – *el padrón real* as Google, the Council of Indies as a database, *el Templo Mayor* as a broadcasting station, or *cruz y campana* as audiovisual media of conquest. Obviously Aztec media of political-religious control and Spanish media of military-religious conquest differ importantly from recent media, and we certainly recognize the risk of the media concept becoming vaporous by overgeneralization. Good analogies can inspire historical research, but good historical research will reveal the limits and qualify those analogies. Scholarship needs both grand comparisons and careful studies. We obviously think it is worth the risk.

Historical comparison can help us better understand our own situation. Digital media are in some ways astonishingly new. But in other ways they just raise the same old challenges. The recent SARS-CoV-2 crisis would be unthinkable without digital systems. It has not only been an epidemiological and economic and political event, but an environmental one as well. The long view reminds us of the sober lesson that new possibilities for the management of space, time, and power do not relieve the old challenges: inequality, domination, the risks of disease and death, and the ability to completely turn our worlds upside down.

In a beautiful philosophical essay called "El tres y el cuatro" the great poet Octavio Paz ponders the legacy of the *letrados* for Mexico, the intellectual bureaucrats with university degrees in law who served as Latin American governors in the many positions assigned by the crown during the colonial period.[34] According to Paz, European settlers in the new world were motivated by the utopian ambition of escaping from history. "To the European mind, America was not only a geographical exception but also a historical and theological one." He details the role played by 16th-century visionaries in the foundation of Mexican culture, *letrados* who brought a potent mixture of Platonic utopianism, Roman stoicism, Christian primitivism, and Renaissance humanism to the task of building New Spain. That violence went together with the building of the new utopia proves Paz's central point, that Mexico is a country of contrasts. In the end what distinguishes Mexican identity for Paz is a tension between warring ideals. Mexico is an experiment to see if two civilizations based on the three (Europe) and the four (Mesoamerica) can live together. There are, he says, two ways to combine the three and the four: addition and multiplication. His conclusion: the identity of Mexico is still up for grabs. "We haven't arrived at either the seven or the twelve: Mexico is still a process."[35]

Paz does not quite connect the strain of national utopianism in Mexican history to its media history, although his interest in numbers as primal cultural organizers is reminiscent of Siegert, and of Friedrich Kittler, Siegert's teacher. Paz's thinking is friendly to the role media play in imagining nationhood.[36] Though writing about English immigrants to the United States, what James Carey says is equally relevant for New Spain:

> The desire to escape the boundaries of Europe, to create a new life, to found new communities, to carve a New Jerusalem out of the woods of Massachusetts, were primary motives behind the unprecedented movement of white European civilization over virtually the entire globe.

The colonial "migration in space was above all an attempt to trade an old world for a new and represented the profound belief that movement in space could be in itself a redemptive act." Carey sees this attitude toward space and movement as permanently giving the US experiment in creating culture at a distance an almost religious sense of mission. US culture has a peculiar attitude toward technology and communication – as devices burdened or blessed with larger political and cultural possibilities. Carey continues:

> The United States was, to flirt with more deterministic language, the product of literacy, cheap paper, rapid and inexpensive transportation, and the mechanical reproduction of words—the capacity, in short, to transport

not only people but a complex culture and civilization from one place to another, indeed between places that were radically dissimilar in geography, social conditions, economy, and very often climate.[37]

Here Carey, following Innis, ties American utopianism to its conditions of communication.[38]

He could have said the same thing about Mexico. America was invented before it was colonized, and the great experiments began already in Europe, in the famous thesis of Edmundo O'Gorman.[39] America was named, after all, after a map-maker, one who may never have visited the new world even if he did manage its facsimile in Seville, and maps are important environing media of imagination and control. As Siegert has pointed out in another essay, maps are not just representations of space but also spaces of representation.[40] By this chiasmus he means that rather than just representing a given world, maps are epistemic objects that construct notions of space and territory in the first place. In the Spanish Empire, as in many others, maps were considered highly classified national secrets that were guarded in particular rooms to which only trusted persons were admitted. America's history is a story of massive confusions between old and new realities – the Aztecs were taken as "moros" or "indios" by the Spaniards and the conquistadores had the luck to arrive in a sacred year of the calendar. The supposed *conquest* by Cortés was aided by a collision of local empires and wars, in which the Spaniards came to take advantage of the aspiration of the rival Tlaxcala to take down the Aztecs.[41] What makes Mexico distinct from the United States and Canada is the collision of two logistical media empires: Spain and the Aztecs. The United States and Canada, of course, have a long, sad, and complicated history with native peoples, but there were no indigenous state-based organizations north of the Rio Grande of comparable complexity. All three countries were shaped by environing media, but each had its own unique path. Perhaps one day Mexico will arrive, as Octavio Paz says, at the seven or the twelve, but in the meanwhile it remains a process, one in which media play an important part.

Notes

Parts of this essay appeared previously in *Critical Inquiry* (2022) Vol. 48, no. 4 as "Media: The Case of Spain and New Spain."
1 Paul N. Edwards, "Infrastructure and Modernity: Force, Time and Social Organization in the History of Sociotechnical Systems," *Modernity and Technology*, eds. Thomas J. Misa, Philip Brey & Andrew Feenberg (Cambridge, MA: MIT Press, 2002), 196.
2 Xiaowei Wang, *Blockchain Chicken Farm: And Other Stories of Tech in China's Countryside* (New York: FSGO x *Logic*, 2020).
3 Joy Elizabeth Hayes, *Radio Nation* (Tucson: University of Arizona Press, 2000).
4 Ruben Gallo, *Mexican Modernity: The Avant-Garde the Technological Revolution* (Cambridge, MA: Cambridge University Press, 2005).
5 Published in part as *Harold Innis's History of Communications: Paper and Printing—Antiquity to Early Modernity*, eds. William J. Buxton, Michael R. Cheney, & Paul Heyer (Lanham, MD: Rowman & Littlefield, 2015).

6 See Harold A. Innis, *The Bias of Communication* (Toronto: University of Toronto Press, 1991).
7 William Melody, Liora Salter, & Paul Heyer (eds.), *Culture, Communication, and Dependency: The Tradition of H. A. Innis* (Norwood, NJ: Ablex Publication Corporation, 1981).
8 For other German media theorists interested in the Hispanic world, see for example: Hans Ulrich Gumbrecht, *Eine Geschichte der spanischen Literatur*, 2 vols. (Frankfurt: Suhrkamp, 1990); Wolfgang Schäffner, "Telematische Representation im 16. und 17 Jahrhundert," *Theatralität und die Krisen der Representation*, ed. Erika Fischer-Lichte (Stuttgart: Springer, 2001); Wolfgang Schäffner, "Die Verwaltung der Endlichkeit Zur Geburt des neuzeitlichen Romans in Spanien," *Die Endlichkeit der Literatur*, eds. Eckart Goebel & Martin v. Koppenfels (Berlin: Akademie Verlag, 2002); Silvia Fehrmann, Irina Podgorny, & Wolfgang Schäffner, "Un Colón para los datos: Humboldt y el diseño del saber," *Redes* 14, no. 28 (Nov. 2008), 77–80.
9 Bernhard Siegert, *Passage des Digitalen: Zeichenpraktiken der neuzeitlichen Wissenschaften, 1500–1900* (Berlin: Brinkmann & Bose, 2003).
10 Adam Wickberg, *Pellucid Paper: Poetry and Bureaucratic Media in Early Modern Spain* (London: Open Humanities Press, 2018).
11 Siegert, *Passage*, 86.
12 Bernhard Siegert, *Passagiere und Papiere: Schreibakte auf der Schwelle zwischen Spanien und Amerika* (Munich: Wilhelm Fink Verlag, 2006), 150.
13 Siegert, *Passagiere und Papiere*.
14 Bernhard Siegert, "Der Nomos des Meeres: Zur Imagination des Politischen und ihren Grenzen," *Politiken der Medien*, eds. Daniel Gethmann & Markus Stauff (Zurich: Diaphanes Verlag, 2005), 39–56.
15 Siegert, *Passagiere und Papiere*, 53, 62, 135. He notes his debt to the work of Roberto González Echeverría, "The Influence of Hans-Ulrich Gumbrecht," *Eine Geschichte der spanischen Literatur*, 2 vols. (Frankfurt: Suhrkamp, 1990), is also clear.
16 Bernal Diaz del Castillo, *Historia verdadera de la conquista de la Nueva España* (Mexico City: Porrúa, 2004), 51–52, 97.
17 Bernal Diaz, *Historia verdadera*, 360.
18 Adam Wickberg, "Plus Ultra: Coloniality and the Mapping of American Nature Culture in the Empire of Philip II," *Necsus: European Journal of Media Studies* 6 (2018): 217.
19 "Contratación, 5197," Minutas de Cartas del Tribunal de la Contratación, Archivo General de Indias, translation by the authors.
20 Bernardino de Sahagún, *Historia General de las Cosas de Nueva España* (1830 [1577]).
21 Ibid., 8.
22 *The Florentine Codex: An Encyclopedia of the Nahua World in Sixteenth-Century Mexico*, eds. Jeanette Favrot Peterson & Kevin Trerraciano (Austin: University of Texas Press, 2019).
23 John Durham Peters, *The Marvelous Clouds: Toward a Philosophy of Elemental Media* (Chicago: University of Chicago Press, 2015), 35–37, 175–177, 225–241, passim.
24 Bernal Diaz, *Historia*, 174.
25 Edward Luttwak, *Coup d'Etat: A Practical Handbook*, revised edition (Cambridge: Harvard University Press, 2016).
26 Barbara Mundy, *The Mapping of New Spain: Indigenous Cartography and the Maps of the Relaciones Geograficas* (Chicago: Perennial Books, 2000).
27 Ibid., 114.
28 Alex Hidalgo, *Trail of Footprints: A History of Indigenous Maps from Viceregal Mexico* (Austin: University of Texas Press, 2019), 42.
29 Ibid., 76.
30 Alexander Koch et al., "Earth System Impacts of the European Arrival and the Great Dying in the Americas after 1492," *Quaternary Science Reviews* 207 (March 2019): 13–36.

31 Clark Erickson, "Amazonia," *Contemporary Archaeology in Theory: The New Pragmatism*, eds. Robert Preucel & Stephen Mrozowski (Hoboken, NJ: Wiley, 2010), 108; Caroline Levis et al. "Persistent Effects of Pre-Columbian Plant Domestication on Amazonian Forest Composition," *Science* 355, no. 6328 (2017): 925–931.
32 Simon Lewis & Mark Maslin, "Defining the Anthropocene," *Nature* 519 (2015): 171–180.
33 Geoffrey Parker, *Global Crisis: War, Climate Change and Catastrophe in the 17th Century* (New Haven, CT: Yale University Press, 2013); Koch et al., "Earth System Impacts," 14.
34 Richard Kagan, *Students and Society in Early Modern Spain* (Baltimore, MD: Johns Hopkins University Press, 1974).
35 Octavio Paz, "El tres y el cuatro," *El laberinto de la soledad* (Madrid: Fondo de Cultura Económica, 2003), 554, 559.
36 See Benedict R. O'Gorman Anderson, *Imagined Communities* (London: Verso, 1983, 1991).
37 James W. Carey, *Communication as Culture: Essays on Media and Society* (Boston, MA: Routledge, 1989), 3, 16.
38 For Carey's tie to Innis, see "Space, Time, and Communications: A Tribute to Harold Innis," *Communication as Culture*, 142–172.
39 Edmundo O'Gorman, *La invención de América* (Mexico City: Fondo de cultura económica 2006).
40 Bernhard Siegert, "The Map is the Territory," *Radical Philosophy* 169 (Sept./Oct. 2011).
41 Matthew Restall, *When Montezuma Met Cortés: The True Story of the Meeting that Changed History* (New York: Ecco, 2018).

References

Buxton, William J., Michael R. Cheney, & Paul Heyer (eds.). *Harold Innis's History of Communications: Paper and Printing—Antiquity to Early Modernity*. Lanham, MD: Rowman & Littlefield, 2015.
Carey, James W. *Communication as Culture: Essays on Media and Society*. Boston, MA: Routledge, 1989.
del Castillo, Bernal Diaz. *Historia verdadera de la conquista de la Nueva España*. Mexico City: Cambridge University Press, 2004.
Edmundo, O'Gorman. *La invención de América*. Mexico City: Fondo de Cultura Económica, 2006.
Edwards, Paul N. "Infrastructure and Modernity: Force, Time and Social Organization in the History of Sociotechnical Systems." *Modernity and Technology*, edited by Thomas J. Misa, Phlip Brey & Andrew Feenberg. Cambridge, MA: MIT Press, 2002: 185–225.
Erickson, Clark. "Amazonia: The Historical Ecology of a Domesticated Landscape." *Contemporary Archaeology in Theory: The New Pragmatism*, edited by Robert Preucel & Stephen Mrozowski. Hoboken, NJ: Wiley, 2010: 104–128.
Favrot, Peterson Jeanette, & Kevin Trerraciano. *The Florentine Codex: An Encyclopedia of the Nahua World in Sixteenth-Century Mexico*. Austin: University of Texas Press, 2019.
Fehrmann, Silvia, Irina Podgorny, & Wolfgang Schäffner. "Un Colón para los datos: Humboldt y el diseño del saber." *Redes* 14, no. 28 (Nov. 2008), 77–80.
Gallo, Ruben. *Mexican Modernity: The Avant-Garde the Technological Revolution*. Cambridge, MA: Cambridge University Press, 2005.
Gumbrecht, Hans Ulrich. *Eine Geschichte der spanischen Literatur*, 2 vols. Frankfurt: Suhrkamp, 1990.

Hayes, Joy Elizabeth. *Radio Nation*. Tucson: University of Arizona Press, 2000.
Hidalgo, Alex. *Trail of Footprints: A History of Indigenous Maps from Viceregal Mexico*. Austin: University of Texas Press, 2019.
Innis, Harold A. *The Bias of Communication*. Toronto: University of Toronto Press, 1991.
Kagan, Richard. *Students and Society in Early Modern Spain*. Baltimore, MD: Cambridge University Press, 1974.
Koch, Alexander et al. "Earth System Impacts of the European Arrival and the Great Dying in the Americas after 1492." *Quaternary Science Reviews* 207 (March 2019): 13–36.
Levis, Caroline et al. "Persistent Effects of Pre-Columbian Plant Domestication on Amazonian Forest Composition." *Science* 355, no. 6328 (2017): 925–931.
Lewis, Simon, & Mark Maslin. "Defining the Anthropocene." *Nature* 519 (2015): 171–180.
Luttwak, Edward. *Coup d'Etat: A Practical Handbook*, revised edition. Cambridge: Harvard University Press, 2016.
Melody, William, Liora Salter, & Paul Heyer (eds.). *Culture, Communication, and Dependency: The Tradition of H. A. Innis*. Norwood, NJ: Ablex Publication Corporation, 1981.
Mundy, Barbara. *The Mapping of New Spain: Indigenous Cartography and the Maps of the Relaciones Geográficas*. Chicago: Perennial Books, 2000.
O'Gorman Anderson, Benedict R. *Imagined Communities*. London: Verso, 1983, 1991.
Parker, Geoffrey. *Global Crisis: War, Climate Change and Catastrophe in the 17th Century*. New Haven, CT: Yale University Press, 2013.
Paz, Octavio. "El tres y el cuatro." *El laberinto de la soledad*. Madrid: Fondo de Cultura Económica, 2003.
Peters, John Durham. *The Marvelous Clouds: Toward a Philosophy of Elemental Media*. Chicago: University of Chicago Press, 2015.
Restall, Matthew. *When Montezuma Met Cortés: The True Story of the Meeting that Changed History*. New York: Ecco, 2018.
de Sahagún, Bernardino. *Historia General de las Cosas de Nueva España*. Mexico City: Alejandro Valdés, 1830 [1577].
Schäffner, Wolfgang. "Die Verwaltung der Endlichkeit Zur Geburt des neuzeitlichen Romans in Spanien." *Die Endlichkeit der Literatur*, edited by Eckart Goebel & Martin v. Koppenfels. Berlin: Akademie Verlag, 2002: 1–12.
———. "Telematische Representation im 16. und 17 Jahrhundert." *Theatralität und die Krisen der Representation*, edited by Erika Fischer-Lichte. Stuttgart: Springer, 2001: 411–428.Siegert, Bernhard. "Der Nomos des Meeres: Zur Imagination des Politischen und ihren Grenzen." *Politiken der Medien*, edited by Daniel Gethmann & Markus Stauff, 39–56. Zurich: Diaphanes Verlag, 2005.Siegert, Bernhard. *Passage des Digitalen: Zeichenpraktiken der neuzeitlichen Wissenschaften, 1500–1900*. Berlin: Brinkmann & Bose, 2003.
Siegert, Bernhard. *Passagiere und Papiere: Schreibakte auf der Schwelle zwischen Spanien und Amerika*. Munich: Wilhelm Fink Verlag, 2006.
———. "The Map is the Territory." *Radical Philosophy* 169 (Sept./Oct. 2011).
Wang, Xiaowei. *Blockchain Chicken Farm: And Other Stories of Tech in China's Countryside*. New York: FSGO x Logic, 2020.
Wickberg, Adam. *Pellucid Paper: Poetry and Bureaucratic Media in Early Modern Spain*. London: Open Humanities Press, 2018.
———. "Plus Ultra: Coloniality and the Mapping of American Natureculture in the Empire of Philip II." *Necsus: European Journal of Media Studies* 6 (2018): 217.

PART 2
Planetary environing media

3
ENVIRONING AND THE HUMAN-EARTH RELATIONSHIP
Synchronizing geo-anthropology

Sverker Sörlin

In September 2009, *Nature* published an article entitled "A safe operational space for mankind". It introduced a new concept, "planetary boundaries", nine dimensions of the Earth system, all with their critical boundaries, eight of which were ascribed defined boundary digits. The article was intended as a novel contribution to the long-standing debate on possible natural limits to the human enterprise on the planet Earth. As it turned out, it did more than that. It also sparked an intense phase of a broader conversation about the new condition for humanity as part of living in the Anthropocene. The article attracted a lot of interest from research, policy, and activism. It had a wide influence, but it also drew criticism, not least from Global South countries that, quite like the situation 1972 after the *Limits to Growth* report, did not want to jeopardize their own future wealth and were uninterested to discuss limits without redressing historical injustices in distribution of global resources and wealth.[1]

In retrospect, the "Planetary Boundaries Framework", as it was termed, can be seen as one of the structuring conceptual elements of a new *human-Earth relationship*, bounded by the life-sustaining interactions of the organic and non-living world. Other such key elements are the *Anthropocene* concept, the climate crisis framing of human-ecological existence, and the *synchronizing temporalities* of the evolving *geo-anthropology*.[2] Ours is a time when the *Earth* itself, and its elemental dimensions such as soils, species, oceans, ice, air, fibers, genetic code, and neural networks, is *entering history and the polity* with a more-than-human presence and is appearing both as *fundamentally contested* in W. B. Gallie's sense, and as a *governable object* on the scale of its properties as planet.[3]

The planetary boundaries article articulated a set of propositions about the transforming human-Earth relationship. However, the human side of the relationship was sorely under-articulated, as Global South critics and multiple other skeptical voices, especially from the humanities and the social sciences, pointed

DOI: 10.4324/9781003282891-5

out. This was also acknowledged in its broadened 2.0 version, published in *Science* in 2015. There, we (I was myself among the authors of both articles) declared that:

> the PB framework does not as yet account for the regional distribution of the impact, nor of its historical patterns. Nor does the PB framework take into account the deeper issues of equity and causation. The current levels of the boundary processes, and the transgressions of boundaries that have already occurred, are unevenly caused by different human societies and different social groups.[4]

Planetary boundaries, just as "Anthropocene", "the Earth", or "the planet", may have considerable strengths as ontological heuristics, providing suggestive conceptualizations of the new human predicament as the largest single geological force. Yet, their quantifications and models depicting the *directions* and *rates of change* of the global environment keep struggling with the complexity of humans, societies, and technologies as they entangle with the rest of the Earth. Numbers, however thick and numerous and however successful in past formations of policy domains,[5] seem insufficient to take on values, morals, and norms concerning the environment. The boundary digits themselves, however carefully calculated, offer little advice on how the leap from the ontological insight, in itself so intuitively compelling, to the normative program for the polity could be conceived or, even harder, pursued in empirically existing societies.

If there ever was a challenge that required a crossing over between vast knowledge domains, this is it. One may, despite the enormous complexity and ambiguity involved, meaningfully use science to *define* planetary boundaries as quantified thresholds or tipping points, beyond which the human enterprise becomes threatened and life conditions distinctly undesirable. *Operating* within those boundaries – defining the "operational space" and how to use it and share it in the real world – is a quite different matter. It is a challenge on what I would like to call a civilizational level, because in order to meet it we need to remake the "operational logic" of our societies. This logic has emerged over a period of several hundred years since the Early Modern period and has given us legal principles, incentives, norms, values, and institutions that have brought tremendous progress but also produced a fundamentally unsustainable human-Earth relationship. The work that is required to change that operational logic is a large societal challenge, and hence a meaningful subject for knowledge in the human sciences.

In what follows I shall approach this topic using the concept of "environing" that has come in wider circulation in recent years. My ambition is to contribute to what has become over the last couple of decades an intense and creative proliferation of concepts and ideas around how the position of humans in relation to their surroundings can be understood. That environ is a verb is not coincidental. I will argue that the environment, or "the planet", is in continual, drastic, and also worrying change due to the environing work that humans do. To state this by now obvious fact is also a way of pointing to the profoundly relational nature of this position. To move beyond the previous dualist ontology of Man versus Nature – a shared ambition in much post-constructivist theory since around the millennium – an additional element is required with which human agency can engage with the natural world. In previous work I have talked about this as "environing technologies", in the plural.[6] Clearly, media belong in these technologies, being a plural in their own right, with a wide repertoire of manifestations, encompassing the observing and recording as well as the communicating and the receiving, emphasizing valuable features of the relational ontology. My approach here is historical as much as conceptual. What I am after is how we can conceptualize what is now a given, namely that there is a human-Earth relationship with profound implications for governance and for the future of both humans and the Earth. To do that, we need a narrative of how it happened and where the concepts come from.

Environment – from object to becoming

The Anthropocene condition haunts academic demarcations. Disciplinary fault lines in the study of nature and culture, dating back to the Renaissance and Early Modern periods, have begun to dissolve. The *nature* that natural scientists study is permeated by human interventions. That is the very essence of the Anthropocene idea: nature is no longer an independent variable; it is part of what humans have already altered. Hence it holds an *added agency*, derived from the human intervention. The *culture* that social scientists study is increasingly subject to added agencies, affordances, and histories of non-human elements. As more scholars begin discussing how to revise the "safe operating space" of the planetary boundaries, it becomes apparent that previous separations of knowledge no longer work. The ontology has changed, the epistemology has to change, too.

One indication of this is that foundational concepts like "the environment", which has a long history, have begun to destabilize. Nature, we might say, already for a long time was not what it used to be. That we are "after nature" and that humans produce "new natures" have been themes in scholarly debates for a couple of decades.[7] A pioneering statement pointing in that direction can be found as far back as in Roland Barthes' *Mythologies* (1957): "Progressive humanism...must always remember to reverse the terms ... constantly to scour nature, its 'laws' and its 'limits' in order to discover History there, and at last to establish Nature itself as historical".[8]

The important word here is "historical". After centuries of work to separate history from nature – once belonging together in the concept *historia naturalis*, used by Pliny the elder in the first century AD – here the two are reassembled again.[9] The culmination of the separation process was reached in the work of R. G. Collingwood, whose *The Idea of History* (posthumous 1946) located history squarely within the human. Only humans had intentionality and agency was therefore exclusive to them. History hence was a history of *actions*, requiring agency. Nature, lacking agency, could only display series of *events*, and therefore could not have history.[10]

Since the late 1950s – Barthes was an early proponent – history, along with the humanities at large, increased its opposition to Collingwood and only gained in "naturalness", although it did so in a non-linear fashion and with considerable differences among disciplines. Environmental history and environmental archaeology formed as sub-fields around 1970. Similar developments occurred in philosophy, sociology, anthropology, in comparative literature with eco-criticism, and in many others. This was a process over several decades still ongoing at the millennium and into the new century. What is pertinent here is that ascribing agency to the non-human emerged only gradually in this process, partly blocked by the growing awareness that nature is increasingly permeated by human action. This latter view had been heralded in the seminal Man's Role in Changing the Face of the Earth conference in Princeton 1955, where some of the foremost luminaries across the natural and social sciences had gathered to take on this grand subject of rising importance. But despite a week-long cavalcade of contributions from more than seventy scholars the analysis rarely left the dualist paradigm. Changing the face of the Earth did not question the ontological status of the Earth as a category fundamentally separate from "Man" or humanity.[11]

A similar conceptual devolution that had already happened to "nature" was now happening to "environment". In fact, establishing "the environment" in the immediate post-World War II years was a major step toward the acknowledgment of the formation of a nature-as-social, i.e., becoming part of the domain of the human.[12] The environment came up as an integrative concept for the increasingly entangled interventions and transformations that humans and their societies wrought on the Earth as a systemic, biogeophysical entity on all scales from the sub-atomic to the macro-spheric (hydrosphere, atmosphere, biosphere, cryosphere, the less common ecosphere,[13] and so on). The transformative moment in this new phase of environmental understanding was embedded in the language of Earth System Science that formed as an institutionalized epistemic community, and as a conceptual innovation, in the 1980s and grew in significance in the following decades, playing a seminal role in the launching of the Anthropocene and the accompanying concept "the Great Acceleration" in the first years of the 2000s.[14]

Historiographical debates and the actual writing of history now focus increasingly on how human societies are part of shaping environments and over time also on ideas about what constitutes "the environment" in the first place and how history "could deal with the non-human part of history".[15] Evidently, environment is not just another word for "nature". It appears to be less a thing and more of a process – turning gradually from fixed object, *environment*, to that which is becoming, through *environing*.[16]

Environing as relational agency

It is as part of these conceptual and epistemic transitions from nouns to verbs – making, becoming, environing that media are recognized as crucial, not only for conducting environmental studies but also for the very notion of what the environment is becoming.

To understand the convergence between environing and media, it may be useful to briefly revisit the modern history of the concept of the environment, and how it has co-evolved with a conceptual expansion of "media". "Environ" migrated as a verb from French to English in the late Middle Ages. The original meaning was "to form a ring around, to surround".[17] Environment would thus be more related to *human action* than to nature itself, and it would expand with human presence and action. So, first is the verb. Then there is the notion of a space, which is encompassed by the environing. In a third instance an agency would be assumed that could be ascribed to this space itself, as a certain property of it. This property could be described as a formative external condition, an idea with deep roots in Antiquity, especially based on Hippocrates' *Airs, Waters, Places* (3rd c. BC), applied by Herbert Spencer in his *On Psychology* (1855) as a creative influence. Later with distinct, perhaps inevitable consequence another strand of the same idea developed into environmental determinism, in particular among geographical and geopolitical authors underpinning racism and imperialism.[18]

The range of the term "environment" grew as it was referring in the first half of the 20th century to influences of climate, place, landscape, or more generally of living conditions, on entire societies and cultures but also on individual people, for examples writers and artists. But it wasn't until after World War II that the concept took on its current meaning of an object, *something* out there, a distinct noun with a set of properties that were defined as a panorama of phenomena for which human agency was responsible but yet also possessed an agency of its own in causing disturbances and concern for humans. In other words, a reciprocal environment, shaped and often domesticated by humans, but capable of a response – or even revenge – of its own. This 180-degree shift of the environment from a quite unspecified psychological influence toward becoming a mighty outside object with added agency derived from the human was a conceptual transformation that helped draw humans into an interventional, relational, and mutually agential position in a wider human-Earth relationship.

This outside category, the environment, was an act of intellectual creation. The outside world was not drastically changed, or rather, that change was always there and ongoing, gradually transforming the natural world. If it wasn't named and ascribed a set of properties, especially its capacity to change in certain directions and at a particular rate of change, "the environment" would not exist. Once it was named and quantified it could be ascribed an agential role, *becoming* many things it hadn't been before: something vulnerable, an indicator of societal morale, a source of risk, something that could strike back, something cherished that needed to be conserved for wise use, or even preserved for posterity. In some respects these were roles previously ascribed for "nature", but with the difference that "the environment" was a concept that could much more readily absorb agency and reduce its naturalness, always a hybrid of the human and the natural.

The environment now possessed qualities that could be measured scientifically to determine its rates and directions of change – toward decline, disaster? It started to fill up with growing strands of expertise that proposed to be able to talk with insight about it, define its health, save it, propose policies for it, and organize conferences on its behalf. It was a revolution of the mind, and one that made further transformations of "Earth" and "planetary" into agential objects possible. Environment was, metaphorically speaking, the heart-lung barrier of the human-Earth relationship. And it was broken, we can see now more than 70 years later, just in the moment when the Great Acceleration began its onset around the middle of the 20th century. This turn in the meaning of environment corresponded to developments of terms like "climate" and "ecology" that conceptualized natural phenomena and systemically connected with elements of the life worlds of humans. Ecological thinking linked nature and society, for example, with regard to Malthusian dilemmas of population growth, economic development, and industrial pollution. Yet, environment held the overarching, integrative function. The other concepts became dimensions of environment, not the other way around.[19]

Environing media infrastructures

With the passing of World War II, ideas about the environment converged with geopolitical realities and the emergence of scientific institutions and international collaborations of researchers such as the International Geophysical Year 1957/1958 and rapid expansion in fields such as oceanography and geophysics. These organizations and their priorities assisted the build-up of integrative concepts and a common globality of anything from nuclear fallout, ocean currents, and an emerging understanding of anthropogenic climate change through the spread of greenhouse gases.[20] Technological advances and the application of machine computing for anything from numerical weather prediction to population dynamics to ecological systems spurred integration of the environment into a wide range of epistemic communities. Computing also underwrote the presumption that the environment had systemic properties that could be depicted using a common mathematical language, which enabled scaling from the local to the global.[21] The spoken language still lacked concepts for many of these large-scale objects, for which we now have found several expressions, such as environmental objects, knowledge objects, governable objects, hyperobjects, or more-than-human realms. These and other distinctions all speak to an ever more qualified and penetrated relational zone of environing.[22]

The collection and processing of quantitative data to make the environment "legible" in James C. Scott's terminology, and hence governable,[23] was a history of reciprocal shaping between Cold War politics, technological advances, and scientific innovations that in turn gave rise to new data processing expertise. The US and Soviet military both launched research programs on oceans, atmosphere, and geophysical conditions, stretching vertically from the seafloor to the stratosphere and horizontally to extreme environments that required special knowledge and equipment for survival.[24] This processed data was of strategic importance for the performance in war, but also added to knowledge, awareness, and what was to become a widespread concern for the environment and activism on its behalf.

The planetary understanding drew heavily on previously military infrastructures of monitoring, in particular orbital satellites and the overviews these enabled of the globe. The extent of ice sheets could be monitored, and changes be traced, month by month to eventually provide records of changes in ice cover spanning decades.[25] These institutional, international, and infrastructural developments suggest that the environment was envisioned and imagined as a networked planet of entangled, interconnected biochemical and geophysical systems of which humans were embedded parts, not external subjective agencies. So, the system-oriented sciences helped undermine Collingwood's dualism. Nature had agency because humans had intervened in it with multiple "environing technologies", literally making it. Media were a significant part of these technologies.

Resulting from the postwar decades of new data processing techniques and massive data collection was the formation of a community of *Earth system science* that made large-scale quantification of environmental phenomena and their aggregation into systemic models their signature project. We may call this growing instrumental arsenal for monitoring and analysis an environing media infrastructure without which the Earth system could not be determined as an empirical phenomenon.[26] The environing media infrastructure and the Earth system theory in alliance owned a remarkable defining power. Coalescing in earnest in the 1980s the Earth system science community also enrolled the systemic approaches of the biological and geological sciences, and could extend into strands of archaeology. They increasingly trusted numbers for modeling, for translating management into crisis frameworks, and for measuring the value of nature *qua* species or ecosystems, sometimes including translating them into monetary terms to allow for market-based forms of governance.[27] A similar fusion came with climate science, which from the 1980s onward began to move from the strategic and security sphere into public environmental discourse. This greening of climate – if I may call it that – is a major example of the capacity of "environment" to serve an integrative function and absorb new knowledge and issue areas.[28]

While the power of the environment in Earth System Science promised problem resolution by science, various groups began to mobilize it for a variety of political causes. The "Earth" of Earth System Science came across ever more clearly as a unit, an environment of environments that could, first of all, be understood as a system and also required management on multiple, including very large, scales. The world of politics and societies, however, was not a system. In parallel to international environmental governance emerged more conflicting perspectives from grass-root initiatives, activists, and non-governmental organizations that would demand a growing presence at environmental conferences. Ideas of environmental justice, the dilemmas of development, and the distribution of responsibility became familiar and entrenched aspects of environmental debates. The United Nations conference on "the human environment" in 1972 attracted a plethora of activist resistance, including a parallel conference in Stockholm called the People's forum and a counter-information press center distributing leaflets headed "Don't trust the UN conference".[29] It was not until the Rio "Earth" Summit of 1992, however, that these formed part of the growing array of actors involved in conference proceedings. The inability of international environmental conferences to deliver political consensus or binding agreements gave these non-governmental organizations a central role in promoting action and local implementation of policies.[30]

At present, the concept of the environment is being eclipsed by other terms, like the Anthropocene or resilience that further emphasize a crisis urgency in the human-Earth relationship. The means and methods of Earth System Science for enumerating, visualizing, and assessing the environment have continued to develop and the infrastructure is more complex than ever. The debate around the Anthropocene indicates that environmental concepts do not lead to closure of debates, nor the dominance of certain groups; rather, it becomes a fault line where rupture emerges and generates creativity and contestation.

The great synchronization – historicizing geo-anthropology

Previous attempts to define what environmental history does were looking at conventional "history" timescales. The interdisciplinary ambitions focused mainly on a thematic, or perhaps better epistemic, hierarchy. For a long time this was productive. Donald Worster identified three strands of work: first, studies of "nature itself"; second, studies of socio-economic interactions between humans and nature; and, third, studies of human thinking about nature. These attempts resulted in numerous synthetic works to make the environment central to history writing, similar to how gender gained significance in mainstream history, as well as case studies that served to bridge environmental history with other disciplines.[31]

The past few decades have seen the emergence of explicitly environmental humanities. Pioneering work was done in Australia, where anthropologists, historians, philosophers, and eco-critical literary scholars, among others, came together to form the field in the late 1990s and the early 2000s. The regular crossing of disciplinary boundaries has resulted in a new identity of these studies as belonging to a knowledge-production whose catch-all phrase is environmental humanities, but that also includes collaborations with arts, sciences, and communicative practices and cross-cutting ways of teaching."[32]

From the early 2000s onward, therefore, humanities scholars have become increasingly involved in expanding the breadth and depth of Earth system science models. These attempts at "big history" help account for human agency, politics, and experience not only in different present-day societies but also those of the past.[33] There are two significant aspects of this emerging historiography. The first is how it expands to include the multiple timescales of the human-Earth relationship. Historiography, traditionally confined to the period of written sources, has discovered the agency acquired by the environment. It has also started, very recently, to take into account "the Earth" in the sense of an Anthropocene ontology. Scientists have been leading the way in this as yet only emerging turn of history, but several historians have followed. Hence, the second main feature of what we may call the new Earth history is that its work is performed both by historians and other practitioners of environmental humanities (geo-humanities, climate humanities, and others), and Earth system scientists, co-exploring new ways of linking past, present, and future, with temporalization, and perhaps especially synchronization of timescales – the rates of change derived from "the environment" – as one of its main features.[34]

This work now brings together different disciplinary strands into a coherent narrative of planetary times, a work that might be called the "Great Synchronization", as a deliberate parallel to the Great Acceleration which is the planetary phenomenon that releases the multiplicity of times that meet in our extended present. Synchronization does not mean putting on the same time in the literal sense; bacterial time of hundreds of millions of years has little to do with the timescales of nuclear fallout or historical revolutions. It is the multiple co-existing times of the Earth System that are becoming a matter of acute concern in the Anthropocene, just as the multiple times of the pre-Holocene world was a concern to philosophies of history in the transition to modernity. The synchronization work conducted by Helge, Herder, and other philosophers of time in the early phases of industrial modernity paved the way for the global world of a common humanity, chiefly an accomplishment of humanist anthropology.[35]

The Great Synchronization can be described as an ongoing timekeeping work of geo-anthropology.[36] During the last ten years, work in the environmental humanities has served to enable an understanding of the Anthropocene that accounts for the role our species collectively have in shifting the geological rules of the planet while at the same time differentiating responsibilities within the human species. In turn, humanists have had to account for no longer having a clear distinction between human history and natural history. In the Anthropocene, humanity disrupts evolutionary and geological timescales, creating for example the compressed timescales of planetary boundaries and carbon budgets, which in turn are devices for action and rescue in the necessary societal transformation in the face of environmental and climate crisis. Societal transformations on the other hand are conditioned by the laws and norms that guide our societies, the large majority of which were conceived without the slightest knowledge about the human-Earth relationship we have now created. The conclusion I can draw is that this predicament requires a deeper reflexivity and an increased complexity of ideas and perspectives. Seeing this predicament clearly can also bring a sense of realism back to our work for the environment.

Environing – beginnings and ends

In our present time the concept of "environment" appears, once again, less as a thing and more as a process of "environing", resembling the Early Modern beginnings of the concept. Like media, environing is formative in both the material and the immaterial domains. The environment is therefore not only the material world "out there" that human activities impact on. The environment also signifies *the knowledge-based representation of the material world in which humans and their actions are entangled*. Hence, environing consists of processes whereby environments appear as historical products, and technologies and media as the tools required for the environing to take place. Consider the copious diversity of distinct features of the environment, from the sub-atomic to the planetary. How would we understand them as a relational entity without the word "environment"? It is the work of environing that turns these features, from rivers to birds, from fungi to soils – or, *Airs, Waters, Places*, in Hippocrates' gracefully inclusive shorthand – into environment as we know it.[37] How can this be? This needs to be acknowledged as a fundamental question about the current human condition.

Essential elements of environing are conceptual (new words), theoretical (new ideas of understanding), visual (new representations), and empirical (based on new data), but even these elements require technologies in turn. Several of these are embodied in media like instruments, storing facilities, technologies of observation, monitoring, collection, calculation, presentation, and multiple others. Importantly, they comprise both environing through perception and understanding and environing through physical changes in nature (terraforming practices). Practice and understanding co-evolve, as so often in the history of knowledge.[38]

Environing that involves physical changes include, for example, technologies related to herding, forestry, irrigation, fishing, or the release of carbon dioxide into the atmosphere. This is also the kinds of technologies that played a key role in pre-industrial agriculture and the ordering and control of land close to the household or village.[39] In Antiquity, we would find architectural constructions like aqueducts, dams, and roads forming cities and landscapes, and in modern times technologies have proven essential in holding empires together and even shaping entire continents, as George Perkins Marsh described in his classic *Man and Nature* (1864), a book almost entirely about physical environing, without ever using the word.[40] Environing *indirectly* altering nature exists in forms such as sensing (seeing, feeling, hearing, smelling), typically aided by technologies and instruments. Often these technologies are connected to writing, as documenting is intrinsic to many activities, and the numerous media and technologies that perform such work. In the category of conceptual environing, we may also put media and technologies involved in painting and photography, measurements, regulations on how to use nature and its resources, economic theory applied to nature – from eco-system services to fishing quotas and estimations of uranium ore assets. Environing media are in this respect crucial for finding things out: first, what the environment is; second, how it became that way; and, third, how to (re-)shape it.

One could say that environing media concern how the human senses perceive and transform impressions of, and data from, the world and turn them into intelligible constructs. These are deeply human, generic activities, common to all human communities, although practiced in very different ways. Some pursue them actively, even professionally. At the same time, we are as humans recipients of the results of these environing activities, insofar as the understanding of environment is in constant flux just as the materially shaped environment is also undergoing ceaseless change. As such, in a fundamental way all humans are environing co-creators of environment. This sounds a noble position to occupy in the world, and for a long time it was how it was chiefly considered, at least in the Western world. To change the face of the Earth was, ultimately, to act on behalf of God. Now it is no longer quite as noble.

The natural world is, in history, being turned through environing into a societal object with the capacity to speak directly to the organization of human knowledge. This process has accelerated enormously since the onset of the industrial revolution and especially since the middle of the 20th century (again: the Great Acceleration). It provides ever more evidence to question the Renaissance dualism between the natural world and the world of culture and suggests instead an interactive, fully mutual human-Earth relationship.

The shift toward environing in environmental history and the wider humanities is congruent with a growing interest for the role of media, and mediation, in the processes of social change. It is in earnest only during the last couple of decades that environmental historians have subjected "the environment" to social theory. Rather than holding nature at a distance, as a thing that can be observed, tamed, or destroyed, the very process of knowing nature – the mediation – is increasingly recognized as part of its making. The importance of media for environment is that they are *significant* with regard to other problems that can be described as political, social, or cultural. For a long time this fundamental dimension of environment was under-theorized in environmental historiography.[41] This is now changing.

The development of super-complex causal chains and the capability of human societies to make, although not control, impacts of planetary dimensions have made absolute distinctions between "human" and "planet" (or even "nature") increasingly untenable. Using an articulation already more than 15 years old:

> The very notion of 'the environment,' as compared to 'nature,' signals a more deep-lying transition. The environment, which seems to be no more than an independent parameter of human existence, actually is its opposite: nature as thoroughly transformed by human intervention. We begin to speak about 'the environment' only once nature, like tradition, has become dissolved.[42]

This seems now a long time ago, and the words (by Paul Warde and myself in 2007) echo the mere beginning of a movement that has taken us a long way into an understanding of "environment" that is ongoing, constantly becoming, and ever more included in the realm of the social and the political. Theorizing the role of technology and knowledge in the environing has been first steps. Environing media in this respect signal a welcome additional unpacking of environment to a wider range of meanings than previously were possible.

The shift from environment to environing and to technologies, including media, that we environ with is a theoretically congruent but quite recent event. It therefore falls upon a number of scholars to trace their interrelationships as part of the aggregated project of renegotiating the human-Earth relationship. To do so will engage the processes of becoming and synchronizing in which media are an essential tool, from the CO_2 detector on the mountain to the buoys in the ocean to the carnival of the streets called Extinction Rebellion or Fridays for Future, represented in mediated narratives.[43] From the Anthropocene viewpoint, they are practices of geo-anthropology making environment.

Notes

1 Frank Biermann & Rakhyun E. Kim, "The Boundaries of the Planetary Boundary Framework: A Critical Appraisal of Approaches to Define a 'Safe Operating Space' for Humanity," *Annual Review of Environment and Resources* 45, no. 1 (2020): 497–521. Jonathan Pickering & Åsa Persson, "Democratising Planetary Boundaries: Experts, Social Values and Deliberative Risk Evaluation in Earth System Governance," *Journal of Environmental Policy & Planning* 22, no. 1 (2020): 59–71.

2 Leah Aronowsky, *The Planet as Self-Regulating System: Configuring the Biosphere as an Object of Knowledge, 1940–1990*, PhD dissertation (Harvard University, mimeo, 2018); Dipesh Chakrabarty, "The Planet: An Emergent Humanist Category," *Critical Inquiry* 46 (September 2019); Sverker Sörlin, "Reform and Responsibility – The Climate of History in Times of Transformation," *Historisk tidskrift* (Oslo) 97 (2018): 1, sections "Who are the architects of time?" and "Social interpretations of the planetary," on 10–15.

3 Bruno Latour and Tim Lenton have discussed these properties focusing especially on the earth's "critical zone" of exchange between quaternary geological strata, productive soils, the human cultural layer, and the atmosphere. See Latour & Lenton, "Extending the Domain of Freedom, or Why Gaia Is So Hard to Understand," *Critical Inquiry* 45 (Spring 2019): 659–680; W. B. Gallie, "Essentially Contested Concepts," *Proceedings of the Aristotelian Society* 56, no. 1 (1956): 167–198. Martin Mahony, "Geographies of Science and Technology II: In the Critical Zone," *Progress in Human Geography* 46, no. 2 (2022): 705–715.

4 Will Steffen, Katherine Richardson, Johan Rockström, Sarah E. Cornell, Ingo Fetzer, E. M. Bennett, Reinette Biggs, Stephen R. Carpenter, Wim de Vries, Cynthia A. de Wit, Carl Folke, Dieter Gerten, Jens Heinke, Georgina M. Mace, Veerabhadran Ramanathan, Belinda Reyers, & Sverker Sörlin, "Planetary Boundaries: Guiding Human Development on a Changing Planet," *Science* 347, no. 6233 (2015): 736–746, on 742.

5 Theodore M. Porter, *Trust in Numbers: The Pursuit of Objectivity in Science and Public Life* (Princeton: Princeton University Press, 1995).

6 Sverker Sörlin & Nina Wormbs, "Environing Technologies: A Theory of Making Environment," *History & Technology* 34, no. 2 (2018): 101–125.

7 Dolly Jørgensen, Finn Arne Jørgensen & Sara B. Pritchard, eds., *New Natures: Joining Environmental History with Science and Technology Studies* (Pittsburgh: University of Pittsburgh Press, 2013); Jedediah Purdy, *After Nature: A Politics for the Anthropocene* (Cambridge, MA: Harvard University Press, 2015).
8 Roland Barthes, *Mythologies* (1957), trans. Annette Lavers (1972), new ed., 25th printing (New York: The Noonday Press, 1991), 101.
9 We may note that Clarence Glacken, in *Traces on the Rhodian Shore: Nature and Culture in Western Thought from Ancient Times to the End of the Eighteenth Century* (Berkeley, CA: University of California Press, 1967), discussed Pliny's work in a chapter entitled "Creating a Second Nature" (esp. on 130, 137), reminding us that a human-made, historical nature was a theme already in Antiquity.
10 Robin George Collingwood, *The Idea of History* (1946), new ed., *The Idea of History: With Lectures 1926–1928* (Oxford: Oxford University Press, 1993).
11 William L. Thomas Jr., ed., *Man's Role in Changing the Face of the Earth* (Chicago & London: The University of Chicago Press, 1956).
12 Paul Warde, Libby Robin & Sverker Sörlin, *The Environment – A History of the Idea* (Baltimore, MD: Johns Hopkins University Press, 2018).
13 C. LaMont Cole, "The Ecosphere," *Scientific American* 198, no. 4 (1958): 83–92; Sabine Höhler, "Ecospheres: Model and Laboratory for Earth's Environment," *Technosphere Magazine*. Dossier: "Spheres." (Berlin: Haus der Kulturen der Welt, June 2018).
14 W. Steffen, W. Broadgate, L. Deutsch, O. Gaffney, & C. Ludwig, "The Trajectory of the Anthropocene: The Great Acceleration," *The Anthropocene Review* 2 (2015): 81–98; R. Costanza, L. Graumlich, & W. Steffen, eds., *Sustainability or Collapse: An Integrated History and Future of People on Earth* (Cambridge, MA: MIT Press, 2007); W. Steffen, K. Richardson, J. Rockström, et al. "The Emergence and Evolution of Earth System Science," *Nature Reviews Earth & Environment* 1 (2020): 54–63.
15 One example of several: Grégory Quenet, "L'Anthropocène et le temps des historiens," *Annales: Histoire, Sciences Sociales* 72, no. 2 (2017): 267–299. Idem, "Environmental History," *Debating New Approaches to History*, eds. Peter Burke & Marek Tamm (London: Bloomsbury, 2018), 75–86, 93–100 (references), on 75.
16 Sörlin & Wormbs, "Environing Technologies".
17 Paul Warde, "The Environment," *Local Places, Global Processes*, eds. P. Coates, D. Moon, & P. Warde (Oxford: Windgather Press, 2016), 32–46; Vin Nardizzi, "Environ," *Veer Ecology: A Companion for Environmental Thinking*, eds. Jeffrey Jerome Cohen & Lowell Duckert (Minneapolis: University of Minnesota Press, 2017), 183–195.
18 E.g., Ellen Churchill Semple, *Influences of Geographic Environment: On the Basis of Ratzel's System of Anthropo-Geography* (New York: Henry Holt; London: Constable, 1911); Ellsworth Huntington, *Civilization and Climate* (New Haven, CT: Yale University Press, 1915). On Spencer, see Warde, "The Environment".
19 Warde, Robin & Sörlin, chapters 1 and 2.
20 Joseph Masco, "Bad Weather: On Planetary Crisis," *Social Studies of Science* 40, no. 1 (2010): 3–30. Idem, "The Age of Fallout," *History of the Present* 5 (2015): 137–168; James R. Fleming, *Inventing Atmospheric Science: Bjerknes, Rossby, Wexler, and the Foundations of Modern Meteorology* (Cambridge, MA: The MIT Press, 2016). Naomi Oreskes, *Science on a Mission: How Military Funding Shaped What We Do and Don't Know about the Ocean* (Chicago & London: The University of Chicago Press, 2021). On the role of the oceans for climate, see Bert Bolin & Erik Eriksson, "Distribution of Matter in the Sea and in the Atmosphere: Changes in the Carbon Dioxide Content of the Atmosphere and Sea due to Fossil Fuel Combustion," *The Atmosphere and the Sea in Motion*, ed. Bert Bolin (New York: The Rockefeller University Press, 1958). Charles H. Langmuir & Wally Broecker, *How to Build a Habitable Planet: The Story of Earth from the Big Bang to Humankind* (Princeton: Princeton University Press, 2012).
21 Alan A. Needell, *Science, Cold War and the American State: Lloyd V. Berkner and the Balance of Professional Ideals* (Amsterdam: Harwood Academic Publishers, 2000); Ronald

Doel, "Constituting the Postwar Earth Sciences: The Military's Influence on the Environmental Sciences in the USA after 1945," *Social Studies of Science* 33 (2003): 635–666; Jacob Darwin Hamblin, *Arming Mother Nature: The Birth of Catastrophic Environmentalism* (New York: Oxford University Press, 2013).

22 Aronowsky, *The Planet*; Timothy Morton, *Hyperobjects: Philosophy and Ecology after the End of the World* (Minneapolis: University of Minnesota Press, 2013). Mahony, "Geographies", on 3 ("more-than-human realms").

23 James C. Scott, *Seeing Like a State: How Certain Schemes to Improve the Human Condition Have Failed* (New Haven, CT: Yale University Press, 1998).

24 Kristine Harper, *Weather by the Numbers: The Genesis of Modern Meteorology* (Cambridge, MA: MIT Press, 2008). Idem, *Make It Rain: State Control of the Atmosphere in Twentieth-Century America* (Chicago & London: The University of Chicago Press, 2017). On the role of computing, especially for climate monitoring and modeling, see Paul N. Edwards, *A Vast Machine: Computer Models, Climate Data, and the Politics of Global Warming* (Cambridge, MA: MIT Press, 2010).

25 Nina Wormbs, "Eyes on the Ice: Satellite Remote Sensing and the Narratives of Visualized Data," *Media and the Politics of Arctic Climate Change: When the Ice Breaks*, eds. Miyase Christensen, Annika Nilsson, & Nina Wormbs (New York: Palgrave Macmillan, 2013), 52–69.

26 "Environing media infrastructure" builds on previous conceptualizations of media infrastructure by John Durham Peters, *The Marvelous Clouds: Toward a Philosophy of Elemental Media* (Chicago & London: The University of Chicago Press, 2015); Nicole Starosielski, *The Undersea Network* (Durham, NC & London: Duke University Press, 2015); and Nicole Starosielski & Lisa Parks, eds., *Signal Traffic: Critical Studies of Media Infrastructures* (Urbana Champaign, IL: University of Illinois Press, 2015).

27 Gretchen Daily, ed. *Nature's Services: Societal Dependence on Natural Ecosystems* (Washington, DC: Island Press, 1997); Robert Costanza, Ralph d'Arge, Rudolf de Groot, Stephen Farber, Monica Grasso, Bruce Hannon, Karin Limburg, et al., "The Value of the World's Ecosystem Services and Natural Capital," *Nature* 387 (15 May 1997): 253–260. A critical discussion of the concept and especially its policy implications in Henrik Ernstson & Sverker Sörlin, "Ecosystem Services as Technology of Globalization: On Articulating Values in Urban Nature," *Ecological Economics* 86 (2013): 273–284.

28 Warde, Robin & Sörlin *The Environment*, ch. 5. The chapter presents the transition of "climate" from weather prediction and several military applications to our contemporary environmental problem of runaway anthropogenic climate change.

29 Eric Paglia, "The Swedish Initiative and the 1972 Stockholm Conference: The Decisive Role of Science Diplomacy in the Emergence of Global Environmental Governance," *Humanities and Social Sciences Communications* 8 (2021): 2. Felicity Scott, *Outlaw Territories: Environments of Insurgency/Architectures of Counterinsurgency* (New York: Zone Books, 2016).

30 Stephen Macekura, *Of Limits and Growth: The Rise of Global Sustainable Development in the Twentieth Century* (New York: Cambridge University Press, 2015); Ken Conca, *An Unfinished Foundation: The United Nations and Global Environmental Governance* (New York: Oxford University Press, 2015); William Kaiser & Jan-Henrik Meyer, eds., *International Organizations and Environmental Protection: Conservation and Globalization in the Twentieth Century* (New York/Oxford: Berghahn Books, 2017).

31 Donald Worster, "Doing Environmental History," *The Ends of the Earth: Perspectives on Modern Environmental History*, ed. D. Worster (New York: Cambridge University Press, 1988), 289–308.

32 David S. Emmett & Robert E. Nye, *The Environmental Humanities: A Critical Introduction* (Cambridge, MA: MIT Press, 2017). Ursula K. Heise, Jon Christensen, & Michelle Niemann, eds., *The Routledge Companion to the Environmental Humanities* (London: Routledge, 2017). Emily O'Gorman, Thom van Dooren, Ursula Münster

et al., "Teaching the Environmental Humanities: A Global Overview and Discussion," *International Journal of Environmental Humanities* 11 (2019): 427–460.
33 David Christian, *Maps of Time: An Introduction to Big History* (Berkeley: University of California Press, 2004).
34 The theme is recurrent in many of the contributions to Anders Ekström & Staffan Bergwik, eds., *Times of History, Times of Nature: Temporalization and the Limits of Modern Knowledge* (New York: Berghahn, 2022). See also Sverker Sörlin & Erik Isberg, "Synchronizing Earthly Timescales: Ice, Pollen, and the Making of Proto-Anthropocene Knowledge in the North-Atlantic Region". *Annals of the American Association of Geographers* 111 (2021): 3, 717–728, and Erik Isberg's contribution to the present volume, "Timing the Ocean Floor: Environing Media and the Swedish Deep-Sea Expedition (1947–1948)".
35 Helge Jordheim, "Introduction: Multiple Times and the Work of Synchronization," *History and Theory* 53, no. 4 (2014): 498–518.
36 The term itself had some, limited previous circulation as a name for the interface of the geological and archaeological sciences, as in J. P. Barker & J. M. Barker, "Geoanthropology," an entry in *General Geology: Encyclopedia of Earth Science* (Boston, MA: Springer, 1988). It has been rekindled in the Anthropocene search for integrative science-humanities approaches to the human-earth relationship. Jürgen Renn & Christoph Rosol, eds., *Towards a Max Planck Institute for Geoanthropology*, Max Planck Institute für Wissenschaftsgeschichte [draft version] (Berlin: Max Planck Institut für Wissenschaftsgeschichte, 2020).
37 Sörlin & Wormbs, "Environing Technologies."
38 Lissa L. Roberts, Simon Schaffer, & Peter Dear, eds. *The Mindful Hand: Inquiry and Invention from the Late Renaissance to Early Industrialisation* (Amsterdam: Koninklijke Nederlandse Akademie van Wetenschappen, 2007).
39 Paul Warde, "The Environmental History of Pre-Industrial Agriculture in Europe." *Nature's End: History and the Environment*, eds. Sverker Sörlin & Paul Warde (Houndmills, Basingstoke: Palgrave Macmillan, 2009), 70–92.
40 From a rich literature, e.g., Daniel R. Headrick, *The Tools of Empire: Technology and European Imperialism in the Nineteenth Century* (Oxford & New York: Oxford University Press, 1981). George Perkins Marsh, *Man and Nature: Or, Physical Geography as Modified by Human Action* (London: Murray, 1864).
41 Sverker Sörlin & Paul Warde, "The Problem of the Problem of Environmental History: A Re-reading of the Field and Its Purpose," *Environmental History* 12 (2007): 1, 107–130, on 111, 118.
42 Sörlin & Warde, "The Problem."
43 Miyase Christensen, Anna Åberg, Susanna Lidström, & Katarina Larsen, "Environmental Themes in Popular Narratives," *Environmental Communication* 12 (2018): 1, 1–6.

References

Aronowsky, Leah. *The Planet as Self-Regulating System: Configuring the Biosphere as an Object of Knowledge, 1940–1990*. PhD dissertation. Harvard University, mimeo, 2018.
Barker, James. , & James. M. Barker. "Geoanthropology." *General Geology: Encyclopedia of Earth Science*. Series editor: Charles W. Finkl. Boston, MA: Springer, 1988.
Barthes, Roland. *Mythologies* (1957), trans. Annette Lavers (1972), new ed., 25th printing. New York: The Noonday Press, 1991.
Biermann, Frank, & Rakhyun E. Kim. "The Boundaries of the Planetary Boundary Framework: A Critical Appraisal of Approaches to Define a 'Safe Operating Space' for Humanity." *Annual Review of Environment and Resources* 45, no. 1 (2020): 497–521.
Bolin, Bert & Erik Eriksson. "Distribution of Matter in the Sea and Atmosphere: Changes in the Carbon Dioxide Content of the Atmosphere and Sea due to Fossil

Fuel Combustion." *The Atmosphere and the Sea in Motion*, ed. Bert Bolin, 130–142. New York: The Rockefeller University Press, 1958.

Chakrabarty, Dipesh. "The Planet: An Emergent Humanist Category." *Critical Inquiry* 46 (September 2019).

Christensen, Miyase, Anna Åberg, Susanna Lidström, & Katarina Larsen. "Environmental Themes in Popular Narratives." *Environmental Communication* 12 (2018): 1–6.

Christian, David. *Maps of Time: An Introduction to Big History*. Berkeley, CA: University of California Press, 2004.

Churchill Semple, Ellen. *Influences of Geographic Environment: On the Basis of Ratzel's System of Anthropo-Geography*. New York: Henry Holt; London: Constable, 1911.

Collingwood, Robin George. *The Idea of History* (1946), new ed., *The Idea of History: With Lectures 1926–1928*. Oxford: Oxford University Press, 1993.

Conca, Ken. *An Unfinished Foundation: The United Nations and Global Environmental Governance*. New York: Oxford University Press, 2015.

Costanza, Robert, Ralph d'Arge, Rudolf de Groot, Stephen Farber, Monica Grasso, Bruce Hannon, Karin Limburg, et al. "The Value of the World's Ecosystem Services and Natural Capital." *Nature* 387 (15 May 1997): 253–260.

Costanza, Robert, Lisa Graumlich, & Will Steffen, eds. *Sustainability or Collapse: An Integrated History and Future of People on Earth*. Cambridge, MA: The MIT Press, 2007.

Daily, Gretchen, ed. *Nature's Services: Societal Dependence on Natural Ecosystems*. Washington, DC: Island Press, 1997.

Doel, Ronald. "Constituting the Postwar Earth Sciences: The Military's Influence on the Environmental Sciences in the USA after 1945." *Social Studies of Science* 33 (2003): 635–666.

Edwards, Paul N. *A Vast Machine: Computer Models, Climate Data, and the Politics of Global Warming*. Cambridge, MA: The MIT Press, 2010.

Ekström, Anders, & Staffan Bergwik, eds. *Times of History, Times of Nature: Temporalization and the Limits of Modern Knowledge*. New York: Berghahn, 2022.

Emmett, David S., & Robert E. Nye. *The Environmental Humanities: A Critical Introduction*. Cambridge, MA: The MIT Press, 2017.

Ernstson, Henrik, & Sverker Sörlin. "Ecosystem Services as Technology of Globalization: On Articulating Values in Urban Nature." *Ecological Economics* 86 (2013): 273–284.

Fleming, James R. *Inventing Atmospheric Science: Bjerknes, Rossby, Wexler, and the Foundations of Modern Meteorology*. Cambridge, MA: The MIT Press, 2016.

Gallie, Walter Bryce. "Essentially Contested Concepts." *Proceedings of the Aristotelian Society*, New Series, 56 (1955–1956): 167–198.

Glacken, Clarence. *Traces on the Rhodian Shore: Nature and Culture in Western Thought from Ancient Times to the End of the Eighteenth Century*. Berkeley, CA: University of California Press, 1967.

Hamblin, Jacob Darwin. *Arming Mother Nature: The Birth of Catastrophic Environmentalism*. New York: Oxford University Press, 2013.

Harper, Kristine. *Make It Rain: State Control of the Atmosphere in Twentieth-Century America*. Chicago & London: The University of Chicago Press, 2017.

———. *Weather by the Numbers: The Genesis of Modern Meteorology*. Cambridge, MA: The MIT Press, 2008.

Headrick, Daniel R. *The Tools of Empire: Technology and European Imperialism in the Nineteenth Century*. Oxford & New York: Oxford University Press, 1981.

Heise, Ursula K., Jon Christensen, & Michelle Niemann, eds. *The Routledge Companion to the Environmental Humanities*. London: Routledge, 2017.

Höhler, Sabine. "Ecospheres: Model and Laboratory for Earth's Environment." *Technosphere Magazine*. Dossier: "Spheres." Berlin: Haus der Kulturen der Welt, June 2018.

Huntington, Ellsworth. *Civilization and Climate*. New Haven, CT: Yale University Press, 1915.

Isberg, Erik. "Timing the Ocean Floor: Environing Media and the Swedish Deep-Sea Expedition (1947–1948)." This volume.

Jordheim, Helge. "Introduction: Multiple Times and the Work of Synchronization." *History and Theory* 53, no. 4 (2014): 498–518.

Jørgensen, Dolly, Finn Arne Jørgensen, & Sara B. Pritchard (eds.). *New Natures: Joining Environmental History with Science and Technology Studies*. Pittsburgh: University of Pittsburgh Press, 2013.

Kaiser, Wolfram, & Jan-Henrik Meyer (eds.). *International Organizations and Environmental Protection: Conservation and Globalization in the Twentieth Century*. New York & Oxford: Berghahn Books, 2017.

LaMont Cole, C. "The Ecosphere." *Scientific American* 198, no. 4 (1958): 83–92.

Langmuir, Charles H., & Wally Broecker. *How to Build a Habitable Planet: The Story of Earth from the Big Bang to Humankind*. Princeton: Princeton University Press, 2012.

Latour, Bruno, & Tim Lenton. "Extending the Domain of Freedom, or Why Gaia Is So Hard to Understand." *Critical Inquiry* 45 (Spring 2019): 659–680.

Macekura, Stephen. *Of Limits and Growth: The Rise of Global Sustainable Development in the Twentieth Century*. New York: Cambridge University Press, 2015.

Mahony, Martin. "Geographies of Science and Technology II: In the Critical Zone." *Progress in Human Geography* 46, no. 2 (2022): 705–715.

Marsh, George Perkins. *Man and Nature: Or, Physical Geography as Modified by Human Action*. London: Murray, 1864.

Masco, Joseph. "The Age of Fallout." *History of the Present* 5 (2015): 137–168.

———. "Bad Weather: On Planetary Crisis." *Social Studies of Science* 40, no. 1 (2010): 3–30.

Morton, Timothy. *Hyperobjects: Philosophy and Ecology after the End of the World*. Minnneapolis: University of Minnesota Press, 2013.

Nardizzi, Vin. "Environ." *Veer Ecology: A Companion for Environmental Thinking*, edited by Jeffrey Jerome Cohen & Lowell Duckert, 183–195. Minneapolis: University of Minnesota Press, 2017.

Needell, Alan A. *Science, Cold War and the American State: Lloyd V. Berkner and the Balance of Professional Ideals*. Amsterdam: Harwood Academic Publishers, 2000.

O'Gorman, Emily, Thom van Dooren, Ursula Münster, et al. "Teaching the Environmental Humanities: A Global Overview and Discussion." *International Journal of Environmental Humanities* 11 (2019): 427–460.

Oreskes, Naomi. *Science on a Mission: How Military Funding Shaped What We Do and Don't Know About the Ocean*. Chicago & London: The University of Chicago Press, 2021.

Paglia, Eric. "The Swedish Initiative and the 1972 Stockholm Conference: The Decisive Role of Science Diplomacy in the Emergence of Global Environmental Governance." *Humanities and Social Sciences Communications* 8 (2021): 2.

Peters, John Durham. *The Marvelous Clouds: Toward a Philosophy of Elemental Media*. Chicago & London: The University of Chicago Press, 2015.

Pickering, Jonathan, & Åsa Persson. "Democratising Planetary Boundaries: Experts, Social Values and Deliberative Risk Evaluation in Earth system governance." *Journal of Environmental Policy & Planning* 22, no. 1 (2020): 59–71.

Porter, Theodore M. *Trust in Numbers: The Pursuit of Objectivity in Science and Public Life.* Princeton: Princeton University Press, 1995.
Purdy, Jedediah. *After Nature: A Politics for the Anthropocene.* Cambridge, MA: Harvard University Press, 2015.
Quenet, Grégory. "Environmental History." *Debating New Approaches to History*, edited by Peter Burke & Marek Tamm. London: Bloomsbury, 2018.
Quenet, Grégory. "L'Anthropocène et le temps des historiens." *Annales: Histoire, Sciences Sociales* 72, no. 2 (2017): 267–299.
Renn, Jürgen, & Christoph Rosol, eds. *Towards a Max Planck Institute for Geoanthropology.* Berlin: Max Planck Institut für Wissenschaftsgeschichte, 2020.
Roberts, Lissa L., Simon Schaffer, & Peter Dear, eds. *The Mindful Hand: Inquiry and Invention from the Late Renaissance to Early Industrialisation.* Amsterdam: Koninkliijke Nederlandse Akademie van Wetenschappen, 2007.
Scott, Felicity. *Outlaw Territories: Environments of Insurgency /Architectures of Counterinsurgency.* New York: Zone Books, 2016.
Scott, James C. *Seeing Like a State: How Certain Schemes to Improve the Human Condition Have Failed.* New Haven, CT: Yale University Press, 1998.
Sörlin, Sverker. "Reform and Responsibility – The Climate of History in Times of Transformation." *Historisk tidsskrift* (Oslo) 97, no. 1 (2018): 7–23.
Sörlin, Sverker, & Erik Isberg. "Synchronizing Earthly Timescales: Ice, Pollen, and the Making of Proto-Anthropocene Knowledge in the North-Atlantic Region." *Annals of the American Association of Geographers* 111, no. 3 (2021): 717–728.
Sörlin, Sverker, & Paul Warde. "The Problem of the Problem of Environmental History: A Re-reading of the Field and Its Purpose." *Environmental History* 12, no. 1 (2007): 107–130.
Sörlin, Sverker, & Nina Wormbs. "Environing Technologies: A Theory of Making Environment." *History & Technology* 34, no. 2 (2018): 101–125.
Starosielski, Nicole. *The Undersea Network.* Durham, NC & London: Duke University Press, 2015.
Starosielski, Nicole & Lisa Parks (eds.). *Signal Traffic: Critical Studies of Media Infrastructures.* Urbana Champaign, IL: University of Illinois Press, 2015.
Steffen, Will, Wendy Broadgate, Lisa Deutsch, Owen Gaffney, & Cornelia Ludwig. "The Trajectory of the Anthropocene: The Great Acceleration." *The Anthropocene Review* 2, no. 1 (2015): 81–98.
Steffen, Will, Katherine Richardson, Johan Rockström, Sarah E. Cornell, Ingo Fetzer, E. M. Bennett, Reinette Biggs, Stephen R. Carpenter, Wim de Vries, Cynthia A. de Wit, Carl Folke, Dieter Gerten, Jens Heinke, Georgina M. Mace, Veerabhadran Ramanathan, Belinda Reyers, & Sverker Sörlin. "Planetary Boundaries: Guiding Human Development on a Changing Planet." *Science* 347, no. 6223 (2015): 736–746.
Steffen, Will, Katherine Richardson, Johan Rockström, et al. "The Emergence and Evolution of Earth System Science." *Nature Reviews Earth & Environment* 1 (2020): 54–63.
Warde, Paul. "The Environment." *Local Places, Global Processes*, edited by Peter Coates, David Moon, & Paul Warde, 32–46. Oxford: Windgather Press, 2016.
———. "The Environmental History of Pre-Industrial Agriculture in Europe." *Nature's End: History and the Environment*, edited by Sverker Sörlin & Paul Warde, 70–92. Houndmills, Basingstoke: Palgrave Macmillan, 2009.
Warde, Paul, Libby Robin, & Sverker Sörlin. *The Environment – A History of the Idea.* Baltimore, MD: Johns Hopkins University Press, 2018.

Williams, Thomas, L. Jr. (ed.). *Man's Role in Changing the Face of the Earth*. Chicago & London: The University of Chicago Press, 1956.

Wormbs, Nina. "Eyes on the Ice: Satellite Remote Sensing and the Narratives of Visualized Data." *Media and the Politics of Arctic Climate Change: When the Ice Breaks*, edited by Miyase Christensen, Annika Nilsson, & Nina Wormbs, 52–69. New York: Palgrave Macmillan, 2013.

Worster, Donald. "Doing Environmental History." *The Ends of the Earth: Perspectives on Modern Environmental History*, edited by D. Worster, 289–308. New York: Cambridge University Press, 1988.

4
PLANETARY ENVIRONING
The biosphere and the Earth system

Giulia Rispoli

Introduction

The biosphere is generally seen as *one among other spheres* of the Earth system whose structure and functioning pertain to Earth system scientists' investigations. Emerging in the early 1980s to study the interactions among the geosphere, the atmosphere, the hydrosphere and the cryosphere, Earth System Science (ESS) has also come to subsume the sphere of life within the realm of its literacy. Yet if we begin to historicize the notion of the Earth system, we see that *environing media* practices that resulted from mid-20th-century science and technology, in particular cybernetics, have led their advocates to falsely construe our planet as a techno-ecological system. In this system, humans are a peripheral driver experiencing the Earth from the *outside*. As a result, a representation of the biosphere as one *part* of the Earth system has emerged as dominant.

This chapter shows that the recognition that human processes have been pushing the Earth into the Anthropocene, imposing new directions on Earth system processes from the *inside*, revives the biosphere as a protagonist of the Earth system, prompting us to re-evaluate historical attempts to conceptualize biosphere genealogies and the history of a human-reconfigured biosphere. Therefore, studying the history of the biosphere as coupled with human history is the first step toward recognizing the predicament of the Anthropocene, which is in turn fundamental to redirecting the pathway toward a more sustainable feature.

A theory of the biosphere addressing the interaction of life with the geophysical and atmospheric environment of the Earth can be dated back to the early decades of the 20th century. In this chapter, I will mostly refer to the ideas of Vladimir Vernadsky, a Russian mineralogist who conceptualized the biosphere as susceptible to change under human global activity. In this early elaboration, the biosphere seems to possess features similar to the contemporary Earth system notion. The inclusion of human factors in Earth System theory and modeling is indeed becoming increasingly fundamental. However, the entanglement, in the 1980s, of ESS with the National Aeronautics and Space Administration (NASA) led to the promotion of the Earth system as a groundbreaking revolutionary concept that incorporates the "biosphere" merely as one of its subsystems. By adopting this narrative, ESS's advocates have provided an often-simplistic reconstruction of a far more complex historical transition from the biosphere to the Earth system theory.[1] In this transition, some features that characterized the early 20th-century elaboration of the biosphere either got lost, were overshadowed or were later incorporated to legitimize ESS as a comprehensive theory of the human-Earth system relationship. In this respect, intellectual history of the concept of the biosphere and the history of environing media can help us understand what led to the bifurcation between the notion of the biosphere and that of the Earth system and how these two concepts came into being. As this chapter shows, a historical reconstruction of the emergence of the biosphere concept offers insights (among other things) into how humanity and nature became conceived of as one tightly interconnected system – how historians and naturalists, in recognizing the human capacity to transform portions and properties of the biogeochemical environment, started a process of self-reflection that brought them to attribute a geological force to humanity. This self-reflection can be seen in other terms at the very core of *environing*, because it is through acting upon and within nature that human perception, experience and representation of the environment develops and changes across time. The process of environing is both material and conceptual. It implies an intervention into nature that is always mediated by pre-existing (technical and intellectual) knowledge. Therefore, environing is a media process that is enabled by certain tools, models, practices and ideas. In the case of the biosphere and the Earth system notions, we will see how different media were at work in building the epistemology of a tightly interconnected system.

The notion of the biosphere is usually used to describe the interdependency of biological communities at large – including human societies – and the surrounding environment. The influence of life sciences on the formation of this object shaped the understanding of the biosphere as a large ecosystem where organisms and environments are plotted by material and energy transfers.[2] This model, scaled up to the planetary level, environed the biosphere as a territory of the Earth that is primarily experienced on the *ground*. In some definitions of the biosphere, the *pedosphere* (the sphere of soil) in fact occupied a prominent role. One example are the investigations of the Russian mineralogist Vasily V. Dokuchaev, whose expeditions across European Russia – conducted with the aim of *ecologizing* agricultural practices to preserve soil functions – led to the environing of the soil's biosphere as a "global natural object" that evolves under the action of climatic and geological but also biotic and anthropogenic forces.[3] The science of the pedosphere, seen as a system that stands in mutual dependence and chemical exchange with the atmosphere and the hydrosphere, emerged from everyday practical experience with the goal of ameliorating aspects of human health and economy.[4] Likewise, new branches of science, such as geography, cartography and mineralogy, received an enormous boost as disciplines necessary for orientation, to conquer new areas and geo-locate resources. At the same time, life sciences (along with systematics and taxonomy) helped situate the point from which to observe the biosphere within the biosphere itself, offering an *inside* perspective of its processes seen in relation to human experience. Geographers like Dokuchaev had to experience the land in order to understand how it works. The development of an *inside* perspective was facilitated primarily by the naturalistic observation during expeditions, thanks to the presence of vast pristine lands. Geographical explorations indeed acted as an environing media practice, which shaped understanding of flora and fauna as ecosystems. Moreover, they triggered the study of the morphology of different soils in relation to changing climatic factors and the coevolving relationship between organisms and their environment.[5]

In contrast to the biosphere notion, the Earth system has primarily been acknowledged as an object to be experienced from the *outside*. At the base of the emergence of the Earth system lies the convergence (in the 1960s and 1970s) of ecology and technology, as embodied, for instance, in the powerful "Spaceship Earth" metaphor. By depicting the Earth as a precarious vessel with limited resources, this metaphor raised awareness of the vulnerability of our environment and the finitude of its resources. Most importantly, however, Spaceship Earth had the side effect of legitimizing a technocratic vision of our planet according to which the sciences shall guide societies to the correct and efficient use and administration of lands, air, waters and the organisms inhabiting them. Together with the iconic images of the Apollo missions, Spaceship Earth became fundamental in generating knowledge about and representations of the Earth as a body observable at a distance. Satellites are instruments placed into orbit that are used for many purposes, but one of their most important applications is taking pictures of the planetary surface to create maps of the Earth or registering events. Satellites not only capture and transmit information but contribute to co-create environments by participating in a process of knowledge formation that becomes the basis for any further comprehension, action and transformation of the environment. In this respect, satellites offered a key demonstration of the act of environing the natural world with the aid of technologies that detach the observer's eye from the human scale.[6]

As the Earth turns into a techno-ecological system experienced from the outside, the biosphere becomes less and less perceivable; however, a separating line between the Earth and the biosphere is harder to draw now than ever before. Considering the biosphere as one part of the Earth system is a misconstruction since the biosphere has turned into a large-scale technological system of human production, for which Peter Haff has proposed the term "technosphere".[7] The biosphere is not simply a part of the Earth system – in the Anthropocene, it is the Earth itself.

This chapter shows how visions of the biosphere and the Earth system that are scientific, economic, social and material have been engendered by specific environing media in the form of instruments, models and discourses used to produce that knowledge. Against this background, our ability to formulate meaningful ideas and strategies to overcome the current predicaments posed by the Anthropocene also depends on our effort to revisit these visions and thus inform our present-day discussions. This is all the more important as historical visions of the biosphere and the Earth system reflect different moments of global environmental knowledge, including at the political and governmental level, that have allowed these notions to propagate and attain international credibility through specific programs. One of the consequences of legitimizing competing environing media is that a perspective that integrates human-biosphere studies and Earth System Science, despite various attempts, has not yet been attained. Realizing this integration is of the utmost importance for devising pathways toward new Earth system futures.

The biosphere as a cosmic medium

Austrian geologist Eduard Suess, one of the founders of tectonics, introduced the biosphere in a book on the geological formation of the Alps in the 1870s. As he portrays it, this celestial body consisting of organic life is situated between the air and rocks and represents the "face of the Earth".[8] Life interacts with both the atmosphere and the lithosphere; however, the former is singled out as an autonomous, concentric system which occupies a specific layer of the Earth, limited in space and time. *Solidarity* among the living populations is a predominant characteristic of the biosphere, but it does not exercise any specific influence on other parts of the Earth.

Suess's understanding of the biosphere was expanded on by Vernadsky a few decades later. The Russian geochemist historicized the biosphere in its role as a transformative driver of the whole Earth. Where Suess sandwiched the *film* of life between the lithosphere and the atmosphere, Vernadsky attributed to the biosphere a more holistic and ubiquitous function. All parts of the Earth, its spaces and physical matters, have been affected by life in some way, which leads to the conclusion that the history of organisms reveals the history of the Earth itself.[9]

In early 20th-century Russia, the predominant form of experiencing nature was naturalistic observation and specimen collection. Vernadsky was not accustomed to working in artificial settings. Already at an early age, he had been exploring nature, observing biogeographical variations of the Russian soil and moving beyond localities to imagine processes that were scalable, stretching out the biosphere as a planetary environment. He inferred that biotic and abiotic components can only be studied with the help of an integrated approach combining biology, chemistry and geology.[10] As Vernadsky saw it, there is barely any area of the Earth that has not been affected by living organisms. The biosphere articulates the overall functioning of the Earth by translating solar energy into biogeochemical *living matter*: it is "the sum total of living organisms that creates innumerable chemical compounds by photosynthesis and extends the biosphere at incredible speed as a thicker layer of new molecular systems".[11]

In this portrayal, the ubiquitous role of the biosphere in the configuration of the Earth is grounded in its capacity to perform a global biogeochemical function which entails the transformation of any element that touches its ground, evaporates in its air and drops back into the ocean. Jacques Grinevald echoes Vernadsky when he writes, "the biosphere has no *geographical boundary*[12] outside the observer's choice. Its extent is defined by the scale of observation" – hence there is nothing small or large in nature.[13] Borders or frontiers (in Russian *granitsa*) are themselves media that translate the biogeochemical information from one sphere to another and among the different *geospheres* as in a process of emergent communication.[14] Gabrys refers in her book *Program Earth* to Gilbert Simondon's concept of mediation. Simondon develops the use of mediation and communication by addressing phases of being and becoming. As an example, he describes a plant communicating and mediating between the cosmic and the mineral, the sky and the ground, taking up and transforming energies and materials through its processes. The *associated milieu* operates as this mediatory space, a transversal ground through which transformations play out and new phases of being emerged.[15] Likewise, in Vernadsky, borders are not meant simply as interfaces that enable the passage of elements. During the transfer of elements from one area of the biosphere to another, there is always a process of creation of new emerging entities. Mediation is always a creative process (that gives rise to something new).

For Vernadsky, the biosphere is as much terrestrial as it is cosmic. It does more than just wrap around the Earth horizontally or define it by the verticality of its relation to the sun. It is a matrix of biogeochemical interactions that involve land, ocean and air with cosmic energy. As the region where solar radiation is intercepted and transformed into active energy by living matter, the biosphere itself can be understood as an environing *medium* connecting the Earth with the cosmos. Radiations across space shaped the surface of the planet and thus our understanding of the role of energy for the existence and perpetuation of life on Earth. Radiation in the form of light, heat and electricity according to its type and wavelength – says Vernadsky – made the biosphere in the way we know it.[16] The immense range of the spectrum of radiation is constantly being extended by scientific discovery; thus, our understanding of the biosphere as a medium between the cosmos and the Earth will be progressively enriched by the science of radiometry, for example. Here again, the concept of mediation and communication through science and technics is particularly relevant to understand the process of environing.

Vernadsky investigated human biogeochemical alteration of the biosphere, which today is referred to as the Earth's "critical zone" – a heterogeneous space of interaction of biogeochemical components. He derived his interest in earthly geochemical interactions from the study of crystals and minerals as dynamic entities. Mineralogy allowed him to construct a view of the Earth as an evolving system subject to historical processes. Specifically, minerals such as aluminosilicates, the most abundant on Earth, are involved in its geological formation, while crystals are solid products of its chemical reactions; all together, they reveal the Earth's history.[17]

The appreciation of crystallography and mineralogy as historical disciplines allowed Vernadsky not only to see the Earth as an evolving system under the influence of endogenous forces, but also to comprehend the biosphere as the arena where those minerals circulate, accumulate, form sediment and get transformed. In this sense, the intervention of living organisms, and specifically humans, is known to act on the very core of the Earth, producing artificial minerals, rocks and new materials that have changed Earth's geochemistry, altering cycles and flows of minerals.

In Vernadsky's time, technologies allowing humans to grow their power at the expense of their surrounding environments generated uneven access to culture, education, wealth and health in different parts of the world. The concept of "environing technologies" developed by Nina Wormbs and Sverker Sörlin[18] is particularly suited in this context. By technology the authors refer to a terraforming practice that is a conceptual and a material process. Indeed Vernadsky has described the development of human technologies as oriented toward the comprehension of the world as a global integrated system, and this comprehension is the precondition for any intervention, being tightly connected to it. For instance, according to Vernadsky, the invention of the printing press made it possible to produce and share knowledge about previously inaccessible areas of the globe. The mastery of new forms of energy – steam, electricity, atomic energy or radioactivity – facilitated the study of the biosphere as a thermodynamic system where solar energy is absorbed and then radiated back in the form of heat, while the penetration into the surface of the Earth by mining, boring and drilling in search of coal, oil and ores made it possible to perceive the profundity of the Earth's crust and the transformative geological capacity of human activities. The invention of telegraph and radio made communication between faraway places possible, shortening distances and contributing to the sense of interconnectedness of our globe. All these and later processes, firmly grounded in human scientific and technological developments, have completely changed the biosphere, which has been heavily reconfigured and redefined both in its own biological components and in the way it interacts with other spheres of the Earth such as the atmosphere and the lithosphere.[19] According to Vernadsky, since the mid-20th century we have been living in a system called the *noosphere*, an epoch in which humans have become aware of their ability to perform a geological role on Earth. At the same time, humans have acknowledged that their power can be disruptive, realizing the urgency of reversing the march of progress that has characterized Western civilization since early modern times.[20] Jürgen Renn has aptly used the concept of "epistemic evolution" to define a new stage of cultural evolution that becomes the dominant process of human history and in which science becomes existential. However, while humans become aware of their power in terraforming the Earth, in effect becoming a geological force, it is plausible that science could emerge and become a dominant factor of our current state without being the necessary result of some initial conditions, but following a process that is also contingent, as in Darwin's theory of evolution.[21]

Similar to the notion of a technosphere, the noosphere is characterized by the increase of Earth's demography; by the transformation and globalization of communication and trade across the planet; by the predominance of humanity's geological role on Earth; by the industrial exploitation of new sources of energy, just to make one example. This concept is reminiscent of the Great Acceleration notion and the resulting Anthropocene model that would emerge later in the 20th century.[22] At the same time, the noosphere appears to have a constructive quality. It is attended by values that could prevent social and environmental catastrophe, namely democracy and equality, creating a real possibility to end malnutrition, hunger, misery and war. Even though humankind's technological force has the potential to irreversibly change the biosphere, this does not have to be the case. These forces must stop or be reoriented toward safe operating thresholds; otherwise, the unintended consequences of human action will generate environmental processes that may expose societies to a full collapse.

Initially, Vernadsky's work did not have a widespread influence on Western narratives of the biosphere. The biosphere theories that emerged in the 1970s, thanks to the work of ecologist Eugene Odum and later chemist James Lovelock, were prompted by different media. The development of technologies in the aftermath of World War II environed the biosphere, remolding its functions. In particular, drawing on cybernetics, new visions of the biosphere emphasized *regulatory aspects* of ecosystems and the *stability* of certain variables that remain constant over change and transformative action.[23] Even in those cases where Vernadsky did exercise an influence on the development of American ecology – for example on limnologist George Evelyn Hutchinson, who was highly fascinated by his biogeochemical approach – the idea that humanity could act as a transforming force of the biosphere was not considered as meaningful, as it lacked scientific basis and empirical evidence.[24]

Odum and Hutchinson promoted a vision of the biosphere as a *self-regulating* system. This definition emerged from the convergence between ecological discourses and cybernetics, which acted as an important trigger to the rise of the Earth system concept in the early 1980s. Following in the footsteps of Hutchinson, Odum claimed in a pioneering article (co-authored with Bernard Patten) that ecosystems *are* cybernetic systems, ushering in a new language which explained the cycling of energy and materials through ecosystems in terms of *input* and *output*, information flow and feedback governing the whole biosphere and the exchange among its parts.[25] Cybernetics mediated an understanding and representation of nature as a complex system to be controlled and managed because nature and society share a universal feedback logic.[26]

Where Vernadsky stressed co-evolutionary processes involving the biosphere and the geospheres as *emergent phenomena* grounded in the convergence of the global biogeochemical function of living matter with the geophysical properties of human technological systems – much like Haff's technosphere – Hutchinson described the biosphere as the place of interaction of two separate entities, organisms and environments, forming one *closed* ecosystem. This can be seen as an *autopoietic* system that reproduces itself from its own properties, shutting out all external perturbations. As Patten would have it, "the *environ*[27] here is delineated as a closely linked structure, a particulate unit of evolution" that introduces a sense of system.[28] Along the same lines Hutchinson proposed the idea of "circular causal system" in ecology, where ecosystems are explained as *networks* of biotic and abiotic components that interact through mechanisms of information feedback.

The notable Macy conferences on Circular Causal and Feedback Mechanisms in biological and social systems, which took place from 1946 to 1953, played a fundamental role in fostering interdisciplinary dialogue under the banner of cybernetics.[29] In 1948, the same year Wiener published his manifesto,[30] Hutchinson, a participant of the Macy conferences, published an article in which he attributed to ecosystems the capability to *self-correct*, arguing that there was little need for concern about anthropogenic increases of carbon dioxide, for example, as the self-regulating mechanisms of the biosphere were capable of correcting imbalances in carbon, whether natural or artificially produced.[31]

The Earth system: Environing from outside

The confluence of cybernetic and ecological discourses embodied in visions of the ecosystem and the biosphere promoted by Hutchinson and Odum, which represents an important catalyst in the rise of ESS, environed natural systems, and the biosphere in particular, as mechanistic entities. In this context, information science offered a solid basis to authorize and legitimize the circulation of concepts ranging from biophysical systems to mind, behavior and technology, unifying them under the epistemic roof of cybernetics as a universal science of control, in turn made possible by the development of the computer and artificial intelligence.[32]

Historian Greg Mitman has emphasized how cybernetics turned ecology into a technoscience in the service of managerial capitalism: "Nature had become a system of components that could be managed, manipulated and controlled. The ecologist's task increasingly became that of environmental engineer" who could monitor and fix the environmental problems created by human society.[33] Along the same lines, David Munns argues that the exigencies of environmental control in the early Cold War turned biologists into technologists, capable of mastering engineering and computer models in order to measure and optimize the climate conditions for a plant to grow in a facility.[34] Along the same lines, as Taylor would put it, Hutchinson and Odum's work in the field of systems ecology, adopts that "technological optimism" that characterizes the social context of the Postwar Years and is constitutive of their methods and research.[35]

The proliferation of terminologies imported by the cybernetic lexicon featured prominently in ecological discourses to explain Earth's responses to changes induced by external perturbations, for example, homeostatic behavior, feedback loops, balance, stability and resilience. Drawing on the interpretation of ecosystem as a cybernetic apparatus characterized by the imperative of energy and information flow, both Hutchinson and Odum – and later, more vigorously, Lovelock, who recognized Hutchinson as a mentor – promoted an understanding of natural systems as entities, comparable with artificial devices, that can both be understood and managed by means of the same cybernetic principles. In Lovelock's view, the ensemble of living organisms – constituting what he, together with Lynn Margulis, named *Gaia*, or the Earth as a living organism – has acted as a single entity to purposefully regulate the chemical composition, surface pH and atmosphere of the Earth. It is these supposed regulatory properties which then led Lovelock to compare the living planet – Gaia – with a gigantic homeostatic system. For physician Walter Cannon, our body is able to keep a physiological stability by buffering perturbations coming from the external environment, a function otherwise ascribed to the *milieu intérieur* theorized by Claude Bernard. Lovelock transferred this capability to the biosphere itself.[36] He maintained that life, since its appearance, has acquired control of the planetary environment via feedback loops.[37]

Cybernetic interpretation of the biosphere made it possible to regard any subsystem involved in its functioning as an equal contributor to the stability and integrity of the whole. One may infer that humans have become part of the Earth's metabolism without bringing any interference to its basic processes, any substantial change. All components regulating this large entity are mutually formative. The only privileged status is ascribed to microbial activity through which the planet has acquired enough resilience, which has in turn equipped the Earth with the ability to transform its gases, like CO_2 and other chemical components, in response to microbial life's metabolic pressure to expand its domain. Gaia is indeed, like Hutchinson's ecosystem, an autopoietic, microbe-centric entity: it is microbial life that controls the global environment.[38]

While many believe that this view of the biosphere has contributed to removing the flaws of anthropocentrism, giving prominence to a human-centered Earth, the vision it has actually propelled is that of a planet that dislodges the *Anthropos* by refusing the very notion of a human species or by denying the possibility of perceiving ourselves as a species.[39] But when humanity fails to recognize its own geological agency and humans are left with no power to change the Earth's processes, they can only act as supervisors who look at the Earth from a distance, adopting a certain neutrality that reinforces, other than dismisses, anthropocentric perspectives. Technologies can therefore be tolerated by the biosphere, as artificial and natural processes are both part of the same entity and do not harm the functioning of the biosphere as a large techno-ecological system.[40]

This position would justify Lovelock's call for engineering efforts to remedy the climate crisis instead of arguing against the fossil fuel economy. At any rate, it is quite curious that those who are still committed to invoking Gaia as a way to awaken global consciousness in a time of anthropogenic impact on the Earth system are doing so at the cost of departing from the original theory.[41]

Visions of the biosphere as a cybernetic system would not have been so compelling had they not been complemented by visions of Earth from outer space, in which the biosphere is hard to spot.

Iconic photographs taken during the Apollo missions such as Blue Marble or Earthrise are environing media that conveyed the vision of a global Earth, or to speak with Elizabeth DeLoughrey, that forged the *American* image of the globe.[42] Moreover, they helped build the narrative of a planet in need of care, which in turn installed the idea of the Earth as an entity requiring *stewardship*.[43]

The integration of cybernetics and ecology that is manifested in the rise of systems and global ecology, along with distant views of the Earth, environed our planet as an "objective" reality. This construed reality became the seed for the emergence of the paradigmatic Earth system notion and the associated science that addresses its functioning.[44] This science had to be characterized by a strong emphasis on self-regulatory functions and on the recognition of the Earth as an integrated entity as well as a system that required new forms of modeling, observations and visual representations, primarily from space.

This view of the Earth found a place in international scientific initiatives of the early 1980s. For example, the International Geosphere-Biosphere Programme (IGBP),[45] launched in 1987, was meant to study how the interaction of human activity with the biological, chemical and physical dimensions of the Earth brought about global change.[46] The program drew on complex models, simulations and especially the Earth Observing System (EOS) to promote a new recognition of the Earth as a system.[47] Despite the intention to pursue ample trajectories that would combine different methodologies and approaches, it was primarily NASA's role to inform the aims and objectives of the program. Breaking off from previous initiatives that were more openly centered around the biosphere,[48] the promoters of the IGBP (e.g.) John Kendrew, Herbert Friedman and Thomas Malone) benefited from the program's scientific and institutional intertwinement with the NASA Earth System Sciences Committee chaired by meteorologist Francis Bretherton, the author of the paradigmatic Bretherton diagram published in 1986. The diagram illustrates one of the primary attempts to include the human dimension in the Earth as a complex system. It was criticized, however, for providing a mechanical description of the Earth system, while the box representing "human activities" was positioned at the margins of the diagram as an external, peripheral force (Figure 4.1).[49]

The IGBP's initial focus on data gleaned from Earth observation satellites neglected local and regional studies as well as land-use problems that were central to sustainability and conservation.[50] The need for the IGBP to embrace wider research trajectories was felt within the communities of ecologists and geographers, as some lamented the lack of focus in the IGBP on the study of landscape heterogeneity and regional developments. The absence of the human sciences stood in contradiction to a program seeking to address anthropogenic interferences with the Earth system.[51] Against this backdrop, NASA Earth system research was thus oriented toward a wide application of space surveillance and monitoring, which in the 1980s constituted the main research line within the IGBP as well.

As Sebastian Grevsmühl has noted, Earth imagery produced by NASA fundamentally promoted Western values of science and nature, eluding questions about the uneven access to the large-scale environmental surveillance infrastructures that grew mostly out of Cold War efforts to monitor the dynamics of the Earth system. Images distributed by the space agency hardly addressed the underlying "geographies of power" so as to avoid highlighting, for example, where the main sources of pollutants came from.[52] Along these lines, Joseph Masco and Elizabeth DeLoughrey have both pointed out that militarism was key to how we map and *visualize* the globe as a planetary biosphere.[53] I would add that militarism, in particular nuclear militarism, created a new environmental and geophysical globalism that consolidated images of the Earth system. These images rendered problems homogeneous, removing discrepancies and the possibility of critical analysis by appealing to the iconic (and rhetorical) image of the Earth as a cybernetic system.

Remote-sensing technologies became environing media that rendered the Earth as a computable planet, as data obtained from remote observations could then be translated into models used, for instance, for climate simulations.[54] As space science was indeed the privileged angle from which to look at the Earth system, life, still very much considered in a cybernetic way, was reduced to its role of controlling the atmosphere and its chemical compounds in order to sustain the Earth's biosphere – Gaia. ESS has therefore circumscribed the role of the biosphere to a regulative dispositive of the planet's atmosphere. The human-reconfigured biosphere as a subsystem of the Earth does not really change, alter or disrupt the Earth's metabolism, and humans do not trigger processes that melt the ice or pollute the oceans.[55] On the contrary, the Earth system became dehumanized and dehistoricized, as it lost human history and scale.[56]

Satellite technologies have defined the scale at which our planet is perceived and conceptualized scientifically.[57] As Schneider and Walsh have pointed out, this *zooming tool* "is a rhetorical trope – both verbal and visual – that manufactures logical and political continuity from what is in reality a diverse and incommensurable set of views".[58] The operation of a scaled-down visualization of the Earth does not easily solve the problem. It neutralizes political tensions of local communities by selling a synoptic picture of global problems. The subjugation of localities to a centralized global picture contributes to *freezing* the planet in space and time. Although images are transmitted *down to Earth* at the speed of light, they seem to be alien to the human history of which they capture fixed instants that correspond in no way to real human events and experience.[59]

Planetary environing 65

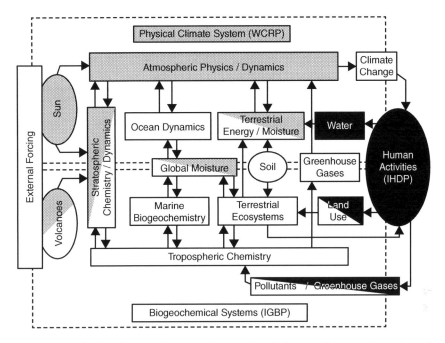

FIGURE 4.1 The Bretherton diagram. Source: Earth System Science Overview: A Program for Global Change. Earth System Sciences Committee, NASA Advisory Council.

A more substantial approach to biosphere studies would mitigate the predominance of geophysical and climatic investigations of the Earth system. Therefore, if the image of the Earth from space opened the way for global environmental consciousness, this rhetoric was conveyed through images of the Earth that once again disregarded human responsibilities.

Efforts of including a terrestrial ecological perspective were pursued in other scientific initiatives insisting on the need to dwell upon a terrestrial dimension of the biosphere but failing to come to an integration with ESS's theoretical basis and methods. A program called *Sustainable Development of the Biosphere*, launched under the aegis of the International Institute of Applied Systems Analysis (IIASA),[60] brought into focus the idea of the biosphere as a system that is no longer *self-governing* in the same way – but undergoes unprecedented processes driven by new components (like new polluting chemicals, new minerals produced within a new fertilization regime, new toxic substances).[61] Therefore, a concerted study of global ecological and geophysical systems in relation to industrial development and resource depletion was strongly emphasized. Such ambitious program, combining regional studies with modeling techniques and geospatial investigation from above in order to study the relationship between humankind and the biosphere, was not easy to achieve considering the resources available for international collaboration, and it came soon to an end.[62] Also, it probably failed to embrace an ESS perspective. However, this initiative showed an alternative way to environ the Earth in a time in which the scenario was primarily dominated by an Earth system approach mediated by the IGBP.

Conclusion

In this chapter I have argued that the emergence and consolidation of ESS is rooted in the idea that all spheres of the Earth are elements of a totality, each contributing to the functioning of the whole system in a mutually reinforcing fashion. The biosphere is seen as one sphere of the Earth that has evolved to keep the Earth's chemical metabolism stable through feedback loops that make the planet habitable.[63] The image and concept of the biosphere has mediated the perception and understanding of the Earth from the outside where the sphere of life, or, as Vernadsky used to define it, the *face of the Earth* is reduced to a regulative function of a larger planetary system. In this process of mediating knowledge about the biosphere, Hutchinson's systems ecology and Lovelock's Gaia theory – which led to the emergence of the Earth system concept – have played a prominent role. These theories acted as environing media in producing an understanding of the biosphere's functioning as restricted and mapped to a biological cybernetic model by which segregated components are seen to contribute to the *stability* of the whole. The theory of *homeostasis* and the use of concepts like *self-regulation* and *control* inscribed in the legacy of cybernetics mediated a narrative of the biosphere in which resilience and adaptation – as well as the autopoietic characteristics of ecosystems – are prioritized over disruption and transformation resulting from human manipulation. I have showed that, contrary to this tradition, the biosphere-noosphere theory elaborated by Vladimir Vernadsky in the first half of the 20th century was based on the awareness that human science and technology are responsible for driving the biosphere toward irreversible changes that dramatically involve all other parts of the Earth system. In this interpretation, human activity is studied in terms of its power to *environ* the Earth while knowledge and awareness resulting from environing technologies further inform our representation of the human-Earth system as a global systemic entity.

While Vernadsky's early biosphere theory was based on the idea that a human-reconfigured biosphere is *reenacting* our planet from the *inside*, Lovelock's biosphere is indebted to the idea of the Earth as visible from the *outside*, where the transformative power of humanity is barely recognizable. This view has environed the Earth as a synoptic whole while contributing to the failure to translate global sources into local knowledge.

The media of satellite technologies and the photographs they produced environed the Earth as a "system". And as the Earth system concept took hold, it obscured the idea of the "biosphere" as a global dynamic process, closing it off as a self-regulating sphere in which microbial life acted to keep the Earth habitable and comfortable in its chemistry and climate. Detached from the *ground*, humans turned into external spectators while the Earth becomes an *objective* reality. Gaia does not recognize the predicament of the Anthropocene but implies that the latter is a "natural" consequence of life's expansion on the planet.

The idea that the biosphere is one part of the Earth system is no longer adequate to explain the state we are in, the Anthropocene. The effect of the biosphere is no longer to reinforce Earth's resilience and stability. And insofar as they are the main actors of the biosphere, humans must be recognized as biogeochemical agents with a major perturbing function in driving the Earth system's parameters. Such an awareness requires current and future initiatives to address the human-reconfigured biosphere as the main driver toward changes in how the Earth system functions.

As Vernadsky's case shows, the rediscovery of visions of the biosphere and the Earth that go beyond the institutional foundation of ESS allows us to study different ways in which humans have environed the planet, in turn allowing us to make sense of the Anthropocene as a historical fact and, mindful of the flaws of anthropocentrism, to highlight human responsibilities in this history.

Acknowledgements

This chapter has been produced in the framework of the project "Planetary Genealogies: Historicizing the Anthropocene" made possible by the Rita Levi Montalcini Award. Moreover, I would like to thank Adam Wickberg, Johan Gärdebo and Pietro D. Omodeo for their precious comments on an earlier version of this essay.

Notes

1 Earth system science: overview – a program for global change/prepared by the Earth System Sciences Committee, NASA Advisory Council Paperback (University of California Libraries, 1986).
2 Arthur J. Tansley, "The Use and Abuse of Vegetational Concepts and Terms," *Ecology* 16, no. 3 (1935): 284–307.
3 V. V. Dokuchaev, "The Place and Role of Current Soil Science in Science and Life," *Russian Chernozem Is More Precious than Gold* (Moscow: Mosk. Gos. Univ., 1994), 195 [in Russian] V. I. Kiryushin, "V. V. Dokuchaev and the Present-Day Paradigm of Nature Management," *Eurasian Soil Science* 39 (2006): 1157–1163.
4 Deborah Coen, *Climate in Motion. Science, Empire, and the Problem of Scale* (Chicago and London: Chicago University Press, 2018).
5 Giulia Rispoli, "Between 'Biosphere' and 'Gaia': Earth as a Living Organism in Soviet Geo-Ecology," *Cosmos and History, The Journal of Natural and Social Philosophy* 10, no. 2 (2014): 78–91.
6 Buckminster Fuller, *Operating Manual for Spaceship Earth* (Carbondale: Southern Illinois University Press, 1969). Kenneth E. Boulding, "The Economics of the Coming Spaceship Earth." *The Environmental Handbook*, ed. Garrett De Bell (New York, 1970). Gardebo Johan, *Environing Technology: Swedish Satellite Remote Sensing in the Making of Environment 1969–2001* (Stockholm: KTH Royal Institute of Technology, 2019). Sebastian Grevsmühl, *La Terre vue d'en haut. L'invention de l'environnement global* (Paris: Seuil, 2014). Sabine Höhler, *Spaceship Earth in the Environmental Age 1960–1990* (Routledge, 2017). Robert Poole, "What Was Whole about the Whole Earth? Cold War and Scientific Revolution," *The Surveillance Imperative Geosciences during the Cold War and Beyond*, eds. S. Turchetti & P. Roberts (London: Palgrave, 2014). Nina

Wormbs, "Sublime Satellite Imagery as Environing Technologies," *Technology and Sublime*, eds. G. Rispoli & C. Rosol, special issue of *Azimuth* 1, no. 12 (2018): 77–93.

7 Peter Haff, "Humans and Technology in the Anthropocene, Six Rules," *The Anthropocene Review* 1, no. 2 (2014): 126–136; Steffen, Will et al., "Global Change and the Earth System: A Planet under Pressure," *Ecology and Society* 9, no. 2 (2004): 2.

8 E. Suess, *Die Entstehung der Alpen* [Origin of the Alps] (Prague: F. Tempsky, 1875). E. Suess, *The Face of the Earth* [Das Antlitz der Erde, 1909], Vol. 4. Translated by H.B.C. Sollas (Oxford: Clarendon Press, 1924).

9 Vladimir Vernadsky, *The Biosphere* (New York: Copernicus/Springer-Verlag, 1998). J. Grinevald & G. Rispoli, "Vladimir Vernadsky and the Co-evolution of the Biosphere, the Noosphere and the Technosphere," *Technosphere Magazine* (20 June 2018): 1–9.

Vladimir Vernadsky, *Scientific Thought as a Planetary Phenomenon* (Moscow: Nongovernmental Ecological V.I. Vernadsky Foundation, 1997). Nicholas Polunin & Jacques Grinevald, "Vernadsky and Biospheral Ecology," *Environmental Conservation* 15, no. 2 (1988): 117–121.

10 Vladimir Vernadsky, *La Géochimie* (Paris: Alcan, 1924).
11 Vernadsky (1998), 50.
12 Emphasis mine.
13 Jacques Grinevald, "Introduction: The Invisibility of the Vernadskian Revolution," in Vernadsky, *The Biosphere* (Springer Science, 1998), 20–32, 25.
14 Vladimir Vernadsky, "O Predelach Biosferii," *Izvestiya Akademii Nauk SSSR*, no.1 (1937): 1–24.
15 Jennifer Gabrys, *Program Earth. Environmental Sensing Technology and the Making of a Computational Planet* (University of Minnesota Press, 2016): 13.
16 Vladimir Vernadsky, *The Biosphere* (New York: Copernicus/Springer-Verlag, 1998).
17 See Vladimir Vernadsky, *Osnovy Kristallografii* [Fundamentals of Crystallography] (Moskva: Mosk. Gosud. Univ., 1904).
18 Sverker Sörlin, & Nina Wormbs, "Environing Technologies: A Theory of Making Environment," *History and Technology* 34, no. 2 (2018): 101–125.
19 Kendall Bailes, *Science and Russian Culture in an Age of Revolutions: V. I. Vernadsky and His Scientific School, 1863–1945* (Bloomington and Indianapolis: Indiana University Press, 1990).

Vladimir Vernadsky, "Scientific Thought as a Planetary Phenomenon," ed. or (2012 [1939]). See also Kendall Bailes, *Science and Russian Culture in an Age of Revolution, V.I. Vernadsky and His Scientific School, 1863–1945* (Bloomington and Indianapolis: Indiana University Press, 1990).

20 Jürgen Renn, *The Evolution of Knowledge. Rethinking Science for the Anthropocene* (Princeton: Princeton University Press, 2020), See also Pietro D. Omodeo, "Bacon's Anthropocene: Epistemological Entanglement of Power, Knowledge, and Nature Reassessed," *Epistemologia & Filosofia Nauki* 58 (2021): 148–170.
21 Giulia Rispoli, "Genealogies of Earth System Thinking". *Nature Reviews Earth & Environment* 1 (2020), 4–5.
22 Odum, Eugene P. & Bernard C. Patten "The Cybernetic Nature of Ecosystems," *The American Naturalist* 118 (1981): 886–895.
23 George Evelyn Hutchinson, *The Biosphere* 223, no. 3 (September 1970), 45–53. See also George S. Levit, *Biogeochemistry – Biosphere – Noosphere: The Growth of the Theoretical System of Vladimir Ivanovich Vernadsky* (Berlin: VWB-Verlag für Wissenschaft und Bildung, Studien zur Theorie der Biologie, 2001).
24 Eugene P. Odum, & Bernard C. Patten, "The Cybernetic Nature of Ecosystems," *The American Naturalist* 118 (1981): 886–895.
25 See Peter J. Taylor, "Technocratic Optimism: H.T. Odum, and the Partial Transformation of Ecological Metaphor after World War II," *Journal of the History of Biology* 21, no. 2 (1988): 213–244.
26 My emphasis.

27 Bernard C. Patten, "Environs: Relativistic Elementary Particles for Ecology," *The American Naturalist* 119, no. 2 (1982): 179–219.
28 *Cybernetics. The Macy Conferences 1946-153*, ed. Claus Pias (Chicago: The University of Chicago Press, 2016).
29 Norbert Wiener, *Cybernetics: Or Control and Communication in the Animal and the Machine* (Paris & New York: Hermann & Cie, MIT Press, 1948).
30 George E. Hutchinson, "Circular Causal Systems in Ecology," *Annals of the New York Academy of Sciences* 50, no. 4 (1948): 221–246. See also Christoph Rosol, 1948 in this volume.
31 Thomas Pringle, "The Ecosystem Is an Apparatus: From Machinic Ecology to the Politics of Resilience," *Machine*, eds. T. Pringle, G. Koch, & B. Stiegler (Lüneberg: Meson Press, 2019), 49–123. See also, William Harold Bryant, "Whole System, Whole Earth: The Convergence of Technology and Ecology in Twentieth-Century American Culture," PhD diss., University of Iowa, 2006.
32 Gregg Mitman, *The State of Nature: Ecology, Community, and American Social Thought, 1900–1950* (Chicago: University of Chicago Press, 1992), 210.
33 David P.D. Munns, *Engineering the Environments. Phytotrons and the Quest for Climate Control in the Cold War* (Pittsburgh: Pittsburgh University Press, 2017). See also the review by Johan Gärdebo, *Technology and Culture* 61, no. 3 (2020): 985–986.
34 Taylor, 1988.
35 James E. Lovelock, *Gaia, a New Look at Life on Earth* (Oxford; New York: Oxford University Press, 1979).
36 J. Lovelock, & L. Margulis, "Atmospheric Homeostasis by and for the Biosphere: The Gaia Hypothesis," *Tellus* 26 (1974): 2–10. See Bruce Clark, *Partial Earth: Lynn Margulis, Systems Theory, and the Evolution of Gaia* (Fall 2020). University of Minnesota Press.
37 Miriam Tola, "Composing with Gaia: Isabelle Stengers and the Feminist Politics of the Earth," *PhoenEx* 11, no. 1 (2016): 1–21.
38 Chakrabarty, Dipesh. "The Climate of History: Four Theses," *Critical Inquiry* 35, no. 2 (2009): 197–222.
39 James Lovelock, *Novacene* (London: Penguin, 2020). Global ecotechnics projects of the 1970s such as *Biosphere 2*, an Earth system science research facility situated in Arizona, have ridden the wave that eventually led to ESS. Backed by NASA, the project served the purpose of space colonization. See John P. Allen, M. Nelson & T.P. Snyder, "Institute of Ecotechnics," *The Environmentalist* 4 (1984): 205–218, Geneva, 1985. John Allen, *Me and the Biospheres* (Santa Fe: Synergetic Press). See Derek Wood, "Terraforming Earth, Climate and Recursivity," *Diacritics* 47, no. 3 (2019): 6–29.
40 T. Lenton & B. Latour, "Gaia 2.0," *Science 361*, no. 6407 (2018): 1066–1068.
41 Elizabeth DeLoughrey, "Satellite Planetarity and the Ends of the Earth," *Public Culture* 26, no. 2 (2014): 257–280.
42 Sebastian Vincent Grevsmühl, "Images, Imagination and the Global Environment: Towards an Interdisciplinary Research Agenda on Global Environmental Images," *Geo: Geography and Environment* 3, no. 2 (2016): e00020. Mike Hulme, "Problems with Making and Governing Global Kinds of Knowledge," *Global Environmental Change* 20 (2010): 558–564. Anton Vidokle & Hito Steyerl, "Cosmic Catwalk and the Production of Time," *E-flux* #82 (May 2017).
43 Poole (2014).
44 W. Steffen, K. Richardson, J. Rockström, et al. "The Emergence and Evolution of Earth System Science," *Nature Reviews Earth & Environment* 1 (2020): 54–63.
45 Thomas F. Malone & Juan J. Roederer (eds.). *Global Change* (Cambridge: Cambridge University Press, on the behalf of ICSU Press, 1985).
46 Steffen et al. (2020); Seitzinger et al. (2016).
47 For instance, the UNESCO Man and Biosphere Programme: https://en.unesco.org/mab.

48 Ola Uhrqvist & Eva Lövbrand, "Rendering Global Change Problematic: The Constitutive Effects of Earth System Research in the IGBP and the IHDP," *Environmental Politics* 23, no. 2 (2014): 339–356.
49 Chunglin Kwa, "The Programming of Interdisciplinary Research through Informal Science Policy Interactions," *Science and Public Policy* 33, no. 6 (2006): 457–467.
50 Robert Kates, "Human Use of the Biosphere," *Global Change*, eds. Malone & Roederer (1985), 491–493.
51 Sebastian Grevsmühl, "A Visual History of the Ozone Hole: A Journey to the Hearth of Science, and Technology and the Global Environment," *History and Technology* (2017): 333–344.
52 Elizabeth DeLoughrey, "Satellite Planetarity and the Ends of the Earth," *Public Culture* 26, no. 2 (2014); Joseph Masco, "The Age of Fallout," *History of the Present* 5, no. 2 (2015): 137–168.
53 Simone Turchetti & Peder Roberts, "Introduction: Knowing the Enemy, Knowing the Earth," *The Surveillance Imperative: Geosciences during the Cold War and Beyond*, eds. Turchetti & Roberts (London: Palgrave, 2014), 1–19; Jennifer Gabrys, *Program Earth, Environmental Sensing Technology and the Making of a Computational Planet* (University of Minnesota Press, 2016); Paul N. Edwards, *A Vast Machine. Computer Models, Climate Data and the Politics of Global Warming* (The MIT Press, 2010).
54 On the Gaia Hypothesis and its use in the context of oil corporations researches projects on the role of organisms in stabilizing climate processes see Leah Aronowsky, "Gas Guzzling Gaia or a Prehistory of Climate Change Denialism," *Critical Inquiry* 47, no. 2 (2021): 306–327.
55 Matthias Heymann, "The Climate Change Dilemma: Big Science, the Globalizing of Climate and the Loss of the Human Scale," *Regional Environmental Change* 19 (2019): 1549–1560.
56 Wormbs, 2018.
57 Birgit Schneider & Lynda Walsh, "The Politics of Zoom: Problems with Downscaling Climate Visualizations," *Geo: Geography and Environment* 6, no. 1 (2019).
58 Trevor Paglen, "Geographies of Times (The last pictures)," *In the Holocene*, ed. João Ribas (Berlin: MIT Press & Stenberg).
59 William C. Clark & Robert E. Munn (eds.). *Sustainable Development of the Biosphere* (Cambridge: Cambridge University Press, 1986).
60 Viktor Kovda, "Biosphere, Soil Cover and Their Changes," *Technology and the Future*, eds. Evgeny P. Velikhov et al. (London: Pergamon Press, 1980).
61 Giulia Rispoli & Doubravka Olšáková, "Science and Diplomacy around the Earth: From Man and the Biosphere Programme to the International Geosphere-Biosphere Programme," *HSNS* 40, no. 5 (2020): 456–481; Jane Lubchenco, et al. "The Sustainable Biosphere Initiative: An Ecological Research Agenda: A Report from the Ecological Society of America," *Ecology* 72, no. 2 (1991): 371–412.
62 T. Lenton, B. Latour, & S. Dutreuil, "Life on Earth Is Hard to Spot," *The Anthropocene Review* (2020): 1–25.

References

Allen, John. *Me and the Biospheres*. Santa Fe: Synergetic Press.
Allen, John P., M. Nelson, & T.P. Snyder. "Institute of Ecotechnics." *The Environmentalist* 4 (1984): 205–218. Geneva, 1985.
Aronowsky, Leah. "Gas Guzzling Gaia or a Prehistory of Climate Change Denialism." *Critical Inquiry* 47, no. 2 (2021): 306–327.
Bailes, Kendall. *Science and Russian Culture in an Age of Revolutions: V. I. Vernadsky and His Scientific School, 1863–1945*. Bloomington and Indianapolis: Indiana University Press, 1990.

Boulding, Kenneth E. "The Economics of the Coming Spaceship Earth." *The Environmental Handbook*, edited by Garrett De Bell. New York: Ballantines Books, 1970.

Bryant, William Harold. "Whole System, Whole Earth: The Convergence of Technology and Ecology in Twentieth-Century American Culture." Dissertation. University of Iowa, 2006.

Buckminster, Fuller. *Operating Manual for Spaceship Earth*. Carbondale: Southern Illinois University Press, 1969.

Chakrabarty, Dipesh. 2009. "The Climate of History: Four Theses." *Critical Inquiry* 35, no. 2: 197–222.

Clark, Bruce. *Partial Earth: Lynn Margulis, Systems Theory, and the Evolution of Gaia*. Minneapolis: University of Minnesota Press, 2020.

Clark, William C., & Robert E. Munn (eds.). *Sustainable Development of the Biosphere*. Cambridge: Cambridge University Press, 1986.

Deborah Coen. *Climate in Motion. Science, Empire, and the Problem of Scale*. Chicago and London: Chicago University Press, 2018.

DeLoughrey, Elizabeth. "Satellite Planetarity and the Ends of the Earth." *Public Culture* 26, no. 2 (2014): 257–280.

Dokuchaev, V. V. "The Place and Role of Current Soil Science in Science and Life." *Russian Chernozem is More Precious than Gold*. Mosk. Gos. Univ., Moscow, 1994, [in Russian] V.I. Kiryushin "V. V. Dokuchaev and the Present-Day Paradigm of Nature Management," *Eurasian Soil Science* 39 (2006): 1157–1163.

Earth System Science: Overview: A Program for Global Change / Prepared by the Earth System Sciences Committee, NASA Advisory Council Paperback. University of California Libraries, 1986.

Edwards, Paul N. *A Vast Machine. Computer Models, Climate Data and the Politics of Global Warming*. Cambridge, MA: The MIT Press, 2010.

Eugene, P. Odum & Bernard C. Patten, "The Cybernetic Nature of Ecosystems." *The American Naturalist* 118 (1981): 886–895.

Gabrys, Jennifer. *Program Earth, Environmental Sensing Technology and the Making of a Computational Planet*. Minneapolis: University of Minnesota Press, 2016.

Gärdebo, Johan. "Review of David P.D. Munns' "Engineering the Environments. Phytotrons and the Quest for Climate Control in the Cold War." *Technology and Culture* 61, no. 3 (2020): 985–986.

———. *Environing Technology: Swedish Satellite Remote Sensing in the Making of Environment 1969–2001*. Stockholm: KTH Royal Institute of Technology, 2019.

Grevsmühl, Sebastian. "A Visual History of the Ozone Hole: A Journey to the Hearth of Science, and Technology and the Global Environment." *History and Technology* (2017): 333–344.

———. "Images, Imagination and the Global Environment: Towards an Interdisciplinary Research Agenda on Global Environmental Images." *Geo: Geography and Environment* 3, no. 2 (2016): e00020.

———. *La Terre vue d'en haut. L'invention de l'environnement global*. Paris: Seuil, 2014.

Grinevald, Jacques. "Introduction: The Invisibility of the Vernadskian Revolution." In Vernadsky, *The Biosphere*. Springer Science, 1998.

Grinevald, J., & G. Rispoli. "Vladimir Vernadsky and the Co-evolution of the Biosphere, the Noosphere and the Technosphere." *Technosphere Magazine* (20 June 2018): 1–9.

Haff, Peter. "Humans and Technology in the Anthropocene, Six Rules." *The Anthropocene Review* 1, no. 2 (2014): 126–136.

Heymann, Matthias. "The Climate Change Dilemma: Big Science, the Globalizing of Climate and the Loss of the Human Scale." *Regional Environmental Change* 19 (2019): 1549–1560.

Höhler, Sabine. *Spaceship Earth in the Environmental Age 1960–1990.* New York: Routledge, 2017.

Hulme, Mike. "Problems with Making and Governing Global Kinds of Knowledge." *Global Environmental Change* 20 (2010): 558–564.

Hutchinson, George Evelyn. *The Biosphere* 223, no. 3 (September 1970): 45–53.

———. "Circular Causal Systems in Ecology." *Annals of the New York Academy of Sciences* 50, no. 4 (1948): 221–246.

Kates, Robert. "Human Use of the Biosphere." *Global Change*, edited by Thomas Malone & Juan J. Roederer, 491–493. Cambridge: Cambridge University Press, on the behalf of ICSU Press, 1985.

Kovda, Viktor. "Biosphere, Soil Cover and their Changes." *Technology and the Future*, edited by Evgeny P. Velikhov et al. London: Pergamon Press, 1980.

Kwa, Chunglin. "The Programming of Interdisciplinary Research Through Informal Science Policy Interactions." *Science and Public Policy* 33, no. 6 (2006): 457–467.

Lenton, T., & B. Latour. "Gaia 2.0." *Science* 361, no. 6407 (2018): 1066–1068.

Lenton, T., B. Latour, & S. Dutreuil. "Life on Earth Is Hard to Spot." *The Anthropocene Review* 7-3 (2020): 248–272.

Levit, George S. *Biogeochemistry – Biosphere – Noosphere: The Growth of the Theoretical System of Vladimir Ivanovich Vernadsky.* Berlin: VWB-Verlag für Wissenschaft und Bildung, Studien zur Theorie der Biologie, 2001.

Lovelock, James E. *Gaia, a New Look at Life on Earth.* Oxford; New York: Oxford University Press, 1979.

———. *Novacene.* London: Penguin, 2020.

Lovelock, J., & L. Margulis. "Atmospheric Homeostasis by and for the Biosphere: The Gaia Hypothesis." *Tellus* 26 (1974): 2–10.

Lubchenco, Jane, et al. "The Sustainable Biosphere Initiative: An Ecological Research Agenda: A Report from the Ecological Society of America." *Ecology* 72, no. 2 (1991): 371–412.

Malone, Thomas F., & Juan J. Roederer (eds.). *Global Change.* Cambridge: Cambridge University Press, on the behalf of ICSU Press, 1985.

Masco, Joseph. "The Age of Fallout." *History of the Present* 5, no. 2 (2015): 137–168.

Mitman, Gregg. *The State of Nature: Ecology, Community, and American Social Thought, 1900–1950.* Chicago: University of Chicago Press, 1992.

Munns, David P.D. *Engineering the Environments. Phytotrons and the Quest for Climate Control in the Cold War.* Pittsburgh, PA: Pittsburgh University Press, 2017.

Odum, Eugene P., & Bernard C. Patten. "The Cybernetic Nature of Ecosystems." *The American Naturalist* 118 (1981): 886–895.

Omodeo, Pietro D. "Bacon's Anthropocene: Epistemological Entanglement of Power, Knowledge, and Nature Reassessed." *Epistemologia & Filosofia Nauki* 58 (2021): 148–170.

Paglen, Trevor. "Geographies of Times (The Last Pictures)." *In the Holocene*, edited by João Ribas. Stenberg, Berlin: MIT Press.

Patten, Bernard C. "Environs: Relativistic Elementary Particles for Ecology." *The American Naturalist* 119, no. 2 (1982): 179–219.

Pias, Claus (ed.). *Cybernetics. The Macy Conferences 1946–153.* Chicago: The University of Chicago Press, 2016.

Polunin, Nicholas, & Jacques Grinevald. "Vernadsky and Biospheral Ecology." *Environmental Conservation* 15, no. 2 (1988): 117–121.

Poole, Robert. "What Was Whole about the Whole Earth? Cold War and Scientific Revolution." *The Surveillance Imperative Geosciences during the Cold War and Beyond*, edited by S. Turchetti, & P. Roberts. London: Palgrave, 2014.
Pringle, Thomas. "The Ecosystem Is an Apparatus: From Machinic Ecology to the Politics of Resilience." *Machine*, edited by T. Pringle, G. Koch, & B. Stiegler, 49–123. Lüneberg: Meson Press, 2019.
Renn, Jürgen. *The Evolution of Knowledge. Rethinking Science for the Anthropocene*. Princeton: Princeton University Press, 2020.
Rispoli, Giulia. "Genealogies of Earth System Thinking". *Nature Reviews Earth & Environment* 1, no. 4–5 (2020): 4–5.
———. "Between 'Biosphere' and 'Gaia': Earth as a Living Organism in Soviet Geo-Ecology." *Cosmos and History, The Journal of Natural and Social Philosophy* 10, no. 2 (2014): 78–91.
Rispoli, Giulia, & Doubravka Olšáková. "Science and Diplomacy Around the Earth: From Man and the Biosphere Programme to the International Geosphere-Biosphere Programme." *HSNS* 40, no. 5 (2020): 456–481.
Rosol, Christoph. "1948". This volume.
Schneider, Birgit & Lynda Walsh. "The Politics of Zoom: Problems with Downscaling Climate Visualizations." *Geo: Geography and Environment* 6, no. 1 (2019): 1–11.
Sörlin, Sverker, & Nina Wormbs. "Environing Technologies: A Theory of Making Environment." *History and Technology* 34, no. 2 (2018): 101–125.
Steffen, W., K. Richardson, J. Rockström, et al. "The Emergence and Evolution of Earth System Science." *Nature Reviews Earth & Environment* 1 (2020): 54–63.
Steffen, Will et al. "Global Change and the Earth System: A Planet Under Pressure." *Ecology and Society* 9, no. 2 (2004): 2.
Suess, E. *The Face of the Earth* [Das Antlitz der Erde, 1909]. Vol. 4. Translated by H.B.C. Sollas. Oxford: Clarendon Press, 1924.
———. *Die Entstehung der Alpen* [Origin of the Alps]. Prague: F. Tempsky, 1875.
Tansley, Arthur J. "The Use and Abuse of Vegetational Concepts and Terms." *Ecology* 16, no. 3 (1935): 284–307.
Taylor, Peter J. "Technocratic Optimism: H.T. Odum, and the Partial Transformation of Ecological Metaphor after World War II." *Journal of the History of Biology* 21, no. 2 (1988): 213–244.
Tola, Miriam. "Composing with Gaia: Isabelle Stengers and the Feminist Politics of the Earth." *PhoenEx* 11, no. 1 (2016): 1–21.
Turchetti, Simone, & Peder Roberts. "Introduction: Knowing the Enemy, Knowing the Earth." *The Surveillance Imperative: Geosciences during the Cold War and Beyond*, edited by Turchetti & Roberts, 1–19. London: Palgrave, 2014.
Uhrqvist, Ola, & Eva Lövbrand. "Rendering Global Change Problematic: The Constitutive Effects of Earth System Research in the IGBP and the IHDP." *Environmental Politics* 23, no. 2 (2014): 339–356.
UNESCO. *Man and Biosphere Programme*. https://en.unesco.org/mab
Vernadsky, Vladimir. *Osnovy Kristallografii* [Fundamentals of Crystallography]. Moskva: Mosk. Gosud. Univ., 1904.
———. "Scientific Thought as a Planetary Phenomenon," ed. or (2012 [1939]).
———. *The Biosphere*. New York: Copernicus/Springer Verlag, 1998.
———. *Scientific Thought as a Planetary Phenomenon*. Moscow: Nongovernmental Ecological V.I. Vernadsky Foundation, 1997.
———. "O Predelach Biosferii." *Izvestiya Akademii Nauk SSSR*, no. 1 (1937): 1–24.
———. *La Géochimie*. Paris: Alcan, 1924.

Vidokle, Anton, & Hito Steyerl. "Cosmic Catwalk and the Production of Time." *E-flux* #82 (May 2017).
Wiener, Norbert. *Cybernetics: Or Control and Communication in the Animal and the Machine.* Paris & New York: Hermann & Cie, MIT Press, 1948.
Wood, Derek. "Terraforming Earth, Climate and Recursivity." *Diacritics* 47, no. 3 (2019): 6–29.
Wormbs, Nina. "Sublime Satellite Imagery as Environing Technologies." *Technology and Sublime*, edited by G. Rispoli & C. Rosol, special-issue of *Azimuth* 1, no. 12 (2018): 77–93.

5
1948

Christoph Rosol

March 24, 1948, New York. 10:00 am. Five speakers assemble in the Grand Ballroom of the Hotel Commodore for a special session on "Advances Significant to Electronics": Norbert Wiener, Claude Shannon, Maurice Deloraine, Isidor Rabi, and John von Neumann. Their talks bear short titles: "Cybernetics," "Pulse Modulation," "Information Theory," "Electronics and the Atom," and "Computer Theory." The panel session is part of the 1948 National Convention of the Institute of Radio Engineers (I.R.E.), the world's largest gathering of electrical engineers to date. According to the organizers, it "appears destined to become known in future years as one of the more important I.R.E. sessions ever to be held."[1] Indeed, the talks at that morning session discuss no less than the very foundations of the coming atomic and digital ages.

The first speaker, Norbert Wiener, believes that a second industrial revolution is imminent. He draws on material from his seminal work *Cybernetics: Or Control and Communication in the Animal and the Machine*, which is about to be published within a few weeks.[2] In it, Wiener, the son of a Polish-Yiddish emigrant and the first Harvard professor for Slavic languages, sets out his vision of self-organizing rhythmic systems, whose governors are distributed over the entire system, regardless of whether this system is a machine or a living organism. While the intellectual concepts of earlier eras mostly corresponded with the principles of mechanical clockworks or thermodynamic steam engines, the present age, he argues, is textured through modalities such as information, communication, organization, and control. However, in order to operate with a structuring entity like "information" a mathematically precise formulation is needed. Later that year, this precise form is provided by Wiener's former student, and son of a German teacher from Michigan, Claude Elwood Shannon. In July and October 1948, the two parts of Shannon's seminal paper "A Mathematical Theory of

Communication" appear in the journal of his employer, Bell Laboratories.[3] Shannon proposes a measure of information known as the bit, which renders the capacities of radio and other information channels universally calculable. The reduction of the concept of communication to measurable and statistically calculable values will supply the technological foundation for what is known today as digitization.

The answer to the question of how to convert the analog, or continuous, world into the discrete signals of the digital world comes from the high-frequency engineer Maurice Deloraine, who emigrated from France just eight years earlier. His idea of pulse-code modulation will pave the way for the micro-temporal sampling and coding of spoken language – no matter whether it is German, French, Russian, or Jiddish – and, soon thereafter, optical images: nothing less than the digital conversion of media itself. The advancement was made possible thanks primarily to work carried out at the MIT Radiation Laboratory, the most important American electronics research facility during World War II. Its sole purpose was to develop high-frequency and radar technology for "remote sensing" on the scale of a global war taking place both in the upper air and deep into the oceans. The deputy director of the "RadLab" was the physicist Isidor Isaac Rabi, an immigrant from Galicia (now southern Poland and western Ukraine). Rabi was also a consultant for the Manhattan Project, an objective of which was to join, as Rabi's talk at the Hotel Commodore put it, "electronics and the atom." For it was precisely the complex computational effort involved in the construction of the atomic and, later, hydrogen bombs that led to the rapid development of the digital computer.

The mathematician most responsible for the liaison between nuclear physics and computer design was John von Neumann, the fifth speaker on the panel and a German-Jewish emigrant from Budapest. While his concise mathematical shortcuts did help to solve the problem of the critical mass needed to initiate a nuclear chain reaction in various types of bombs with the help of analog punch-card computers, increased computational demands led to the development of the first general-purpose digital computer, the Electronic Numerical Integrator and Computer (ENIAC), an effort which also produced the logical basis of the computer architecture still in use today.

It is unknown whether and to what extent the audience at the Hotel Commodore fathomed the import and the monumental implications of the talks, which, judging by the speakers' backgrounds, must have been delivered in heavy European accents.[4]

★★★

The same day, March 24, 1948, 2,000 km to the south. Representatives of 56 nations sign the Havana Charter. The agreement stipulates the establishment of an international trade organization, an "International Clearing Union," and a supranational unit of account known as the bancor to promote a global trade system. But none of the proposals come to pass because of the refusal of the US

Congress to ratify the charter.[5] As a result, the General Agreement on Tariffs and Trade (GATT), a partial treaty that came into force on January 1, 1948, will remain in effect for a long time to come. Even though GATT is intended as just a stopgap, it will cement the dominance of Western industrialized countries in world trade for decades.

★★★

April 21, 1948, Haifa, Palestine. The Jewish paramilitary organization Haganah seizes the port refineries and the terminal of the British-built Kirkuk-Haifa oil pipeline, securing what was shaping up to be the world's most important strategic commodity and instrument of power.[6] The move marks a turning point in the 1947–1949 Palestine War. By the beginning of the Arab revolt in 1936 – the greatest revolt against British colonial rule in the 20th century – the newly built pipeline had become a target of multiple attacks and acts of sabotage. For its protection, the British established a militia of armed Jewish settlers. The militia makes up the core of the Zionist army that takes control of Palestine in April 1948, which leads to the creation of the state of Israel only three weeks after the conquest of Haifa.

On the same day that the head of the pipeline falls into the hands of the Haganah, Iraqi workers revolt at the K3 pumping station near Haditha. K3 is a strategically important junction where the pipeline delivering crude oil from the Kirkuk oil fields splits into two: one line going to the Lebanese city of Tripoli; the other, to Haifa. The strike is part of a wave of protests that erupted after the nationwide anti-colonial al-Wathbah uprising led by students and the young but influential Iraqi Communist Party was put down in January. The blockade lasts until May 25, when the besieged strikers decide to march on Baghdad and soon afterward become ensnared in a trap. By the end of 1948, the Communist Party is in shambles and its leaders are in prison. Supporters of pan-Arabism argue that the movement is no longer credible after it followed Moscow's doctrine in recognizing the State of Israel and thus gave up on exploiting the oil reserves for themselves.

After the end of World War II, the United Kingdom withdraws from the Middle East on account of their crushing war debt. This allows the United States to emerge as the new dominant power in the region. In the early 1930s, American companies had already secured concessions for oil exploration in all of Saudi Arabia and Bahrain and in half of Kuwait. In 1948, Texaco and Standard Oil of California, the joint owners of the Arabian American Oil Company, or Aramco for short, take on two new partners: Standard Oil of New Jersey (later to become Exxon) and Socony Vacuum (later to become Mobil). In June of that year, the northern part of the Ghawar oil field is discovered near the Persian Gulf. Between 1948 and 2000 an estimated 65% of total Saudi oil production will come from Ghawar, the largest onshore oil field ever discovered. Owing to the enormous quantity of oil found at Ghawar, Aramco becomes the world's most profitable company, and remains so today, accounting for roughly 5% of accumulated global CO_2 equivalent emissions since its establishment.

Mostly because of the extraordinary jump of Middle East oil imports from 1,000 barrels per day in 1947 to 75,000 per day in 1948 US oil imports exceed its exports for the first time that year. Already in January 1948, the Secretary of Defense James Forrestal meets with Brewster Jennings, the president of Socony Vacuum, to discuss how best to handle the coming oil glut from the Middle East. In an effort to keep raw materials scarce and profits high, they encourage American automobile manufacturers to develop inefficient, gas-guzzling engines.[7] In less than a decade, the average horsepower of automobiles produced for the US market will double and be accompanied by an explosive growth in the number of vehicles on the road and the petro-libidinal suburban lifestyles they make possible. Between 1948 and 1972, US oil consumption will triple in an economy that aims no longer to satisfy needs but to increase consumption.

In Europe, meanwhile, the Organization for European Economic Cooperation (or OEEC, the precursor to today's OECD) is created in April 1948 to superintend the Marshall Plan, an initiative recently enacted by the US Congress for the economic recovery of Western Europe. As part of the initiative and in response to the severe energy shortages that befall Europe in 1946 and 1947, the OEEC promotes the switch from coal to imported oil. Around 20% of Marshall Plan dollars go straight to the purchase of oil and oil-processing facilities. The reconstruction of Europe and the rise in oil production in the Middle East go hand in hand.[8]

Meanwhile, a delegation of Venezuelan officials tours the Middle East in 1949 to convince the kingdoms to demand at least a 50-50 split of revenues in their oil concessions to American companies. The blueprint was the 50% profit sharing model implemented by legislation in Venezuela in 1948, itself an outcome of negotiations in which Venezuela originally wanted more (60:40), but had to concede to the powerful interests of big oil. A 50-50 agreement presented an increase in revenue for most Middle Eastern states, however. The eventual adoption essentially helped to cement the presence of foreign oil producers in the region, acting as states within states. At the same it showed how collective action of third-world countries could drive concessions. The Venezuelan delegation visit of 1949 thereby encouraged the way of cartel formation that led to the foundation of the Organization of the Petroleum Exporting Countries (OPEC) in 1960 and the eventual rise of a post-colonial energy world order in which not only Western oil tycoons but also kings, dictators, and ruling elites from petro-states sought to reap the benefits of exploiting Earth's million-year-old chemical energy reservoirs.

★★★

May 26, 1948, South Africa. The Herenigde Nasionale Party wins the majority of seats in the parliamentary elections with a minority of the popular vote. In the same year, it begins to enforce systematic racial segregation in all areas of public and private life. It is the start of institutionalized apartheid. Organized by the state apparatus and its arsenal of media technologies of registration, classification, and territorialization, the withdrawal of rights becomes law. Working through the decades of white supremacist rule that follow and subsequent rudiments of reconciliation will only be possible by using similar media techniques: cases, files, databases, microphones, questionnaires, hearings.[9]

★★★

August 31, 1948, Moscow. At a hastily organized session of the Lenin Academy of Agricultural Sciences, its president, Trofim Denisovich Lysenko, delivers an address titled "On the Situation in the Biological Sciences." The powerful agronomist decries Western genetics as an anti-socialist and false doctrine, and endorses instead a neo-Lamarckian view in which the inherited properties of organisms are shaped by their environmental conditions. Even before the end of the meeting, he makes clear that the Soviet Politburo had already approved his speech.[10] In fact, Josef Stalin, himself a passionate hobby gardener and mimosa breeder, personally edited Lysenko's manuscript. In the wake of great famines in 1946 and 1947, the new program aims to increase agricultural yields and put a stop to the bourgeois determinism of Western genetics. This understanding of biology will soon prove to have grave consequences as crop failures ravage not only the Soviet Union, but also the young People's Republic of China that also adopts Lysenko's methods.

In the West, scientists are also working on programs to increase yields. One of their main objectives is to prevent the spread of communism among agrarian countries in the south. The Mexican Agricultural Program of the Rockefeller Foundation established in 1944 under the direction of Norman Borlaug (with money from Standard Oil founder John D. Rockefeller) becomes a global operation in 1947, when embarking on the programmatic goal of the "Green Revolution," which, starting in the 1960s, will fundamentally transform agriculture especially on the Indian subcontinent. Farmers combine newly bred high-yield varieties of rice, wheat, maize, and beans with large quantities of mineral fertilizers and pesticides such as DDT.[11] The industrial-scale strategy proves an effective means of feeding the rapidly growing populations in developing nations – while causing lasting damage to the environment. Amid the burgeoning Cold War, science must enter the service of ideology, even with something as seemingly innocuous as crop breeding. The laboratory-based "green" revolution is meant to act as a bulwark against the power struggle of the "red" revolution.

The genetics that Lysenko spoke out against began in earnest when, in 1944, the Canadian doctor Oswald Avery isolated deoxyribonucleic acid, or DNA, at the Rockefeller University Hospital in New York – just a few blocks north of the Hotel Commodore. The work on molecular genetics was spearheaded by the Rockefeller Foundation, under the direction of Warren Weaver, the head of its natural sciences department – the same Warren Weaver who, in 1949, will co-edit Claude Shannon's collected essays on information theory. Based on Erwin Chargaff's work in 1947, Alfred Hershey and Martha Chase will prove in 1952 that DNA is responsible for the transmission of genetic information. One year later, James Watson and Francis Crick will use X-ray crystallography to develop a double-helix model for the structure of the DNA molecule. The rise of molecular biology culminates in what Watson calls its "central dogma": the hypothesis, still essentially valid today, that describes the sequential copying, transcriptions, and translations of the information encoded in genes by DNA, ribonucleic acid (RNA), and proteins. The process not only recalls text-based media and communication but also very materially represents the idea of a universal, symbolically coded order of living organisms. It is an idea that will later go on to shape theories of language and culture.[12]

Meanwhile, Lysenko's star in the Soviet Union continues to fall as further attempts to deploy socialist Lamarckism fail. One is a scheme to reforest the steppe. The idea is to plant trees close together based on Lysenko's assumption that collectivism will help the saplings survive and grow under the steppe's harsh conditions. On October 20, 1948, just two months after his speech at the Lenin Academy, the Council of Ministers of the Soviet Union pass the "Plan for planting shelterbelts, introduction of grassland crop rotation and construction of ponds and reservoirs to ensure high sustainable crop yields in steppe and forest-steppe areas of the European USSR." Later renamed the "Great Stalin Plan for the Transformation of Nature," the plan comprises a series of large-scale projects, from the planting of 70,000 km of wood belts to the diversion of entire river systems.[13] The Promethean hybris of improving nature by means of a "technocratic ecology" soon spreads to the Central Asian region.[14] Eventually, however, all projects will be abandoned. Only around half of the planned areas will be reforested, and a majority of the seedlings planted between 1949 and 1953 will die.

★★★

October 3, 1948, Göteborg, Sweden. After 15 months of circumnavigating the water planet called "Earth," the Swedish Albatross research vessel returns to its port of registry. On board are more than 200 sediment cores raised from the sea depths of up to 7,900 m from around the equatorial line. Wrapped in parchment, stoppered in aluminum tubes filled with paraffin wax, and cooled to 5°–8°C, they hold geologic and climatic records of the last 3 million years. Thanks to the newly designed "piston corer," cores of unseen lengths of up to 20 m were obtained, storing continuous and undisturbed paleoenvironmental information of the entire Quaternary. An entirely new deep-time vista opens up for deep-sea oceanography.

Almost exactly one month later, a paper by the nuclear chemist Harold C. Urey appears in the journal *Science* showing how the ratio of different oxygen isotopes found in geological sampling material can reveal temperatures at the time of its formation.[15] Just a little earlier, Urey's colleague at the University of Chicago Willard Libby had already proposed a method for dating organic materials by measuring their content of carbon-14 (14C or C-14), a radioactive isotope of carbon. The German-Danish physicist Hilde Levi, who visited Libby and Urey for several months in early 1948, carried this method to Copenhagen, establishing the Copenhagen Isotope Colloquia series in the same year and the first C-14 lab on European soil in 1951.[16]

However, the radiocarbon dating method extends only back to archaeological and prehistorical times, not geological. Here, correlations between different dating and proxy methods are of essence. With high-resolution sediment cores available from the deep sea and the new technique of deriving "paleotemperatures" through measuring isotope compositions Cesare Emiliani, a micropaleontologist and oceanographer hired by Urey, will be able to meticulously chronicle the dramatic ice age temperature swings before Neolithic humans came to dominate the surface of the planet.

★★★

Two days later, October 5, 1948, Fontainebleau, France. The International Union for the Protection of Nature (IUPN) is founded at the renaissance castle of Fontainebleau. The international organization is a building block in the co-emergence of international bureaucracy, transnational science, and the idea of a "global environment" in the aftermath of World War II.[17] A dispute arises among its founders about whether nature should be *protected* from human interference or be strategically *conserved* as a warehouse of raw materials for agriculture, the production of goods, and future conflicts. Two publications published in 1948 by individuals involved in the dispute give the modern environmental movement of neo-Malthusian imprint a fulminant start: William Vogt's *Road to Survival* and Fairfield Osborne's *Our Plundered Planet*.[18] Ultimately, the conservationist attitude prevails, and in 1956 the IUPN will be renamed the International Union for the Conservation of Nature and Natural Resources (IUCN).

Meanwhile, another dispute about protection finds a home in Fontainebleau, this time focused on the specter of nuclear war and the total annihilation of all of higher life on Earth: in 1952, the command of the Allied Forces Central Europe of NATO (founded in 1949) established their headquarters in the French castle. However, it was not only the global strategic risks of atomic warfare that featured prominently in the discussions of these Cold War strategists, much of whose thinking was informed by the scenario planning groups of the RAND corporation (founded in 1948), and their embracing of game theory as well as operations research and linear programming (which found its first real-world application in the Berlin Airlift of 1948–1949). The decade following the end of World War II is also the heyday of environmental warfare scenario planning, turning the newly established concept of the environment not in an outside object to be protected but to be used against other humans. Various military considerations of crop destruction through pests, contamination of strips of land through radioactive waste, and weather and climate modification are fueled by a frenzy of lab experiments and thought experiments among industrial scientists, many of whom give rather hyperbolic assessments of their potential application. Crucially, the imminent threat of environmental manipulation prompts the rise of "catastrophic environmentalism" and the understanding of resilience and security as something gained through conserving ecosystem variety and complexity.[19] The International Geophysical Year of 1957–1958, in which scientists from East and West work together and share a hitherto unseen wealth of environmental data, extends that view up to the planetary scale. It helps to propel a systems-oriented understanding of the global environment as a space in which radioactive tracers can cycle as much as biogeochemical substances through Earth's varied reservoirs such as the biosphere, atmosphere, and hydrosphere.[20] In turn, this understanding raises the question of how such cycles can be artificially altered – and this time not by intended interventions but through the unintended consequences of human activities.

★★★

October 1948, Arnhem Land, Northern Territory, Australia. A team of American and Australian scientists complete what is now widely considered the last of the great expeditions: an eight-month exploration of Arnhem Land, located at the upper tip of Australia's Northern Territory. They return from the journey with thousands of plant and animal species along with other data such as indigenous tools and bark paintings, but also 16 mm film recordings and color photographs documenting the Yolngu tribe and other Aboriginal peoples who have lived there for tens of thousands of years. Despite the use of modern media, the expedition is an anachronistic undertaking, a kind of historical re-enactment of the natural and ethnographic explorations of the 19th century.[21]

It soon becomes apparent that the expedition is likely to be the last opportunity to study a pre-modern human ecosystem on the continent. A good ten years earlier, the cane toad, a species native to South America, was introduced in Queensland in an effort to control pest infestations on sugar cane plantations. The measure was unsuccessful, but the cane toad thrived. An invasive species with poison glands, few natural predators, and a high rate of reproduction, the toad spread exponentially, displacing other species and threatening the survival of monitor lizards and other predators. The amphibian species will reach Arnhem Land within two decades. Today, the toads' distribution extends from Northern Australia to New South Wales and CRISPR gene editing efforts – descendant techniques of the molecular biology paradigm of the mid-20th century – are underway to detoxify the toad and put an artificial end to the environmental havoc created by the artificial introduction of the toad into the Australian gene pool.[22]

The Western Pacific is a melting pot of geo-historical time in 1948. In January the aforementioned Albatross expedition has taken samples from the deep-sea floor in the western Pacific to chronicle a natural history of that region before the advent of humans. Just a few weeks later the Arnhem Expedition set out to study the result of tens of thousands of years of prehistoric migrations in that same region, investigating a confined area still largely untouched by modern extractive cultures and technologies. At the same time, less than 2,500 miles away from Arnhem and just a few hundreds of miles north of the Albatross route, around 10,000 American army employees and scientific personnel prepare for bantering natural history in turning an entire area into an experimental site for high-tech investigation. On Enewetak Atoll, they relocate the indigenous population, raze the islands of Enjebi, Aomon, and Runit, and build a causeway for running cables between a test site on Aomon and the control station on the neighboring island of Bijire. As part of Operation Sandstone, the army conducts three nuclear weapons tests on Enewetak between April and May 1948. Unknowingly and quite narrowly, the Albatross expedition had managed to capture the very last instance of ocean history free of contamination with artificial plutonium.[23] The inhabitants of the Marshall Islands, meanwhile, embark on the intergenerational traumas of nuclear colonialism, not being permitted to return to Enewetak until 1980, when radiation levels still remain dangerously high.

The primary purpose of the Sandstone tests is to update the design of the "Fat Man" bomb, the implosion-type nuclear device that exploded over Nagasaki on August 9, 1945 after a similar model was tested at the Trinity site in New Mexico. It was none other than John von Neumann who, working at the Los Alamos National Laboratory, calculated the density of the fissile material needed to prompt a nuclear chain reaction in Fat Man and determined the detonation height for maximum destruction. Fat Man ended the Pacific War only to usher in a new war against the Pacific ecosystem and its human and non-human inhabitants.

The nuclear tests of Operation Sandstone will lead to significant improvements in bomb design and efficiency. Forty more tests will follow, including, in 1952, the detonation of the first hydrogen bomb, which will completely destroy Elugelab, another island in the atoll. By that time, the mass production of nuclear weapons that ignited the Cold War arms race is already on. On June 1, 1948, the Soviets have begun the manufacturing of weapons-grade plutonium at the Mayak plant near Chelyabinsk. One year later they detonate a bomb based on the Fat Man design in the unforestable steppes of Kazakhstan. Over the following decades, the US and the Soviet Union will carry out some 500 aboveground nuclear tests. The resulting global radioactive fallout will spell the end of the Holocene epoch.[24]

★★★

December 4, 1948, Barnhill, Scotland. George Orwell sends the completed manuscript of *Nineteen Eighty-Four* to his publisher.

The Crystallization of the Technosphere

The year 1948 is a historical magnifying glass of the present. It is a moment in history that condenses a diffuse period chronicling the transition into the planetary situation of today. The various historical-geographical vignettes outlined above chart a strikingly similar origin and mutual unleashing of the digital, the nuclear, and the environmental age. They show the synchronous rise of electronic computation, molecular genetics, of petro power and petro chemistry, the commodification and universalization of global relations under the West's domination, as well as the emergence of new concepts of humans in nature and new concepts of engineering as information engineering. The numerous technoscientific fragments left by a modernity torn asunder during two world wars recombined into a new, mutually reinforcing technological, scientific, cultural, and global environmental order, which surpasses previous waves of globalization, greatly accelerating the merciless, destructive, and unstoppable drive of the juggernaut of modernity.[25] The year 1948 – or, more accurately, the period spanning from 1945 to 1950 – marks a decisive moment not only for the reconstitution of the *world* as a hypermodern and geopolitical project. More than that, it is a moment in which the *Earth* became a guinea pig in humanity's experiment with an industrialized global economy, resulting in many unintended "geopolitical" consequences that our societies are now stuck with when facing the multiple crises of the Anthropocene.

Looking back at this historical inflection point, it is then possible to see how the planet became a space activated by technology, and media technologies in particular. Until about the middle of the 20th century, the Earth bore mainly the traces of geophysical, biological, and biogeochemical activity. Since then, however, a new, technical-industrial force unfolded, whose impact finds no equivalent in the history of the Earth. The fusing of several rapid and unchecked technological advancements helped to crystallize a new player in the planetary metabolism: a technosphere interlacing with and rivaling the great natural spheres like the biosphere or hydrosphere. Technologization in conjunction with a social contract that bound the fate of populations, elections, and five-year plans to an extractivist program to "plunder the Earth" (Osborne), locked in a path in which humanity has become a decisive factor in the current making of geological history.

The ensemble of graphs tracking the Great Acceleration – the exponential growth across a range of parameters measuring socioeconomic activities and their effects on the Earth system since around 1950 – paint a diagrammatic signature portrait of this watershed moment. At no previous moment in human history did anthropogenic impact on the environment grow as explosively and has had effects on a planetary scale as it did since the middle of the 20th century AD. Fossil-fuel-powered machines undertook the extraction, converting and scattering of hitherto unimaginable amounts of raw materials and thereby dissipated critical elements globally; artificial radionuclides and huge quantities of synthetics and chemicals began to accumulate in the geosphere; the carrying capacities of the planetary ecosystem commenced their rapid decline, headed by a human-led degradation of the biosphere, essentially initiating a sixth mass extinction in Earth history; the burning of fossil fuels enabled humans to break through the photosynthetic energy barrier, only to catapult Earth's climate into regimes last seen millions of years ago.

The technosphere, this amorphous ensemble of global resource and energy infrastructures, built environments, transport systems, financial institutions, state-led bureaucracies, and human workforces dramatically reconfigured the earthly circulation of matter and energy. It did so, mainly, by exploiting the lithosphere, biosphere, atmosphere, and hydrosphere as an energy source and a waste dump at the same time. But it is one decisive part of the technosphere, namely the media systems that orchestrate, manipulate, and culturally encode all these anthropogenic structures and energy conversions, that has remodeled not only the quasi-stable environment of the Holocene Earth but also the epistemic representation of the environment – both the global and the varied local articulations of it – as such to the technosphere's liking. Even expressing "Nature" in terms of spheres and systems that circulate and converse energy, like just done, gives witness to this epistemological remodeling.

Knowledge about the environment and the technosphere are enmeshed or "moored" together: they condition and serve, sustain and propel each other. Without a modern scientific approach to natural resources and forces there would be no technosphere; without the technosphere there would be no contemporary knowledge. On the one hand, natural science and engineering allows for the theoretical understanding and technical mastery of energy and matter, both living and inert, and thus the existence of a technosphere. On the other hand, it is the technosphere that enables modern science and engineering to exist.

Such knowledge, however, is always contained and available in some form of media and socio-technical arrangement. Current science and engineering are linked to the devices and metrics of a fleet of technical media, of certain institutional configurations and methodologies: data formats, building technology, patents, impact factors, remote sensing satellites, greenhouses, campuses, curricula. Ultimately, these kinds of technospherical practices, instruments, and facilitations of knowledge creation and management are also the ones that form the basis of our understanding of the environment and its cardinal changes that are underway.

Coming back to the pivot point 1948, it seems only logical that the Anthropocene Working Group – the group of geologists, geochemists, paleobiologists, archaeologists, and Earth system scientists that is tasked with reviewing the evidence for and against an Anthropocene boundary in recent Earth strata – identified the mid-20th century as the most likely starting date of the new epoch.[26] Their preferred method? The very same isotope analysis pioneered in the late 1940s by fusing nuclear chemistry with geology and oceanography. If one takes into account the further fact that also climate and Earth system modeling grew out of developments starting in that very same period – namely the origins of general circulation models spearheaded by John von Neumann's fusing of computer design and numerical weather forecasting in Princeton between 1946 and 1955 – and the rise of cybernetic-styled global systems ecology, the beginning of the Anthropocene and the beginning of its scientific realization are stunningly coeval.[27] Around 1948 a new sense of planetary affairs is "environed" through mass spectrometry, general circulation models, piston corers, nuclear tracers, chemical pollutants, and human-led alterations of biogeochemical cycles.

One almost paradoxical constellation is worth mentioning here: the role of the minute and small in leveraging the big and systemic. As much as measuring isotope compositions and running digital bits of information on electronic computers were instrumental in creating vistas on a changing planetary environment, human activity's large-scale effects on the planetary condition became possible only because of the manipulation of small-scale, elementary building blocks: genes, atoms, bits, and molecules. What is true for monitoring Earth system change is also true for driving these changes. Propelled by capitalist and communist ideologies – themselves shaped by two centuries of extensive industrialization as well as several hundred years of internal and external colonialism – the new technical mastery of the microscopic world produced enormous economies of scale. The control of nuclear fission, the digitalization of symbolic representations, the functional design of molecular polymer chains, and the manipulation of genetic material enabled self-reinforcing operations of ceaseless multiplication and duplication. Atomic bombs became produced en masse, Saudi oil became consumed en masse, data became calculated en masse while interconnected in multiplying networks: a technosphere xeroxing itself.[28]

The revolution in microelectronics initiated by the invention of the point-contact transistor at Bell Labs in December of 1947 gave rise to a drive for miniaturization which itself became an empirical law, Moore's law. Today, human agency is scarcely conceivable without the, maybe, octillions (1048) of transistors photolithographed onto integrated circuits. In the chemical sector, the most momentous change was the development of a global hydrocarbon system extending from oil fields and refineries to internal combustion engines and food additives. The precise breakdown and recombination of simple carbon-based chemical compounds and their respective polymerization products brought about the "molecular mobilization" of fuels and plastics.[29] Although this process began before 1948, it did not experience an explosive expansion until after World War II and the advent of "Hydrocarbon Man."[30]

Other large-scale consequences of the radical discretization of the world into smallest, mass-duplicated units[31] began to occur outside science. The supranational currency bancor was the premature attempt to create a global transaction space structured by the circulation of universal markers or tokens, intended to standardize nothing less than a global economy. What was ultimately left of it, GATT, produced the trade policy framework of the Great Acceleration, along with a host of political, economic, and cultural imbalances that favored the North. Alongside it arose other efforts to order Earth as an industrial-bureaucratic space. The most obvious examples are standardization systems such as the International Standard Industrial Classification of All Economic Activities, introduced by the UN in 1948 to classify statistical data across various economic areas. But they also include codifications of values such as the Universal Declaration of Human Rights, which was also adopted in 1948.

These examples of manipulation at the micro-level and its massive effects at the macro-level are tied to technologies that increasingly populate and saturate the planet as a whole. The historical result of this technological autopoiesis is that not only economic output and growth but also culture, politics, and science reoriented themselves to supporting the structural formation of the technosphere.[32] The crises we face today were born of this operational closure between the technosphere and the former "natural" spheres such as the biosphere, atmosphere, and lithosphere. The massive investment in research and technology that accompanied World War II catalyzed enormous creative power based on a capital-fueled market logic and East-West antagonisms. Though intellectuals in the immediate postwar era already remarked on this development,[33] the political will over the last decades to curb it has so far failed – too great are the infrastructural and political path dependencies of the technosphere and its ever-deepening grooves in the new planetary metabolism of humans and machines.

What the five speakers addressed at the Hotel Commodore[34] in March 1948, therefore, represented a major medial turn as part and parcel of a still larger turn of earthly matters. In close association with the global availability and distribution of raw materials and goods, with the development of nuclear weapons and defense systems, with an oil-based Pax Americana, with globalized science, and with international bureaucracy, the turn birthed a technology and a way of thinking that did much more than just optimizing electronic components. Engineers and CEOs alike fell gradually for the charms of the new cultural technique of digitally automated number processing whose credo is the representation of highly complex processes in binary circuit logic. Now it moves the world, effectively steering material and energetic flows within a technosphere spanning the globe from satellite orbits 40,000 km above the Earth's surface to 10 km into the lithosphere. Founded on the fundamental asymmetry between coded information and its physical effects – micro-energy inputs leveraging macro-energy impacts in the material world – digital media technologies have had a tremendous stake in the unleashing of Anthropocene drivers.[35]

At the same time, these media constitute the very same technologies that are key to detecting and understanding this transition. Monitoring and modeling the human-impacted Earth system are today squarely performed by digital technologies, but also shaping scientific, cultural, political, and even legal perception and the sense of place of living on a planet that has already transgressed its "boundaries of a safe operating space for humanity."[36]

Shortly after the turn of the new millennium, many believed that we had entered a new scientific era, one in which nanotechnology, biotechnology, information technology, and cognitive science would converge into a single, unified program. While this outlook may have been fueled by a megalomanic techno-optimism, the reality today is not far from what they predicted: bioinformatics, gene editing techniques like CRISPR, the creation of synthetic organisms and the engineering of metabolic pathways, new functional materials, synthetic minerals and chemical compounds, algorithms that code real-world phenomena and everything else that powers the dreams of post-cybernetics, from the buzz words of yesterday like Industry 4.0 and the Internet of Things to the buzz words of today like smart farming and the coming climate-tech economy. What we are witnessing now, in other words, is the gradual fusion of developments that were made possible in and around 1948. We are at the provisional end of a cascading process that started to gain momentum in the middle of the 20th century. The confluence of events in and around the year 1948 established a technical and social lock-in situation. Despite the astonishing speed of technological progress, the LP whose cover bears this epoch-making and hitherto neglected year continues to play.[37]

Notes

1 1948 I.R.E. National Convention Program, *Proceedings of the IRE* 36, no. 6 (1948): 754.
2 Norbert Wiener, *Cybernetics or Control and Communication in the Animal and the Machine* (Cambridge, MA: MIT Press, 1948). Wiener came up with the idea for the book during a meeting with the publisher Enrique Freymann, who operated a small bookstore at the Sorbonne. Under contract with Freymann, Wiener wrote his most famous work for the small publishing house Hermann et Cie. It was only later that MIT Press acquired the rights.
3 Claude E. Shannon, "A Mathematical Theory of Communication," *Bell Labs Technical Journal* 27 (1948): 379–423; 623–656. The complete essay appeared one year later with a general introduction by Warren Weaver in Claude E. Shannon & Warren Weaver, *The Mathematical Theory of Communication* (Urbana: University of Illinois Press, 1949).
4 Twenty years later, on the occasion of the anniversary of the founding of the Association for Computing Machinery, Jay Forrester – the inventor of the magnetic-core memory for computer RAM and the founder of the Institute for System Dynamics at MIT, entrusted with simulating the "limits of growth" for the Club of Rome – spoke of the disconnect between Old World intellectualism and Yankee engineering:

> Many years ago, I found myself seated at the end of a table about this wide at lunch and on one side was John von Neumann and on the other side was Norbert Wiener and they totally ignored me but they spent the…entire lunch discussing how you would translate modern tabloid headlines into four letter renaissance English words

(*ACM Annual Meeting*, Computer Oral History Collection, Archives Center, National Museum of American History, Washington, D.C., Transcripts, 1969–1973, 1977, Box 2, Folder 3).
5 In early 1948, Louis Bean, a Lithuanian-born advisor in the US Department of Agriculture, published the book *How to Predict Elections*. Using a novel approach based

on statistical observations of election cycles, he correctly predicted – contrary to the projections of America's political pundits – that Harry Truman would be reelected and that the Democrats would take control of Congress. It was the very same Democrat-led Congress that did not allow a vote on the Havana Charter, which proposed restrictions on the global trade of agricultural goods to protect local farming communities and ensure regional diversity.

6 See Timothy Mitchell, *Carbon Democracy: Political Power in the Age of Oil* (London & New York: Verso, 2011), 100ff.
7 See Mitchell, *Carbon Democracy*, 41f.
8 See Daniel Yergin, *The Prize: The Epic Quest for Oil, Money & Power* (New York: Simon & Schuster, 1991), 409 and 422ff.
9 Anne Fleckstein, "'Nothing but the Truth': Bezeugen in der südafrikanischen Wahrheitskommission," *Politik der Zeugenschaft*, eds. Sibylle Schmidt, Sybille Krämer, & Ramon Voges (Bielefeld: Transcript, 2014), 311–330.
10 See Nils Roll-Hansen, "Wishful Science: The Persistence of T. D. Lysenko's Agrobiology in the Politics of Science," *Osiris* 23, no. 1 (2008): 115–135.
11 The Swiss chemist Paul Hermann Müller was awarded the 1948 Nobel Prize in Medicine for discovering DDT's insecticidal properties. Also in that year, the Nobel committee considered giving Josef Stalin the Nobel Peace Prize but ultimately decided not to name a recipient.
12 See Hans-Jörg Rheinberger & Staffan Müller-Wille, *Vererbung: Geschichte und Kultur eines biologischen Konzepts* (Frankfurt am Main: Fischer, 2009), 248.
13 See Paul Josephson, "The Stalin Plan for the Transformation of Nature, and the East European Experience," *The Name of the Great Work: Stalin's Plan for the Transformation of Nature and its Impact in Eastern Europe*, ed. Doubravka Olšáková (New York: Berghahn Books, 2016), 1–41. See also Paul R. Josephson, *Industrialized Nature: Brute Force Technology and the Transformation of the Natural World* (Washington, D.C.: Island Press, 2002).
14 Stephen Brain, "The Great Stalin Plan for the Transformation of Nature," *Environmental History* 15, no. 4 (2010): 670–700.
15 Harold C. Urey, "Oxygen Isotopes in Nature and in the Laboratory," *Science* 108, no. 2810 (1948): 489–496. On this episode see Christoph Rosol, "Hauling Data. Anthropocene Analogues, Paleoceanography and Missing Paradigm Shifts," *Historical Social Research* 40, no. 2 (2015): 37–66.
16 Emily M. Kern, "Archaeology Enters the 'Atomic Age': A Short History of Radiocarbon, 1946–1960," *The British Journal for the History of Science* 53, no. 2 (2020): 207–227, here 221f.
17 See Perrin Selcer, *The Postwar Origins of the Global Environment: How the United Nations Built Spaceship Earth* (New York: Columbia University Press, 2018). See also Paul Warde, Libby Robin, & Sverker Sörlin, *The Environment. A History of the Idea* (Baltimore: Johns Hopkins University Press, 2018), 53ff.
18 Warde et al., *The Environment*, 20ff.
19 Jacob Darwin Hamblin, *Arming Mother Nature: The Birth of Catastrophic Environmentalism* (London: Oxford University Press, 2013).
20 A key paper for such understanding is George Evelyn Hutchinson's 1948 paper: "Circular Causal Systems in Ecology," *Annals of the New York Academy of Sciences* 50, no. 4 (1948), 221–246.
21 As the Australian historian Martin Thomas observes, the expedition is its own "*genre*…a distinctive and self-perpetuating mode of moving, acting, organizing and writing," Martin Thomas, "Expedition as Time Capsule: Introducing the American-Australian Scientific Expedition to Arnhem Land," *Exploring the Legacy of the 1948 Arnhem Land Expedition*, eds. Martin Thomas & Margo Neale (Canberra: ANU Press, 2011), 18.

22 Elizabeth Kolbert, "CRISPR and the Splice to Survive," *The New Yorker*, January 11, 2021, URL: https://www.newyorker.com/magazine/2021/01/18/crispr-and-the-splice-to-survive
23 The residues from nuclear weapons testings serve as prime markers in identifying a distinct stratigraphic boundary for the start of the Anthropocene. See, for instance, several contributions in the "Nuclear Anthropocene" dossier at *Anthropogenic Markers: Stratigraphy and Context*, eds. Christoph Rosol and Giulia Rispoli (online at Anthropocene Curriculum, 2022), URL: https://www.anthropocene-curriculum.org/anthropogenic-markers/nuclear-anthropocene
24 See Jan Zalasiewicz et al., "When Did the Anthropocene Begin? A Mid-Twentieth Century Boundary Level Is Stratigraphically Optimal," *Quaternary International* 383 (2015): 196–203.
25 The metaphor of modernity as a heavy, unstoppable juggernaut derives from Anthony Giddens, *The Consequences of Modernity* (Stanford: Stanford University Press, 1990).
26 See ibid. and Will Steffen et al., "The Trajectory of the Anthropocene: The Great Acceleration," *The Anthropocene Review* 2, no. 1 (2015): 81–98.
27 Cf. Christoph Rosol, "Which Design for a Weather Predictor? Speculating on the Future of Electronic Forecasting in Post-War America," *Cultures of Prediction in Atmospheric and Climate Science. Epistemic and Cultural Shifts in Computer-based Modelling and Simulation*, eds. Matthias Heymann, Gabriele Gramelsberger & Martin Mahony (London: Routledge, 2017), 68–84; Christoph Rosol, "Data, Models and Earth History in Deep Convolution. Paleoclimate Simulations and Their Epistemological Unrest," *Berichte zur Wissenschaftsgeschichte* 40, no. 2 (2017): 120–139.
28 On October 22, 1948, the Haloid Company revealed its xerography technology. One year later, it rolled out the world's first commercial photocopier, the XeroX Model A.
29 Benjamin Steininger, "Petromoderne Petromonströs," *Technology and the Sublime*, eds. Giulia Rispoli & Christoph Rosol, special issue, *Azimuth* 12, no. 2 (2018), 23.
30 Yergin, *The Prize*, 541.
31 No wonder that even the famous "$\alpha\beta\gamma$-paper," explaining the origin of the building blocks of the universe through big-bang nucleo-synthesis, was published in 1948: Ralph A. Alpher, Hans Bethe, & George Gamow: "The Origin of Chemical Elements," *Physical Review* 73, no. 803 (1948).
32 For more on the concept of technological autopoiesis, see Bronislaw Szerszynski: "Vom Werkzeug zur Technosphäre," *Technosphäre*, eds. Katrin Klingan & Christoph Rosol (Berlin: Matthes & Seitz, 2019), 48–63.
33 See, for instance, Robert Jungk's travel reports from the farms, laboratories, and offices of the American model in *Tomorrow Is Already Here* (New York: Simon & Schuster, 1954).
34 Indeed, the Hotel Commodore is itself a symbol of hypercapitalist continuity. Opened in 1919 and located next to the Grand Central Station, the hotel was named after "Commodore" Cornelius Vanderbilt, the founder of the New York Central Railroad. Donald Trump acquired the run-down hotel in the late 1970s under dubious circumstances. It was his first major project as a developer and the start of his real-estate empire. However, his business partner in the deal, Hyatt Hotels, would later outmaneuver him, buying his stake in the hotel in 1996.
35 For more on that topic cf. Christoph Rosol et al., "On the Age of Computation in the Epoch of Humankind," *Nature Outlook* 563, no. 7733 (2018): 1–5.
36 Will Steffen, "The Planetary Boundaries Framework: Defining a Safe Operating Space for Humanity," *The Safe Operating Space Treaty. A New Approach to Managing Our Use of the Earth System*, eds. Paulo Magalhães, Will Steffen, Klaus Bosselmann, Alexandra Aragão, & Viriato Soromenho-Marques (Cambridge: Cambridge Scholars Publishing, 2016), 23–46.
37 The Hungarian-American engineer Peter Carl Goldmark and his team at Columbia Records developed a 33 1/3 rpm long-playing disc made of polyvinyl chloride (PVC). Its introduction in 1948 marked the end of shellac records and the advent of the vinyl era.

References

Alpher, Ralph A., Hans Bethe, & George Gamow. "The Origin of Chemical Elements," *Physical Review* 73, no. 7 (1948): 803–804.
Bean, Louis. *How to Predict Elections*. New York: Alfred A. Knopf, 1948.
Brain, Stephen. "The Great Stalin Plan for the Transformation of Nature," *Environmental History* 15, no. 4 (2010): 670–700.
Computer Oral History Collection, Archives Center. *ACM Annual Meeting*. National Museum of American History, Washington, D.C., Transcripts, 1969–1973, 1977, Box 2, Folder 3.
Fleckstein, Anne. "'Nothing but the Truth': Bezeugen in der südafrikanischen Wahrheitskommission." *Politik der Zeugenschaft*, edited by Sibylle Schmidt, Sybille Krämer, & Ramon Voges, 311–330. Bielefeld: Transcript, 2014.
Giddens, Anthony. *The Consequences of Modernity*. Stanford: Stanford University Press, 1990.
Hamblin, Jacob Darwin. *Arming Mother Nature: The Birth of Catastrophic Environmentalism*. London: Oxford University Press, 2013.
Hutchinson, George Evelyn. "Circular Causal Systems in Ecology," *Annals of the New York Academy of Sciences* 50, no. 4 (1948): 221–246.
I.R.E. National Convention Program. *Proceedings of the IRE* 36, no. 6 (1948): 754.
Josephson, Paul. *Industrialized Nature: Brute Force Technology and the Transformation of the Natural World*. Washington, D.C.: Island Press, 2002.
Josephson, Paul. "The Stalin Plan for the Transformation of Nature, and the East European Experience." *In the Name of the Great Work: Stalin's Plan for the Transformation of Nature and its Impact in Eastern Europe*, edited by Doubravka Olšáková, 1–41. New York: Berghahn Books, 2016.Jungk, Robert. *Tomorrow Is Already Here*. New York: Simon & Schuster, 1954.
Kern, Emily M. "Archaeology Enters the 'Atomic Age': A Short History of Radiocarbon, 1946–1960," *The British Journal for the History of Science* 53, no. 2 (2020): 207–227.
Kolbert, Elizabeth. "CRISPR and the Splice to Survive," *The New Yorker*, January 11, 2021, URL: https://www.newyorker.com/magazine/2021/01/18/crispr-and-the-splice-to-survive
Mitchell, Timothy. *Carbon Democracy: Political Power in the Age of Oil*. London & New York: Verso, 2011.
Rheinberger, Hans-Jörg & Staffan Müller-Wille. *Vererbung: Geschichte und Kultur eines biologischen Konzepts*. Frankfurt: Fischer, 2009.
Roll-Hansen, Nils. "Wishful Science: The Persistence of T. D. Lysenko's Agrobiology in the Politics of Science," *Osiris* 23, no. 1 (2008): 115–135.
Rosol, Christoph, "Hauling Data. Anthropocene Analogues, Paleoceanography and Missing Paradigm Shifts," *Historical Social Research* 40, no. 2 (2015): 37–66.
Rosol, Christoph, "Data, Models and Earth History in Deep Convolution. Paleoclimate Simulations and Their Epistemological Unrest," *Berichte zur Wissenschaftsgeschichte* 40, no. 2 (2017): 120–139.
Rosol, Christoph, "Which Design for a Weather Predictor? Speculating on the Future of Electronic Forecasting in Post-War America." *Cultures of Prediction in Atmospheric and Climate Science. Epistemic and Cultural Shifts in Computer-based Modelling and Simulation*, edited by Matthias Heymann, Gabriele Gramelsberger & Martin Mahony, 68–84. London: Routledge, 2017.
Rosol, Christoph, Benjamin Steininger, Jürgen Renn & Robert Schlögl. "On the Age of Computation in the Epoch of Humankind," *Nature Outlook* 563, no. 7733 (2018): 1–5.

Selcer, Perrin. *The Postwar Origins of the Global Environment: How the United Nations Built Spaceship Earth*. New York: Columbia University Press, 2018.

Shannon, Claude E. "A Mathematical Theory of Communication," *Bell Labs Technical Journal* 27 (1948): 379–423; 623–656.

Shannon, Claude E. & Warren Weaver. *The Mathematical Theory of Communication*. Urbana: University of Illinois Press, 1949.

Steffen, Will. "The Planetary Boundaries Framework: Defining a Safe Operating Space for Humanity." *The Safe Operating Space Treaty. A New Approach to Managing Our Use of the Earth System*, edited by Paulo Magalhães, Will Steffen, Klaus Bosselmann, Alexandra Aragão, & Viriato Soromenho-Marques, 23–46. Cambridge: Cambridge Scholars Publishing, 2016.

Steffen, Will, et al. "The Trajectory of the Anthropocene: The Great Acceleration," *The Anthropocene Review* 2, no. 1 (2015): 81–98.

Steininger, Benjamin, "Petromoderne Petromonströs." *Technology and the Sublime*, edited by Giulia Rispoli & Christoph Rosol, special issue, *Azimuth* 12, no. 2 (2018): 15-29.

Szerszynski, Bronislaw. "Vom Werkzeug zur Technosphäre." *Technosphäre*, edited by Katrin Klingan & Christoph Rosol, 48–63. Berlin: Matthes & Seitz, 2019.

Thomas, Martin. "Expedition as Time Capsule: Introducing the American-Australian Scientific Expedition to Arnhem Land." *Exploring the Legacy of the 1948 Arnhem Land Expedition*, edited by Martin Thomas & Margo Neale, 1-30. Canberra: ANU Press, 2011.

Urey, Harold C. "Oxygen Isotopes in Nature and in the Laboratory," *Science* 108, no. 2810 (1948): 489–496.

Warde, Paul, Libby Robin & Sverker Sörlin. *The Environment. A History of the Idea* (Baltimore: Johns Hopkins University Press, 2018).

Wiener, Norbert. *Cybernetics or Control and Communication in the Animal and the Machine*. Cambridge, MA: MIT Press, 1948.

Yergin, Daniel. *The Prize: The Epic Quest for Oil, Money & Power*. New York: Simon & Schuster, 1991.

Zalasiewicz, Jan, et al. "When Did the Anthropocene Begin? A Mid-Twentieth Century Boundary Level Is Stratigraphically Optimal," *Quaternary International* 383 (2015): 196–203.

PART 3
Elemental environing media

6
WINDS, MIASMA, POLLUTION
Pathologies of the air as an environing medium

Eva Horn

As I was starting to write this text in the spring of 2020, most of the world was in lockdown because of the COVID-19 pandemic.[1] In my home town of Vienna, citizens were cautioned to stay in isolation but allowed to go to the supermarkets and for runs or strolls while observing the rules of social distancing. Spring had come unusually early, mid-March, yet with intermittent spells of frost. As the trees in the city's parks started blooming, people, despite the curfew, left their houses, not just, like me, for solitary walks, but for picnics, conversing with neighbors, or to take the kids to the playground. Friends were sharing a bag of chips, young men were standing together smoking. Kids were playing in groups. Enjoying the arrival of spring, the smells, the sunshine, and the being-together with strangers and friends, play-mates and neighbors, people were taking the air, as one says. Cautiously jogging past these groups, I realized, as if it was at the very moment of its disappearance, that sociality consists in being in the air together, sharing a common air. All of a sudden, this sharing of air now came with a novel risk: the risk of contagion.

As an airborne disease, the virus SARS-CoV-2 is transmitted by "dissemination of either airborne droplet nuclei or small particles in the respirable size range containing infectious agents that remain infective over time and distance".[2] Research has shown that the virus can travel through the air in aerosols (droplets smaller than 5 μm) as they are produced by normal or heavy breathing.[3] Carriers of the virus not only eject it in droplets from coughing and sneezing but also emit it by simply exhaling. In a pandemic brought forth by an airborne disease such as COVID-19, the air has become the very medium of pathogens. Now, breathing together, that is, being social, is a risk. All of a sudden, the eeriness of this airborne disease brought into focus an aspect of air that we seem to have forgotten, in spite – or maybe because – of the complexity and immensity of political issues such as pollution and climate change. Air is a medium of the social – a medium of communication but also of contagion.

DOI: 10.4324/9781003282891-9

Elements and environments

Air is not just matter that can be analyzed chemically and broken down into its contents such as the composition of gases (including the growing quantity of greenhouse gases) as well as particulate matter such as dust, ash, sulfur, pollen, and aerosols of organic and inorganic origin. Air should, as I have suggested elsewhere, be understood as a *medium*: a medium of biological life, of metabolism, perception, movement, and of the physical structure of all organisms; but also, more specifically, a medium of the social life of humans.[4] Treating air as a medium does not mean pinning down what it *is*, but looking at, or telling a story about, *what it does*.[5] Air as a medium is a condition of existence and of being-alive, yet also of social life, precisely by environing humans and shaping their lifeworld, at once connecting and separating them. "Environments", writes John Durham Peters, are "media. Water, fire, sky, earth, and ether are elements – homey, sublime, dangerous, and wonderful – that sustain existence, and we still haven't found out how to care for them; our efforts to do so constitute our technical history".[6] However, media are not simply "natural"; no matter, no object is a medium in itself, rather "media are ensembles of natural element and human craft".[7] Understanding air as an "elemental medium" means two things. First (1), it implies understanding air as an element in the ancient sense, an omnipresent "root" of the world.[8] Second (2), it means telling a story about how air, for the longest time in Occidental thought, was thought of as an "environing medium", a medium connecting bodies with bodies, bodies with locations, locations with spaces, and all of these to the cosmos.

(1) Elements in the Ancient sense were "considered profoundly animate, social, and even divine – whether in the guise of localized bodies, purposeful forces, or powerful deities".[9] They were in a constant dynamic of exchange, opposition, mixture, and separation, they possessed agency and life. Elements create a cosmos that cannot be broken down into "pure matter" or into the modern dichotomy of "organism" and "environment". Telling a story of air as an element involves reconstructing the ways in which air was understood as a force shaping landscapes and livelihoods, as an agent transmitting health and disease, entering and exiting the body, forming and deforming it, linking the individual body to a *genius loci*, a community, and a cosmic order. The elements stand for a world in which the environment is *in* the organism, as much as the organism is *in* the environment.

"For millennia", Jeffrey Jerome Cohen and Lowell Duckert write, the "elements offered a mode of conceptualizing materiality that conveys how difference underlays all substance, how nature covets entanglement, how entropy promises universal ruin as well as unceasing regeneration".[10] An elemental understanding of the world – and, more specifically, of nature, as David Macauley argues – requires "anamnesis", a "loss of forgetfulness"[11] of ancient, seemingly obsolete conceptualizations of nature and humans. These may help rethink modern notions of the environment in a way that is more attuned to the

Anthropocene as the epoch of an inextricable entanglement of the human and the non-human, the organic and the inorganic. This would involve taking into account human interventions into nature but also recalling seemingly obsolete notions of "nature" or "world" that have granted agency, movement, and life to non-human, non-organic entities. Elemental thought might be a helpful tool for conceiving of a new being-in-the-world that transcends the modernist separation between history and nature, organism and environment.

(2) The notion of "environing media" implies a similar gesture of anamnesis. It means retrieving an older understanding of "medium" as "the in-between". A medium in this sense is the surrounding or connecting agent, the necessary condition for perception and for the transmission of influx and force.[12] In this pre-modern sense, the concept of "medium" is not primarily about communication technologies or data processing but almost synonymous with "nature", "environment", "milieu", or "ambiance". While such a conception does not exclude technology, it focuses rather on the topology and materiality of media, that is, on the question as to how things are situated and transferred within space, and what material exchanges between organisms and their surroundings are possible. Peters defines media as "infrastructures of being" or "modes of being". They are "the habitats and materials through which we act and are. This gives them ecological, ethical, and existential import".[13]

From this perspective, speaking of an "environing medium" almost amounts to a tautology. Environments *are* media. Looking at the history of the two concepts, "medium" and "environment", one cannot help but notice the similarity of their meanings in the early stages of their emergence. Both are essentially *topological*. "Medium" is the in-between, "environment" is that which surrounds. Air, Bronislaw Szerszynski has argued, is a medium that carries the "signal of life" – an abiotic aliveness that keeps the Earth's atmosphere, unlike that of other planets, in a dynamic, far-from-equilibrium state.[14] In turn, understanding environment as a medium means to observe and describe how it *operates* as an infrastructure or condition of possibility, of existence, exchange, transport, and influence. Sverker Sörlin, in this volume, emphasizes the transitive structure of the concept. Environments are best described as an activity – *to environ* – not a noun.

> Literally all the distinct features of the environment, from the sub-atomic to the planetary, can't be described and understood without the word. It is the work of environing that turns these features, from rivers to birds, from fungi to soils – or, *Airs, Waters, Places*, in Hippocrates' gracefully inclusive shorthand – into the environment as we know it.[15]

Air as an environing medium thus has a conceptual history. Theories, stories, fictions, metaphors, and the practices of observation, measurement, and control of the surroundings all contribute to the constitution of the different historical states of knowledge about the air. How could an elusive entity such as the air be conceptualized as an environing medium? What is the relation between the surroundings and that which is surrounded, between the environment and the environed, e.g., a body, a society, a state, a house? How is it, at a particular historical juncture, understood?

While the focus on air as an *elemental medium* means dealing with its materiality, its contents, and its internal dynamics and agency (including its dangers), thinking about the air as *environing medium* means tracing the practices and cultural techniques that create types of knowledge, generate data, and devise models of the air as environment. Throughout history, air, conceived as an all-pervasive element, has been turned into an environment by means of perception, observation, data gathering, and eventually politicizing. The history of perception and conceptualizations of air, however, is far from continuous. A historical perspective on *air as an environing medium* involves tapping into a tradition that has not only fallen into oblivion but today strikes us, in many of its concepts and core ideas, as pre-modern, outdated, and epistemologically untenable. It is a story about the air being understood as a medium of the social, a shared environment that forms and transforms human beings while, in turn, also being altered and constituted by them. It is also a story about how this medium becomes the object of a specific form of attention and concern, of practices of "care", designed to record, prevent, and control its influences and dynamics.

If such stories strike us, today, with an uncanny topicality, it is because they are about the air's *pathologies* or disruptions. It is in its disruption or disturbance that the medium itself becomes perceptible. I will focus on three of such pathologies: fever-carrying winds, miasmas, and the long history of air pollution. It may not be by chance that one of the first texts on air pollution, John Evelyn's *Fumifugium* (1661), addresses the "aer" as an "omnipresent, and, as it were, universal Medium".[16] What these pathologies of the air have in common is that the air is not only perceived as a medium of harmful influences on individual bodies. Rather, they force us to think about the social as a communal being-in-the-air, being-in-the-medium. Indeed, it is through the harm that the air can impose on both the individual and the social body, that its nature as an environing medium becomes all the more perceptible. In the form of illness and pollution, the air is subject to historically specific forms of knowledge about what it means to "environ" and to be "environed" by such an elusive, yet hazardous medium as the air.

Winds

For a long time, fevers and other diseases were thought to be carried by the air. In his book on *Epidemics* I, Hippocrates describes the onset of certain epidemic diseases as the result of an unusual course of the seasons:

> In Thasus, about the autumn equinox, and under the Pleiades, the rains were abundant, constant, and soft, with southerly winds; the winter southerly, the northerly winds faint, droughts; on the whole, the winter having the character of spring. ... The whole constitution of the season being thus

inclined to the southerly, and with droughts early in the spring, from the preceding opposite and northerly state, ardent fevers occurred in a few instances, and these very mild, being rarely attended with hemorrhage, and never proving fatal. Swellings appeared around the ears, in many on either side, and in the greatest number on both sides, being unaccompanied by fever so as not to confine the patient to bed; in all cases they disappeared without giving trouble, neither did any of them come to suppuration, as is common in swellings from other causes.[17]

What sounds like the opening of a novel is in fact an account of the climatic, meteorological, and astrological factors that led to an epidemic of fever and swollen glands (presumably mumps) which befell the inhabitants of Thasus. With the fall being exceptionally wet, the winter too warm, the spring particularly dry, and the winds blowing mostly from the South, the epidemic fever for Hippocrates can be attributed to this specific meteorological constellation. This is why his detailed descriptions of widespread diseases in an area are always framed by information about the season in which they emerge. As the air invariably affects everyone living in a given area, the weather and prevailing winds explain why certain diseases grow in frequency at certain times of the year (I.II, 2). In the Hippocratic tradition, health was conceived as a balance (*eucrasia*) between the bodily fluids (*humors*) that stood in relation to the four elements: air, water, Earth, and fire. So if one of the elements or its corresponding quality, i.e., dryness, dampness, coldness, or heat, is in excess in the body's environment, the internal balance of the humors would be disturbed.[18] In his famous treatise on local climates, *Airs, Waters, Places*, Hippocrates emphasizes the importance of knowing "the warm and cold winds, both those common to every country and those peculiar to a particular locality".[19] The state and the movements of the air (along with other environmental factors such as water quality, soils, and staple foods) shape the inhabitants' physical constitution and illnesses, as well as their mentalities and cultures.[20]

While diet and other health practices can follow individual choices, the air and its varying states are inescapably common to all those who live in the same location. People breathe the same air, are exposed to the same winds, the same temperatures, degrees of moisture or pollution. This is why winds or the irregularities of the seasons, according to the Hippocratic logic, account for epidemic illnesses. The air explains the similarities within a given population – be it the same mentalities, illnesses, bodily constitution, or cultural practices. "Climate" in a narrower, geographical sense – as the slant of the sun's rays in a given location – accounts for the general environmental conditions of a location. The winds and the seasons, however, are the agents of change in the course of the year. They bring the bounties of harvest, but also the misery of winter or danger of epidemics. Certain winds are to be avoided, others sought to regularly freshen private houses. In many cultures there is considerable folklore about the deleterious influences of winds. In Chinese, fever is *shangfeng*, "wounded by the wind",[21] and even today in Indonesian a common cold is *masuk angin* – "the wind has entered". Germans are famously intolerant to drafts. In Europe, the Mediterranean Sirocco or the Alpine Föhn are notorious for their deleterious effects on physical and mental health: the Sirocco is supposed to bring pestilence, madness, and even violence and crime; the Föhn meanwhile brings endemic irritability and migraine. In the influence of the winds, physical, psychological, and social aberrations mix.[22]

In the course of the 18th and 19th centuries, when the Hippocratic tradition was revived, the changing states of the air became an object of research, observation, and data gathering. A "meteorological medicine" was established which meticulously studied "The effects of Air on Human Bodies", as a famous treatise by the doctor and satirist John Arbuthnot is aptly titled.[23] In the endeavor to observe and archive the relation between illnesses and the weather, both researchers and private citizens started taking measurements and collecting meteorological data. By gathering and processing environmental data which together produce a particular understanding of climate and humans, the air is turned into an environing medium. On the one hand, these data served the methodological study of climate and weather phenomena, including a statistical understanding of the link between the occurrence of certain illnesses and air pressure, rain, winds, temperature, etc.[24] On the other hand, these acts of data gathering became increasingly sophisticated documents of physical and mental states. Thinking about the weather was a source of reflecting on one's self, specifically the subject's individual sensitivity to the states of the air. As doctors and their patients started keeping weather diaries, observing the air and its variations became a practice of personal and general healthcare.[25] The human body, as Jan Golinski has shown, became itself an instrument of weather sensing, each diarist being a "human barometer".[26] In accordance with each person's specific weather susceptibility, he or she will react to its impacts and changes differently.

As the dynamics and disturbances of the air as elemental medium, winds thus affect humans *at a given place*. However, this conception of an impact of the weather, winds, or seasons on the human body is based on a perspective on the body as an individual single body with its particular constitution and sensitivity. If wind and weather exert an influence, they constitute, as it were, an "individual environment" affecting the body as singular entity. If they bring epidemics, it's not because they *transport* illnesses from one body to the other. Rather, they are supposed to influence each and everybody in the same way in a given area. According to this conception of air, climate and weather are shared conditions but they are not "social". In meteorological medicine, every human being braves the weather alone.

Miasma

The social dimension of air makes its entrance with the concept of "miasma", the most persistent theory of the air's dangers in European medical history.

"Miasma" was thought to be a noxious substance emanating from the soil, from processes of decay, stagnant water, or intensely odorous substances. Literally meaning "stain", "miasma" can refer both to a toxic substance and to moral guilt, the stain of spilt blood.[27] In both cases – most famously in Sophocles' *Oedipus Rex* – the miasma brings *loimos*, pestilence. The air carries the pathogenic "stain" and affects all people in a given area by entering the body through respiration. To cite Hippocrates:

> Whenever many men are attacked by one disease at the same time, the cause should be assigned to that which is most common, and which we all use most. This it is which we breathe in. ... But when an epidemic of one disease is prevalent, it is plain that the cause is not regimen but what we breathe, and that this is charged with some unhealthy exhalation.[28]

Leaving the aspect of moral guilt behind, in the post-Hippocratic tradition of medicine, airborne miasmas became shorthand for the origin of any illness that may afflict the body. Miasmas could stem from tombs, water, all processes of organic decomposition, animal and human feces, but also from fertile soils, sultry weather, and even from the fumes emanating from the Earth in volcanic eruptions and earthquakes. While with the winds, the air is an elemental medium which directly affects the body, in the theory of miasma the air operates as an environing medium which mediates pathogens.

At the beginning of the 18th century, air thus became a source of universal physical endangerment. It was seen as a medium which carries an infinite list of hazardous matters: dust and soil, smells, water, salt, oil, greasy particles, sulfur, vegetable vapors, sweat, flatulence and exhalation of humans and animals, volcanic ash, insect eggs, maggots, pollen, seeds, etc.[29] These mixtures accounted for the singular conditions of a given place. Arbuthnot writes:

> The air near the surface of the earth, in which all animals live and breathe, contains the steams, effluvia, and all the abrasions of bodies on the surface of the earth, when they are so small and light as to float in it; from whence it is evident, that the contents of it must be different in different places of the surface of the earth.[30]

As air is constitutive of all processes of life, it is, according to the medicine of the time, contained in any organic matter. The body ingests air not only by inhalation but also through the skin and with food. Since air is both outside and inside every living organism, the body's health and sickness depend on it. As the author of a *Guide to Health* published in 1744 wrote: "Distempers seldom arise from any other cause than the air, for either it is too much or too little, or abounds with infectious filth".[31]

Not surprisingly, a particular danger stems from urban air. Cities are aggregations of excrement, garbage, and physical proximity. Urban air is, as it were, *social air*. In one of his essays on 19th century Vienna, the Austrian poet Adalbert Stifter illustrates the dangers of social contact in a succinct image:

> Our forefathers built this city so densely, that it happens at times, when I open my window in the morning to let in fresh air, that all I get is the night air from my neighbor's bedroom, who also has opened his window and wishes me a good morning.[32]

City dwellers breathe each other's exhalations. The air is a medium of the social – however in the form of unwanted, disgusting, and toxic closeness, perceptible in the smelly and lukewarm fumes from the neighbor's house.

By the end of the 18th century, the air and its quality became the object of constant concern. The sources of miasmas had to be eliminated or – as in the case of tanneries or graveyards – exiled outside the cities; sewer systems were built; frequent ventilation of houses became mandatory. Alain Corbin has vividly described the new attention paid to the sense of smell, the fears of being sickened by odors, but also the fascination with which doctors and scientists started investigating the olfactory nuances of putrefaction or feces.[33] These concerns about the air lead to the development of an early version of "environmental medicine", the hygiene movement.[34] Hygiene is less concerned with curing illnesses then with preventing and eliminating risk. It comprises many different practices ranging from diet, exercise, and cleanliness, to ways of keeping the noxious influences of bad air at bay and seeking healthier air in mountain and seaside resorts.

At the core of the hygiene movement is a specific conception of environment, captured in the term coined by the French doctor and health reformer Jean Noël Hallé: "*circumfusa*". Literally, it means everything that "flows around" a given body. The term captures not only the mediality of air but also its specific dynamics – its flowing nature that allows it to absorb, influence, surround, and penetrate everything, from bodies to food and solid materials. Air has a dynamic of its own, a flow – and the hygienist's task is to help control or avoid being overpowered by these flows. Air as a *circumfusum* is a medium in the sense that it transports substances and forces from the environment to the beings living in these environments. It is so all-encompassing that it is not just a source of life but also a threat to it, an object of permanent vigilance and concern.

An inextricable influence and influx, air is intensely, even overwhelmingly perceptible by the senses. The most immediate way of sensing the air and its contents might be by its smell, which, in itself, can kill or badly harm a person's health. The air can also be felt by the tactile sense of the skin that perceives the quality of the winds: dry or moist, cold, cooling, balmy or torrid, cutting or mild, dusty or sandy, thick or clear. In a more indirect way, air can also be seen – in the obscurity of fog and smoke or in the pellucidity of pure mountain air. While the body itself is open and permeable to the specific environment it dwells in, the environment, in turn, is defined – as in Hippocrates' famous formula of "airs, waters, and places (*topon*)" – as the *topos*, a specific place that imprints its mark on its inhabitants. The air as an elemental medium marks the particularity of this location. Vladimir Janković has emphasized the "topocentric approach" of Hippocratic and neo-Hippocratic theories of the air and climate, its general attention to the environmental specificity of a given location, "Living well and feeling healthy was identified with the properties of one's existential coordinates. The locus of illness moved from the individual body to the space between bodies".[35] As the medium that inescapably binds life to its dwelling place and society to its location, air was, as it were, the spirit of the place, the *genius loci*.

Jean-Baptiste Fressoz has pointed out that the notion of *circumfusa* is much broader than the concept of "environment" today. It includes everything that influences the body, and is based on the idea of a fundamental "physical analogy of man with the objects that surround him/her", as the physiologist Pierre-Jean-Georges Cabanis puts it.[36] As in the notion of "air" or "climate", *circumfusa* is an environment which profoundly shapes the human being but in turn is also altered by humans. "The power of the 'circumfusa' is unclear and disquieting", writes Fressoz: "Environmental modifications that seemed benign could turn out to have terrible consequences".[37] Fressoz cites the example of an epidemic on the Dutch Molucca islands which was attributed to the destruction of the local clove trees. In the absence of the cloves whose aromatic scents were believed to sanitize the air, the noxious fumes of a nearby volcano could bring the disease. Thinking of the air as an environing medium thus not only highlights its inherent dangers and invasiveness. It also emphasizes the air's fragility. Seen from a medical standpoint, the air is the carrier of noxious vapors and epidemic diseases. At the same time, the air can also be seen as endangered by the fumes and emissions of modern civilization.

Pollution

Today we think of pollution as the introduction of noxious substances (gases such as carbon dioxide, carbon monoxide, ammonia, sulfur dioxide, and particulates such as ashes, dust, and soot) into the atmosphere through industrial processes such as the burning of fossil fuels, waste treatment, or agricultural activities. Yet, in early concepts of air pollution, nature and culture, weather conditions and industrial emissions, fog and smoke are not treated as separate categories. One of the first texts decrying the pollution of London air by the smoke emitted by various industries, Evelyn's *Fumifugium*, refers to the air as an element which affects health through the "humours" but also the "passions of the soul".[38] The soot from brewers, soap-boilers, and lime-burners poisons not just the air Londoners breathe but also soils clothes and skin, and kills animals and humans. The reforms Evelyn suggests to King Charles II consist in banning these industries from the city center and to surround London with a ring of fragrant plants. Yet Evelyn's text, which has often been understood as one of the first environmental manifestos, can also, as Mark Jenner has suggested, be read as a political treatise addressing the king as the chief cleanser of the political order in the wake of the Restoration.[39] Furthermore, the city of London is not just treated as a specific geographical location vulnerable to the impact of bad air, as in the case of miasma. In Evelyn's treatise, London is an imperial capital whose glory – despite its climatically superior location – is sullied by the filth of unchecked, insalubrious industrial activities. In the case of pollution, nature and politics merge.

In the following centuries, the discourse on air pollution "politicizes" nature by intricately connecting meteorological phenomena with industrial, economic, and social questions. While smoke was initially used as an antidote to the poisonous miasma of decomposing matter, in the course of the industrial revolution it started to be understood as a threat not only to the health of the city's inhabitants, it also threatened the plants and animals, the surfaces of buildings and monuments, and ultimately the social order.[40] During the spells of heavy fog in London from the last decades of the 19th century well into the middle of the 20th century, death rates due to breathing difficulties and bronchitis temporarily rose by up to 40%.[41] The thickness of London air filled with smoke and fog made vision so hard that it became, as a popular magazine noted in 1855, "a carnival of petty larceny" where thieves, cloaked in the fog, would "contrive to relieve you of any loose cash, pocket-book, or tempting 'ticker', with a dexterity you cannot but admire".[42] Air pollution is an environmental condition that sows not only petty crime and accidents caused by the lack of visibility, it separates – as in the caricature from *Punch* 1870 – citizens from one another by its murkiness.

Pollution also separates the classes. While the poor are forced to live in the parts of the city most directly affected by industrial emissions, the more affluent could choose to either live in healthier surroundings or move outside of the city altogether. A journal article from 1855 complains that the

> smoke-charged atmosphere leads to moral results of a most unfortunate kind, in as far as it sends away the rich to dwell apart from the poor, who are thus deprived of the neighborly sympathy ... and edification which they might otherwise obtain from their more fortunate and better-educated brethren.[43]

Smoke – and its deleterious effects on health and longevity – marks the difference between the classes.

As environing medium, city air thus becomes an environment which is a hybrid of meteorological conditions and human making. The famous London "smog" – the suffocating combination of foggy weather with industrial smoke and acidic aerosols – became the epitome for a specifically insalubrious weather. This kind of weather is not a natural given but man-made, as Henry A. Des Voeux, who coined the term "smog" in 1904, emphasized.[44] Charles Dickens remarked that country fog "was grey, whereas in London it was, at about the boundary line, dark yellow, and a little within it brown, and then browner, until at the heart of the city ... it was rusty-black".[45] Cities, as observed by Luke Howard as early as 1818, have their own climate – the famous "urban heat island" – that distinguishes them from their surrounding countryside.[46] City air thus produces an environment that is no longer defined, on the model of the miasma, as a specific location haunted by the neighbor's exhalations and the sewer's vapors. The city is, in contrast, a wide area of very specific climatic and meteorological conditions presenting an amalgam of nature and civilization. Urban climate is a man-made climate, and it is social not just in the sense of physical proximity but in the sense that it reproduces – and even enforces – socio-economic inequality.[47]

Climatically, the city is thus not only a system in itself, where industry, inhabitants, traffic, heating, plants, animals, and climatic conditions form a network that contributes to very specific states of the air. The city also influences and changes its surroundings through its expansion, emissions, and its need for resources. In the discourse of pollution, city air is no longer the expression of a *genius loci*, as the winds and miasmas, but evinces a much further-reaching influence. It is an environment with its own metabolism and its own very specific pathologies, distinct, yet in constant exchange with other environments (such as the suburbs, the countryside, the rest of the nation, and, ultimately, the globe). In Great Britain, pollution from the big cities was soon understood to affect the entire country's agriculture and public health. Pollution as a pathology of the air is thus not just the object of medical and biopolitical measures – as in the case of the *circumfusa* – but an environmental problem that is political from the very moment of its discovery.

The disappearance of the air

In the pathologies of the air – winds and weathers, miasmas, and pollution – the mediality of the air as environing medium comes into the foreground. The three models of air as a medium which I have sketched out each stand for a very specific relation between an entity which is surrounded (the body, the individual, a society) and the surrounding medium. The winds – changing weather, seasons, and the "airs, waters, and places" with which they are associated – deal with the influences of a geographical location on human bodies, their constitution and their illnesses. Here the air, as a single, jet pervasive element, is an individual environment affecting each body specifically, depending on its constitution and susceptibility. Winds and seasons also stand for the impact of temporality on human lives: ephemeral, ever-changing weather, the cycle of the seasons and their irregularities. The element is turned into an environment through cultural techniques such as observation, recording, and individual prevention. The perspective of meteorological medicine calls for practices of perception and registering, for prevention, protection and adaptation – both of the world of the elements and of the self.

The concept of miasma, in contrast, creates a granular, local, highly differentiated environment made out of whatever emanates from the processes of life and death. Decay and breathing, morning dew and night smells, soil and water, sickness and health – everything can be understood as producing a vapor affecting every living being in the immediate surroundings. Miasmas are the signature of being entangled in a web of life and death, of metabolism and morbidity. This is why, in the concept of miasma, notions of sociality and biology merge. If miasma in its archaic sense is the stain of moral guilt, in its early modern sense it is the stain that accompanies social proximity, the dangerous proximity of life and death. The conception of miasma or, in its 18th century version, *circumfusa*, accordingly calls for constant measures of data gathering, prevention, sanitization, and control. *Circumfusa* and the practices of hygiene dedicated to them are thus biopolitical: they politicize the practices of healthcare and disease prevention, they call for a sanitization of urban space and social life – from the elimination of risk sources (such as abattoirs, graveyards, or stagnant waters) to the tight control of insalubrious habits (such as overheated or overcrowded rooms, gaslighting, and lack of exercise).

While the notion of miasma and circumfusa addresses environment on a very small scale – the sewer, the neighbor's night air, the vapors from the nearby river – the concept of pollution involves, first and foremost, a massive spatial *scaling up*. For a long time, pollution – just as miasma – was seen as an amalgam of natural factors and human practices. Yet it addresses much larger spaces than the intimate environments of miasmas. Pollution is about cities and their surroundings, about a capital and the empire, about a nation and its chief industrial to towns. Pollution is not caused by cycles of life and death but by developments in technology. It refers to a "nature" that is non-natural, man-made – epitomized in the word "smog". In pollution, the environing medium air becomes a technologically crafted medium. For a long time, smoke and industrial emissions have been the hallmark of modernization in all its ambivalence of progress and destruction. Pollution thus involves a notion of environment as an intricate conjunction of nature, technology, economy, and politics. No wonder that pollution would become one of the first issues of environmental politics, rapidly shifting from a local and regional problem to a national and transnational scale.

Yet all these conceptualizations of air as an environing medium still strike us as strangely outdated. This is because they are at odds with many fundamental distinctions we are taught to make when thinking about bodies and their environments. In order to understand them, Fabien Locher and Jean-Baptiste Fressoz write, "we need to shake off our innate/acquired, body/environment, living/inert, or nature/society dichotomy-based classifications to think our way into a now defunct epistemological realm … where technique, political form, environment, and bodies all overlapped".[48] What the three models presented here have in common is that the distinction between nature and culture in each case collapses – yet each time in a very different way. The same holds true for the distinction between organism and environment – human life is, in all of these models, permeated, shaped, afflicted, and endangered by the very environment that sustains it. As a result, humans have not just the possibility, but the duty to "care" for this environment, that is, to control it, transform it, adapt to it, protect themselves against it – and to determine the scope of their own interference with it. Humans, as the old climate theory succinctly puts it, are shaped by climate, but they can also change (local) climates – and thereby ultimately change themselves.[49] The air, as environing medium, is both overpowering and fragile – as are humans in relation to nature. What all three models finally have in common is that they conceive of air and its various states as being extremely perceptible. The air strikes, enters, affects, transforms, and sickens the body, yet it does so very palpably through smells, drafts, temperature, moisture, murkiness, or the ways it soils skin, lungs, clothes, buildings, and plants.

All this comes to an end with the onset of modern science. Modern meteorology, while extremely adept at collecting and computing weather data all over the world, all but eliminated the "human barometer" in favor of standardized methods of measurement. The body and its health issues are no longer the reason for trying to understand and keep track of the vagaries of weather and wind. Today, meteorological medicine is marginalized as a rather obscure branch somewhere between psychosomatic and environmental medicine. For the most part, illnesses are attributed solely to individual constitutions – not to the winds and the weathers. While meteorology today is able to predict weather with impressive accuracy, its medical aspects are reduced to a small set of data on the daily levels of ozone and fine particulate matter. Whoever gets a migraine from certain winds or feels depressed by the darkness of winter is referred to a psychotherapist rather than a practitioner of meteorological medicine.

What the development of modern meteorology in the late 19th and the 20th century did for the Hippocratic notion of airs, waters, and places, germ theory did for the notion of miasma. While the miasma theory attributes illness to the environing medium air, everything seemingly changes with a concept of contagion defined as the transmission of disease directly from person to person. This transmission happens through infectious particles that are transferred by direct contact or various modes of transmission. Since the bacteriological discoveries of Louis Pasteur and Robert Koch, these particles are not some ominous vapors but organisms with a life cycle of their own. While miasma theory attributes illnesses to a slightly fuzzy constellation of bodily predisposition and environmental influences, germ theory nails down the cause to one single agent, a pathogenic organism. An organism, however, that cannot be sensed by smell, murkiness, temperature, or some other perceptible warning sign. In spite of their epistemic differences, however, germ theory and miasma theory co-existed for a very long time and were often rhetorically lumped together. Maybe the alternative "miasma vs. germ theory" not only is historically inaccurate. With COVID-19 as a disease transmitted through the air, some aspects of miasma theory gain a new appeal.[50]

Pollution is the pathology of air which can best be integrated into modern concepts of the environment and its endangerment by human interference. It has, one could say, just been scaled up from a notion of environment as regional and national to a global environment. Pollution is no longer an amalgam of human and natural causes – but, as we like to say, "anthropogenic" – in the sense that the planetary environment is now, in the Anthropocene, marked by human interference. The chief polluting agents are no longer smoke, acid rain, and soot but greenhouse gases. The true heir of the concept of pollution as a politicization of nature today is climate change. Climate change has elevated the notion of environment to a planetary scale – and the idea of air to the abstract, highly complex and imperceptible notion of the atmosphere that contemporary science is dealing with.

The air as a medium has disappeared. Not that it's no longer there – but, along with models that framed it as an environing medium, it has withdrawn from our perception and our consciousness. The relation between body and weather is relegated to alternative medicine, personal anecdotes, and abstract meteorological information about threats we cannot see or feel or smell. Germs, we have learned, rarely warn us of their presence through foul smells or visible fumes – they have become the epitome of health dangers that are imperceptible. Climate is no longer a category that explains the relation of societies to the places they dwell in – it has become an abstract composite of planetary averages we observe with a mix of awe and incomprehension. Climate is now treated as something "out there", an externalized entity, an abstract set of data, graphs, images, and complex information. Pollution – in the ancient sense – is equally reduced to data: measures of particulates on a scale of 2.5 (the most dangerous) to 10.0, ozone levels, and nitrous oxides. Yet they are imperceptible unless one lives in airs as noxious as in Delhi, Beijing, or Doha. Likewise, casting the air as a social medium has become a quite complicated task. The neighbor's night air feared by Adalbert Stifter is, today, caused by our own car, the lack of CO_2 taxes, the ever-rising emission curve. Politicizing it will not be done by means of a letter to the King.

Ironically, what brought back the air in the sense I have described was COVID-19. All of a sudden, the air became once more a "matter of concern", of private concerns about the density of our face masks, the distribution of virus-laden aerosols in the air, the probability of getting infected in public transport or at the office, and last but not least, the psychic effects of weeks spent apart from family, friends and colleagues. But it also became the object of public concern – in the debates about the statistical distribution of infections, the economic costs of a general quarantine, the financial value of human life, the collapse of national health systems. As an airborne disease, COVID-19 brought back the vigilance of the age of hygiene and cast us into a state of being afraid of the very air we breathe. The pandemic has made the air social again. And even political, as we soon learned from the curfews, closed borders, and ever-changing governmental decrees about shopping or social contact. Maybe COVID-19 presents – among many other things – the revenge of the air, reminding us that it is both immediately dangerous and in immediate danger. As the air is social and political, we must start to sense it again, and fear it.

Notes

1 This text has been long in the making. It was started in spring 2020, but finalized during my fellowship at the Wissenschaftskolleg zu Berlin in 2021/2022 which gave me time, ideas, and air to breathe. Besides this, I am grateful for input from Benjamin Robinson, Adam Wickberg, Johan Gärdebo, and Jürgen Renn.
2 Jane D. Siegel, Emily Rhinehart, Marguerite Jackson, & Linda Chiarello, "Healthcare Infection Control Practices Advisory Committee," *2007 Guideline for Isolation Precautions: Preventing Transmission of Infectious Agents in Healthcare Settings*, Update July 2019, 19, https://www.cdc.gov/infectioncontrol/guidelines/isolation/index.html
3 Neeltje van Doremalen, Trenton Bushmaker, & Dylan H. Morris, "Aerosol and Surface Stability of SARS-CoV-2 as Compared with SARS-CoV-1. Letter to the Editor," *New England Journal of Medicine* (March 17, 2020), DOI: 10.1056/NEJMc2004973 (no pages).
4 Eva Horn, "Air as Medium," *Grey Room* 73 (2018): 6–25.
5 Tim Ingold, "An Ecology of Materials," *Power of Material – Politics of Materiality*, ed. Kerstin Stakemeier & Susanne Witzgall (Berlin/Zurich: Diaphanes, 2014), 59–65, 63.
6 John Durham Peters, *The Marvelous Clouds. Toward a Philosophy of Elemental Media* (Chicago: University of Chicago Press, 2015), 2.
7 Ibid., 3.
8 Empedocles laid the foundation of the theory of the four elements in the 5th century B.C.E. and called the elements the "roots" (rhizomata) of the world. M. R. Wright, *Empedocles: The Extant Fragments* (London: Gerald Duckworth, 1995).
9 David Macauley, *Elemental Philosophy: Earth, Air, Fire and Water as Environmental Ideas* (New York: SUNY Press, 2010), 334.
10 Jeffrey Jerome Cohen & Lowell Duckert, *Elemental Ecocriticism: Thinking with Earth, Air, Water, and Fire*, ed. Jeffrey Jerome Cohen & Lowell Duckert (Minneapolis: University of Minnesota Press, 2015), 103.
11 Macauley, *Elemental Philosophy*, 2.
12 Peters, *The Marvelous Clouds*, 46–49. For a comprehensive history of the 'media' concept, see Stefan Hoffmann, *Geschichte des Medienbegriffs* (Hamburg: Felix Meiner, 2002) and John Guillory, "Genesis of the Media Concept," *Critical Inquiry* 36, no. 2 (Winter 2010): 321–362.
13 Peters, *The Marvelous Clouds*, 14–15.
14 See Bronislaw Szerszynski, "Life in the Open Air," *Issues in Science and Theology: What Is Life?* eds. Dirk Evers et al. (Basel: Springer, 2015), 27–42.
15 Sverker Sörlin, "Medias in Res" (in this volume).
16 John Evelyn, *Fumifugium or the Inconveniencie of the Aer and Smoak of London Dissipated Together with Some Remedies* (London: Godbid, 1661), 3. Italics in the original.
17 Hippocrates, *Of the Epidemics I*, 1. Transl. Francis Adams, in the Internet Classics Archive by Daniel C. Stevenson, http://classics.mit.edu/Hippocrates/epidemics.mb.txt
18 As a brilliant introduction to elemental thought, see Gernot Böhme & Hartmut Böhme, *Feuer, Wasser, Erde, Luft. Eine Kulturgeschichte der Elemente* (Munich: Beck, 2014).
19 Hippocrates, *Airs, Waters, Places*, paragraph 1.1., *Hippocratic Writings*, ed. Geoffrey Ernest Richard Lloyd, trans. John Chadwick & William Neville Mann (Harmondsworth: Penguin, 1978), 148–169, 148.
20 The effect of climate on the spirits and culture of humans is the subject of the second half of the treatise. Hippocrates, *Airs, Waters, Places*, paragraphs 12–24, 159–169.
21 Cf. the excellent chapter on winds in Shigehisa Kuriyama, *The Expressiveness of the Body and the Divergence of Greek and Chinese Medicine* (New York: Zone Books, 1999), 234.

22 As for the Ancient theories of the transmission of disease, see William Vernon Harris, "Contagion and Ancient Thinking about Disease," *Mediterraneo Antico*, XXIV, 1–2, 2021, 11–26.
23 John Arbuthnot, *An Essay Concerning the Effects of Air on Human Bodies* (London: J. Tonson, 1733).
24 See George C. D. Adamson, "Private Diaries as Information Sources in Climate Research," *WIREs Climate Change* 6 (2015): 599–611.
25 See Jan Golinski, *British Weather and the Climate of Enlightenment* (Chicago and London: University of Chicago Press, 2007), 143ff., Patrick Ramponi, "Wetterfühligkeit und Diätetik. Skizzen zur literarischen Wissensgeschichte eines kulturellen Symptomleidens 1800/1900," *L'alimentation et le temps qu'il fait. Essen und Wetter, Food and Weather*, ed. Karin Becker, Vincent Moriniaux, & Martine Tabeaud (Paris: Herrmann Éditeurs, 2015), 39–56.
26 Golinski, *British Weather*, 151.
27 Jacques Jouanna, "Air, Miasma and Contagion in the time of Hippocrates and the Survival of Miasmas in Post-Hippocratic Medicine", Jacques Jouanna, *Greek Medicine from Hippocrates to Galen. Selected Papers*, ed. Philip van der Eijk (Leiden: Brill, 2012), 121–136, 122.
28 Hippocrates, *Nature of Man*, ch. IX, p. 25, 10–27, 47, Hippocrates Volume IV, transl. W.H.S. Jones, *Loebs Classical Library* 150 (Cambridge: Harvard University Press, 1931).
29 Vladimir Jankovic, *Confronting the Climate: British Airs and the Making of Environmental Medicine* (New York: Palgrave Macmillan, 2010), 17.
30 On the "ingredients of the air" see, e.g., Arbuthnot, *Essay*, 3–14, 3.
31 Bernard Lynch, *A Guide to Health through the Various Stages of Life* (London: Cooper, 1744), 134, quoted in Jankovic, *Confronting the Climate*, 17.
32 Adalbert Stifter, "Wiener Wetter," *Wien und die Wiener* (Vienna: Amalthea Signum), 151. My translation.
33 See Alain Corbin, *The Foul and the Fragrant: Odor and the French Social Imagination* (Cambridge, MA: Harvard University Press, 1986).
34 Cf. Ludmilla Jordanova, "Earth Science and Environmental Medicine: The Synthesis of the Late Enlightenment," *Images of the Earth. Essays in the History of the Environmental Sciences*, eds. Ludmilla Jordanova & Roy Porter (Oxford: British Society for the History of Science, 1997), 127–152.
35 Jankovic, *Confronting the Climate*, 3.
36 Pierre-Jean-Georges Cabanis, *Rapport du physique et du moral de l'homme* (Paris: Caille et Ravier, 1805), 135. My translation. On *circumfusa* see Jean-Baptiste Fressoz: "Circonvenir les circumfusa. La chimie, l'hygiénisme et la libéralisation des « choses environnantes » : France, 1750–1850," *Revue d'histoire modern et contemporaine* 56, no. 4 (2009): 39–76, 41.
37 Fressoz takes this anecdote from Jérôme Richard, *Histoire naturelle de l'air et des météores* (Paris: Saillant, 1770, vol. 2): 412, Fressoz, Circonvenir, 41. My translation.
38 Evelyn, *Fumifugium*, 22.
39 Mark Jenner, "The Politics of London Air: John Evelyn's 'Fumifugium' and the Restoration," *The Historical Journal* 38, no. 3 (1995), 535–551, 541.
40 Peter Thorsheim, *Inventing Pollution. Coal, Smoke, and Culture in Britain since 1800* (Athens: Ohio University Press, 2006).
41 Thorsheim, *Inventing Pollution*, 28.
42 "Observations in a London fog," *Hogg's Instructor* 5 (1855), 53–55: 55, quoted in Thorsheim, *Inventing Pollution*, 15.
43 "Dr. Arnott on Smokeless Fires and Pure Air in Houses," *Chambers Journal*, 15 September 1855, 174–176, 175.
44 Harold Antoine Des Voeux, "Letter to the Editor," *Times* (London), 27 December 1904, 11a.
45 Charles Dickens, *Our Mutual Friend* (Oxford: Oxford university Press, 1989), 420.

46 See Luke Howard, *The Climate of London, Deduced from Meteorological Observations, Made at Different Places in the Neighbourhood of the Metropolis* (London: W. Phillips, 1818).
47 For a similar approach to contemporary city environments, see Henrik Ernstson & Sverker Sörlin (eds.), *Grounding Urban Natures. Histories and Futures of Urban Ecologies* (Cambridge, MA: MIT Press, 2019).
48 Fabien Locher & Jean-Baptiste Fressoz, "Modernity's Frail Climate. A Climate History of Environmental Reflexivity," *Critical Inquiry* 38, no. 3 (2012): 579–598, 581.
49 Johann Gottlieb Herder, *Outlines of a Philosophy of the History of Man*, trans. T. Churchill (London, 1800), 176.
50 Appourva Mandavilli, "In the W.H.O.'s Coronavirus Stumbles, some Scientists See a Pattern," *New York Times*, 9 June 2020, https://www.nytimes.com/2020/06/09/health/coronavirus-asymptomatic-world-health-organization.html?referringSource=articleShare

References

Adamson, George C. D. "Private Diaries as Information Sources in Climate Research." *WIREs Climate Change* 6 (2015): 599–611.
Arbuthnot, John. *An Essay Concerning the Effects of Air on Human Bodies*. London: J. Tonson, 1733.
Böhme, Gernot & Hartmut Böhme. *Feuer, Wasser, Erde, Luft. Eine Kulturgeschichte der Elemente*. Munich: Beck, 2014.
Cabanis, Pierre-Jean-Georges. *Rapport du physique et du moral de l'homme*. Paris: Caille et Ravier, 1805.
Chambers Journal. "Dr. Arnott on Smokeless Fires and Pure Air in Houses." *Chambers Journal*, 15 September 1855, 174–176, 175.
Cohen, Jeffrey Jerome & Lowell Duckert(ed.). *Elemental Ecocriticism: Thinking with Earth, Air, Water, and Fire*. Minneapolis: University of Minnesota Press, 2015.
Corbin, Alain. *The Foul and the Fragrant: Odor and the French Social Imagination*. Cambridge, MA: Harvard University Press, 1986.
Dickens, Charles. *Our Mutual Friend*. Oxford: Oxford University Press, 1989.
van Doremalen, Neeltje, Trenton Bushmaker, & Dylan H. Morris. "Aerosol and Surface Stability of SARS-CoV-2 as Compared with SARS-CoV-1. Letter to the Editor." *New England Journal of Medicine* (17 March 2020), DOI: 10.1056/NEJMc2004973 (no pages).
Ernstson, Henrik & Sverker Sörlin (eds.). *Grounding Urban Natures. Histories and Futures of Urban Ecologies* (Cambridge, MA: MIT Press, 2019).
Evelyn, John. *Fumifugium or the Inconveniencie of the Aer and Smoak of London Dissipated Together with Some Remedies*. London: Godbid, 1661.
Fressoz, Jean-Baptiste. "Circonvenir les circumfusa. La chimie, l'hygiénisme et la libéralisation des « choses environnantes » : France, 1750–1850." *Revue d'histoire modern et contemporaine* 56, no. 4 (2009): 39–76.
Golinski, Jan. *British Weather and the Climate of Enlightenment*. Chicago and London: University of Chicago Press, 2007.
Guillory, John. "Genesis of the Media Concept." *Critical Inquiry* 36, no. 2 (Winter 2010): 321–362.
Herder, Johann Gottlieb. *Outlines of a Philosophy of the History of Man*, trans. T. Churchill. London, 1800.
Hogg's Instructor. "Observations in a London Fog." *Hogg's Instructor* 5 (1855): 53–55.

Howard, Luke. *The Climate of London, Deduced from Meteorological Observations, made at Different Places in the Neighbourhood of the Metropolis.* London: W. Phillips, 1818.

Hippocrates. *Airs, Waters, Places, Hippocratic Writings,* ed. Geoffrey Ernest Richard Lloyd, trans. John Chadwick & William Neville Mann. Harmondsworth: Penguin, 1978, 148–169.

———. *Of the Epidemics I,* 1. Transl. Francis Adams, in The Internet Classics Archive by Daniel C. Stevenson, http://classics.mit.edu/Hippocrates/epidemics.mb.txt

———. *Nature of Man.* Hippocrates Volume IV, transl. W.H.S. Jones. Loebs Classical Library 150. Cambridge: Harvard University Press, 1931.

Hoffmann, Stefan. *Geschichte des Medienbegriffs.* Hamburg: Felix Meiner, 2002.

Horn, Eva. "Air as Medium." *Grey Room* 73 (2018): 6–25.

Ingold, Tim. "An Ecology of Materials." *Power of Material – Politics of Materiality,* edited by Kerstin Stakemeier & Susanne Witzgall, 59–65. Berlin and Zürich: Diaphanes, 2014.

Jankovic, Vladimir. *Confronting the Climate: British Airs and the Making of Environmental Medicine.* New York: Palgrave Macmillan, 2010.

Jenner, Mark. "The Politics of London Air: John Evelyn's 'Fumifugium' and the Restoration." *The Historical Journal* 38, no. 3 (1995): 535–551.

Jordanova, Ludmilla. "Earth Science and Environmental Medicine: The Synthesis of the Late Enlightenment." *Images of the Earth. Essays in the History of the Environmental Sciences,* edited by Ludmilla Jordanova & Roy Porter, 127–152. Oxford: British Society for the History of Science, 1997.

Jouanna, Jacques. "Air, Miasma and Contagion in the Time of Hippocrates and the Survival of Miasmas in Post-Hippocratic Medicine." *Greek Medicine from Hippocrates to Galen. Selected Papers,* edited by Philip van der Eijk, 121–136. Leiden: Brill, 2012.

Kuriyama, Shigehisa. *The Expressiveness of the Body and the Divergence of Greek and Chinese Medicine.* New York: Zone Books, 1999.

Lloyd, Geoffrey Ernest Richard (ed.). *Hippocratic Writings.* Trans. John Chadwick & William Neville Mann. Harmondsworth: Penguin, 1978.

Locher, Fabien, & Jean-Baptiste Fressoz. "Modernity's Frail Climate. A Climate History of Environmental Reflexivity." *Critical Inquiry* 38, no. 3 (2012): 579–598, 581.

Lynch, Bernard. *A Guide to Health through the Various Stages of Life.* London: Cooper, 1744.

Macauley, David. *Elemental Philosophy: Earth, Air, Fire and Water as Environmental Ideas.* New York: SUNY Press, 2010.

Mandavilli, Appourva. "In the W.H.O.'s Coronavirus Stumbles, Some Scientists See a Pattern." *New York Times,* June 9, 2020, https://www.nytimes.com/2020/06/09/health/coronavirus-asymptomatic-world-health-organization.html?referringSource=articleShare

Peters, John Durham. *The Marvelous Clouds. Toward a Philosophy of Elemental Media.* Chicago: University of Chicago Press, 2015.

Ramponi, Patrick. "Wetterfühligkeit und Diätetik. Skizzen zur literarischen Wissensgeschichte eines kulturellen Symptomleidens 1800/1900." *L'alimentation et le temps qu'il fait. Essen und Wetter, Food and Weather,* edited by Karin Becker, Vincent Moriniaux, & Martine Tabeaud, 39–56. Paris: Herrmann Éditeurs, 2015.

Richard, Jérôme. *Histoire naturelle de l'air et des météores.* Paris: Saillant, 1770, vol. 2, 412.

Siegel, Jane D., Emily Rhinehart, Marguerite Jackson, & Linda Chiarello. "Healthcare Infection Control Practices Advisory Committee." *2007 Guideline for Isolation Precautions: Preventing Transmission of Infectious Agents in Healthcare Settings,* Update July 2019, 19, https://www.cdc.gov/infectioncontrol/guidelines/isolation/index.html

Sörlin, Sverker. "Medias in Res" (in this volume).

Stifter, Adalbert. "Wiener Wetter." *Wien und die Wiener* (Vienna: Amalthea Signum, 1988).
Szerszynski, Bronislaw. "Life in the Open Air." *Issues in Science and Theology: What Is Life?,* edited by Dirk Evers et al., 27–42. Basel: Springer, 2015.
Thorsheim, Peter. *Inventing Pollution. Coal, Smoke, and Culture in Britain since 1800.* Athens: Ohio University Press, 2006.
des Voeux, Harold Antoine. "Letter to the Editor." *Times* (London), 27 December 1904, 11a.
Wright, M. R. *Empedocles: The Extant Fragments.* London: Gerald Duckworth, 1995.

7
OCEAN ENVIRONING MEDIA
Datafication of the deep sea

Susanna Lidström, Adam Wickberg and Johan Gärdebo

Introduction: The mediated ocean

Our knowledge about the ocean is perhaps more conditioned by technological mediation than that of any other environment on Earth. As Stacy Alaimo points out in an introduction to "blue humanities," "most aquatic zones, species and topics exist beyond human domains, requiring the mediation of science and technology."[1] Likewise, in *Wild blue media*, Melody Jue emphasises the importance of mediation for knowing the marine environment: "in order to study the ocean – especially the deep ocean – scientists need a variety of instrumentation, satellites, remotely operated vehicles (ROVs), submersibles, sonar, and other technical prostheses for sampling and sensing," meaning that "the (deep) ocean emerges as an object of knowledge only through chains of mediation and remote sensing."[2] Developing these observations, ocean historian Helen Rozwadowski has further noted the central role that this mediated knowledge plays in shaping human relationships to "this vast, trackless and opaque place," enabling people to "exploit marine resources, control ocean space, extend imperial or national power, and attempt to refashion the sea into a more tractable arena for human activity."[3] Governance, exploitation and knowledge of the ocean are thus all fully dependent on processes of mediation, and this is increasingly true as the pace by which the ocean is mapped, sensed and datafied rises and the ocean becomes an environed space rather than a wilderness.

With mediation, we refer to the processes of gathering, processing and disseminating environmental data and information. While our empirical focus is on the development of the Argo program, the autonomous floats that gather and supply global marine data, we place this practice in a longer environing media history, showing how data gathering and processing has been key to producing the ocean as we know and understand it over long periods of time.

DOI: 10.4324/9781003282891-10

We understand environing to mean the process of both knowing and changing the environment, and environing media to mean the technical means by which this process can take place. Taken together as a theoretical concept, environing media refers to the production of environmental epistemologies understood as an ongoing continuous process with historical roots. It also highlights the fact that an environmental object – such as the world ocean – has been in a process of change throughout Earth's history and that in the very latest part of this history humans have come to have considerable impact on these processes of change. Anthropogenic impacts have evolved through scaling up and accelerating the ways in which humans make use of planetary resources, the ontological precondition of which are environing media. With this theoretical framework, this chapter studies the technological mediation of the marine realm and how specific media technologies condition our understanding of what the ocean is, how it changes and what is considered essential and "actionable" ocean knowledge.

Different historical phases of knowing the ocean can be characterised with reference to developments in and application of sensing technologies. Following a long history of increasing exploration and innovation, the arguably most influential contemporary infrastructure for how the ocean is known and mediated is the Argo program, which has been in operation since the early 2000s. Argo consists of a fleet of around 4,000 autonomous instruments, floating with ocean currents in the upper 2,000 m of the water column, recording key variables such as temperature and salinity, and providing fundamental input for oceanographic research as well as for broader Earth system sciences, including, importantly, climate change models.[4] As such, the Argo floats act as data gatherers and are the first-level interface in the mediation process of knowledge about the Earth system from the oceanic part of the hydrosphere.

The Argo program has been described as arising "opportunistically from the combination of great scientific need and technological innovation."[5] This chapter follows up on that statement by placing Argo in the context of environing media technologies used to study and understand the ocean since the start of the modern period. In this way, we aim to show how a gradual accumulation of ocean data and developing mediating technologies have informed and shaped the Argo program, but also how the modern floats introduce a new era of knowing and mediating the marine environment and, by association, the planetary system as an integrated whole. We discuss how Argo floats and the data flows they generate mediate specific forms of knowledge, with implications for how and in what terms the ocean is perceived as well as for how ideas and practices around ocean governance are formulated. We also consider the reverse; how a perceived need for monitoring and evaluating the ocean influences future developments of the Argo program, to make the ocean fully accounted for in the broader notion and project of the mediated planet.

The chapter begins with two sections looking back at the history of how the ocean has been explored, mapped and known. We first review the most important developments taking place from early modern times and throughout the 19th century, before looking more closely at the technologies that emerged around the mid-20th century that ventured further beneath the surface than before and advanced oceanography as a scientific discipline central to Earth system governance. We then examine the beginnings and nature of the Argo program as emerging from this history, including how the new program was presented, envisioned and motivated. In the penultimate section, we discuss the wider datafication of the marine environment that Argo is at the heart of, and the novel views of the ocean that digital environing media enable. To conclude, we suggest some implications of this digital way of knowing the ocean for ocean governance and stewardship.

Connecting and controlling the continents

Argo emerged as a scientific project in the late 1990s. The initial design described a distribution of floats in a 3° × 3° array in the upper 2,000 m of the ice-free and open ocean between 60°N and 60°S.[6] The theoretical premises for a global grid, encircling not only land but also oceans, can be traced back to the early modern period and Ptomely's projection of the spherical surface of the Earth onto a two-dimensional map, an essential environing medium from the 1500s onwards.[7] The early modern European colonialist expansions were essentially naval operations, and hence completely dependent on constructing accurate ocean knowledge. While humans across the globe had long lived with and by the sea, a radical disruption in human-ocean relations took place during the 1500s with the transoceanic colonial enterprises, which demonstrated the connection of the world oceans. While the history of colonialism has mostly focused on territorial conquests, its true condition of possibility was the combination of scientific advances and navigational practices, often promoted by the same institutions, as was the case in Spain. The Spanish empire worked to increase the number of skilled navigators who could facilitate the transoceanic enterprise by mastering the complexities of a new mathematised system of celestial navigation and the associated instruments and tools.[8] In 1552, the House of Trade in Seville established a formal school with a chair of cosmography through which every navigator and pilot had to pass. The school drew its resources and rationale from aiding the colonial aims, which became a model also for maritime communities across Europe in the following centuries.[9]

It was the pursuit of global colonialist ambitions that confronted competing European state powers with the issue of knowing vast oceans adequately enough to navigate and exploit them – Helen Rozwadowski has noted how scientists were tasked with "creating charts and other representations of the ocean that could be used to extend imperial power."[10] The rise of Spanish, Dutch and British empires was made possible by a spatial revolution that transitioned navigation from approximation to precision in a quest for exactness.[11] Early modern mapping and sensing of the world ocean relied on mechanical instruments, mathematics and continuous first-hand documentation of ocean currents, tides and wind patterns registered in rutters and nautical charts.[12] While finding the latitude of a place is fairly straightforward by measuring the angle between the horizon and the polar star or sun in zenith with an astrolabe or quadrant, longitude is more difficult to establish and is calculated from the difference between local time of a prime meridian and the local time of place, which was unknown at sea. The problem of longitude determination was the most-researched aspect of oceanic life in the early modern period and could not be properly solved until the 18th century, after a long history of transnational efforts. This issue was due to the fact that the only available timekeeping devices – necessary to adequately determine the ship's position at sea – were pendulum clocks that constantly lost their beat due to the rolling of the ship on the ocean. The problem was solved after John Harrison's invention of the marine chronometer, a timepiece that could withstand the motion and temperature shifts of sea voyages. With a reliable timepiece set to a fixed location, like Greenwich (GMT), navigators could calculate their geographical position at sea using the time difference of the ship's local time, since each hour corresponds to 15° (360° divided by 24 hours). With longitude and latitude in place, the understanding of oceanic space could be constructed as a grid with exact addresses. The effects of this transition in spatial perception still form the ontological and epistemological basis for planetary environing media today.

The 19th century saw the beginnings of explorations into ocean depths and the efforts of knowing the sea in all its dimensions that continue today. Scale and opacity made this knowledge production particularly difficult. It was first driven by the booming whaling industry which sought new ocean areas after depleting the whale populations of shallower waters. Early ocean environing media include sounding with lead devices attached to lines, which were hauled after touching bottom and counted in fathoms (1.8 m). Records kept by whalers and navigators formed the basis of scientific progress in knowing the deeper ocean. The Gulf Stream, for instance, was well known to whalers long before any scientists started inquiring into the phenomenon.[13]

The science of oceanography emerged from mid-1800s as part of state initiatives for, and public interest in, transatlantic telegraph cables and other communication media infrastructures being successfully installed at the bottom of the ocean.[14] Rather than as occasional experiments, soundings were now performed on the request of governments and with a clear goal in mind: to find a suitable pathway for cables across the Atlantic seabed. The first bathymetric chart of the North Atlantic basin, reflecting results from about 90 soundings, was completed by Matthew Fontaine Maury, an American hydrographer and naval officer, in 1853.[15] In addition, broken cables that had been laid over the seafloor were recovered with a multitude of unfamiliar creatures attached to them, thus also putting an end to the until then prevailing notion that no life could exist below 300 fathoms. The scientific progress and discoveries made in relation to the cables led to an increased interest in the ocean and the second half of the 19th century saw several cruise ships setting out to further investigate, equipped with dredges, trawls and nets to sample the depths. The most well known is the British 1872–1876 *Challenger* expedition, whose results, eventually documented in 50 volumes, provided a foundation for the new science to build from.[16]

Beneath the surface

In the 20th century, acquiring new ocean knowledge became tightly interwoven with military aims, as sonar and submarines became central wartime technologies. Before the Second World War the ocean floor was little known and perceived as a commons by both scientists and naval officers, but after the war the mapping of ocean depths instead became tied to secrecy and nationalistic ends. A great surge in military support for the Earth sciences emerged in this context, and most oceanographic research efforts depended on these ties, and scientific data became relevant to national security. In 1957 Bruce Heezen and Marie Tharp of Columbia University's Lamont Geological Observatory published the first map of the seafloor of the North Atlantic, followed by seafloor maps of all Earth's ocean basins.[17] After Pentagon classified ocean depth data for security reasons, Heezen and Tharp created a physiographic map to avoid the restriction on bathymetric maps, which also turned out to have great advantages for portraying the seafloor.[18] This mapping program provided critical evidence for the theory of plate tectonics, which became accepted in the 1960s and changed the understanding of Earth's geology. These new insights that resulted from the Heezen–Tharp seafloor maps built on new data points created with new and improved instruments, including sounding devices and automated depth recorders, which were financed by US defence agencies.

The International Geophysical Year (IGY) of 1957–1958 saw a fundamental transition in ocean environing media. The program organised the first globe-spanning set of oceanographic expeditions and included coordinated measurements from a dispersed network of sensors. Through the IGY, scientists managed to create the largest and most thorough dataset on oceanic phenomena to date.[19] The systematic and global-scale collection of geophysical data was made possible not only through new technologies for observing and sensing the ocean, but also through the growing technological capacity of storing and processing data with early supercomputers, which meant that the collected data could be used to mediate the marine environment in entirely new ways. Together, the different new technologies formed the conditions of possibility for global biogeochemical and biogeophysical models that together could visualise an *integrated* planetary environmental system, which increasingly included the oceanic realm.[20] The attempt at an integrated vision of the whole ocean, dependent on a grid-based view of dispersed sensors and data points, was profoundly different than sample-based views of the sea, which also developed around the mid-20th century through technological inventions such as the bathyscaphe and scuba diving equipment. While these technologies made possible novel ways to explore and encounter the marine environment, they were only able to provide individual snapshots of mostly coastal oceans. Monitoring technologies represented a fundamentally different scientific approach.

One critical technology developed within the IGY was the first version of a neutrally buoyant float, invented by British oceanographer John Swallow.[21] The IGY also saw the development of another key technology for studying ocean circulation, the bathythermograph, developed in the US for ship-based temperature measurements. As Lehman notes, both technologies "have enduring legacies"; the bathythermograph is still in use, and the Swallow floats pioneered a series of further developments of floats that were eventually able to perform many more measurements than simply the tracking of currents.[22] After Swallow's initial design, several research groups and institutions contributed to improvements and specialisations of the technology.[23] By the 1970s, the floats could provide a range of scientific measurements, significantly improving understanding of oceanic eddy fields as well as circulation within different ocean basins. A major breakthrough was made in the 1980s, when so-called Profiling Autonomous Lagrangian Circulation floats, or P-ALACE floats, were designed to include added sensors that could collect more data.

The P-ALACE floats were also able to transmit their data directly to satellites when they surfaced, which allowed them to operate without depending on acoustic tracking and data reception by associated ships, as earlier floats had done. The P-ALACE floats were also able to descend and surface repeatedly, which significantly reduced the need for maintenance and re-deployment. This development signified a consequential shift for ocean observing, from relying on expensive and labour-intensive research cruises towards becoming a remote and autonomous operation, a shift that has only become more pronounced in the decades since. The P-ALACE floats were equipped with sensors collecting high-quality data on conductivity, temperature and salinity (CTD), and the oceanographic community quickly recognised them as a key technology for global ocean monitoring, including for climate studies. The P-ALACE floats are the most immediate predecessor to the original Argo floats.

While the technologies developed as part of the IGY helped "to generate an unprecedented amount of oceanographic data" in the late 1950s, they were still only able to sample a miniscule part of the global ocean.[24] This remained true in the following decades, even as attempts were made to follow up on the IGY and increase ocean measurements and observations through other large-scale collaborations and initiatives, including improved designs of the neutrally buoyant floats. Following on these continuous efforts, in the 1990s two sampling programs were initiated within the WCRP to gather measurements on a bigger scale: the Tropical Ocean Global Atmosphere program (TOGA, 1985–1994), and the World Ocean Circulation Experiment (WOCE, 1990–2002), a one-time global hydrographic survey and the first of its kind. Both TOGA and WOCE were primarily motivated by the need for data that could be used to improve and extend climate change predictions, which required more detailed observations of global ocean circulation, a key factor in ocean-atmosphere interactions.

WOCE was envisaged as establishing a baseline against which future changes in circulation could be measured, but the results were not as expected.[25] Rather than a baseline, or "snapshot," of global ocean circulation, the project resulted in a realisation of the extent to which the ocean was characterised by variability, complexity and change; a central insight of the decadal research project was that "it may not be possible to know the ocean on a planetary scale."[26] However, this insight, rather than an impasse, led to new ways of thinking about the ocean. In Lehman's description, it constituted a discovery of "productive limits," in the sense that "ocean variability both prompted new forms of knowledge and the development of a global knowledge infrastructure that is contingent, uneven, and fully entwined with geopolitical dynamics."[27] In other words, from the limits encountered, new avenues of research opened up, including the Argo program.

The period around the turn of the millennium, when WOCE was being conducted, was also the time when practices of "satellite oceanography" took off.[28] While the P-ALACE floats were to an extent part of a satellite-based network of observing technologies, in general satellite oceanography focused on the surface of the ocean. In 1992, the US National Aeronautics and Space Administration (NASA) launched its second major satellite TOPEX/Poseidon, where TOPEX stood for "ocean topography experiment." The TOPEX/Poseidon satellite measured the height of sea levels, as a way to deduce the ocean's heat content, providing an entirely new kind of data for ocean science. The successor to the TOPEX/Poseidon satellite, called Jason, was launched in 2001. While satellites vastly increased the proliferation and coverage of ocean data, as Höhler points out, they "could not 'see' in depth,"[29] which created a strong motivation for a below-the-surface complement to satellite measurements: "The need to observe the global subsurface ocean, together with a fit-for-purpose revolutionary autonomous technology [...], led to a multinational proposal for a global subsurface ocean observing system."[30] This proposal was the Argo program, which was both named and viewed as a partner program to the first Jason satellite mission.

The limitation in knowledge extraction and production encountered by WOCE is an important dimension of all environing media; the quest for knowledge about the Earth and its interconnected systems have, since it took off in earnest during the early modern era, time and again encountered limitations of knowing the environment, both in general, and for the oceans and atmosphere in particular. This limitation has often led to new ideas and technologies being innovated that have subsequently added to and built environmental epistemologies. A central limitation that has come to play a key role in both science and policy in recent decades is the practical impossibility to fully model or predict the climate system, a limitation that has been exploited by some to delay climate change mitigation by referring to uncertainties in scientific knowledge. Limitations or biases of knowledge also come through choice; in many cases military technology developed for strategic geopolitical purposes, not least during the cold war, have later become fundamental to scientific inquiry into the Earth system, as was the case with meteorology.[31] For oceanography, several studies have shown how military aims have fundamentally shaped scientific knowledge about the ocean, making the point that limitations in knowledge are not only the result of technological capacity, but also of factors such as funding and geopolitics.[32]

In addition to the influence of military programs, from around the time of the conceptualisation of the Argo program, oceanography has been shaped by increasing concern for how people are changing the planetary environment, including the global ocean; from having been studied as a "matter of fact," scientists, research funders and policymakers increasingly conceived of the ocean also as a "matter of concern."[33] In a study of a satellite-based infrastructure for environmental surveillance, also called "Argos," Etienne Benson has for example shown how that program, initiated in the 1970s, after its first decade of operation underwent a change from being merely focused on collecting environmental and ecological data, towards becoming more "environmental" in its nature, by having its observations directly tied to questions such as pollution and the tracking and protection of biodiversity.[34] The Argo program studied in this chapter, designed in the late 1990s, was explicitly environmental from the start, foremost in its relevance for predictions of climate change.

Scaling up: The Argo program

The Argo program was proposed in 1998 by a team of researchers led by Dean Roemmich at Scripps Institution of Oceanography (SIO) in the US. Their plan is explained in a 35-page report titled "On the design and implementation of Argo: a global array of profiling floats." The document notes the limitations of ship-based studies of global ocean features, pointing out that "WOCE required seven years and the combined resources of many nations to obtain a single sparse realization of temperature, salinity, velocity (T, S, v) and geochemical tracers."[35] The proposal highlights the important institutional as well as technological experiences gained within TOGA and WOCE, as well as the TOPEX/Poseidon mission, but also notes their shortcomings. They validate Lehman's argument that the previous programs encountered "productive limits" by motivating Argo specifically as a strategy for overcoming existing "sampling limitations."[36] Rather than an expensive, one-time ship-based snapshot of a stable ocean, as had been the goal and strategy of WOCE, Argo would coordinate an array of continuously operating profiling floats that would be able to obtain an extended stream of data, reflecting an ocean in constant flux.

Two research networks were responsible for developing the new Argo framework: the Climate Variability and Predictability (CLIVAR) component of the WCRP (also responsible for TOGA and WOCE), and the Global Ocean Data Assimilation Experiment (GODAE), initiated just two years earlier, in 1996. The members of the "science team," later Argo Steering Team (AST), listed as authors of the original proposal were appointed at a workshop in Tokyo in July 1998

122 Susanna Lidström et al.

convened jointly by CLIVAR and GODAE. The objectives of the new program were clearly identified from the start, including the number of floats imagined to be necessary, the parts of the ocean they would be able to reach, and how the data would be received and managed:

> Based on the information available now, it is proposed that Argo should comprise around 3,300 floats, each profiling through 0–2,000 m around 25 times per year over an estimated lifetime of 3–4 years. Each float will measure both temperature and salinity and will provide estimates of current velocity at the parking depth of the floats (probably around 1,500 m). All data will be telemetered in real time and will be available (and widely distributed) within 1–2 days of capture (or sooner if practical). The quality of the data will be ensured through the establishment of data assembly centres for float data.[37]

The proposal notes that recent technological advancements with regards to float designs, notably the addition of censors and the prolonged lifetime of each float, made the proposed program "a very cost-effective option."[38]

The strategy for deployment focused on expanding existing nodes where floats were already present, before extending the array to new areas. Existing floats operated primarily in the North Atlantic and eastern tropical Pacific Ocean. The Indian and Southern Oceans were identified as initial areas for expansion, with deployments predicted to begin within two years, in 2000. The plan was to reach global coverage as soon as possible, with the central AST coordinating small-scale national or regional contributions of floats to avoid overlaps and fill in gaps, "ensuring global coverage and adequate resolution."[39] The proposal notes that though some regions would be challenging to reach, even with autonomous floats, the program was both doable and necessary:

> It is clear global coverage will not be easy to achieve and it is likely a consortium-like approach will be needed to ensure adequate sampling in data sparse regions. There are also several outstanding technical issues that need to be addressed. However, our best advice at present suggests none of these issues represent an insurmountable obstacle for Argo.[40]

The most important scientific contribution that Argo was forecasted to make was to improve the accuracy of climate prediction models. Interactions between the ocean and the atmosphere are one of the most central dynamics in the climate system, and even more so as the climate changes, as the ocean takes up excess heat and carbon from the air to reach a new equilibrium. The process changes the marine environment, both locally and globally, as added carbon leads to acidification and higher temperatures expands the volume of the water and causes deoxygenation, while also affecting how different water masses move, mix and interact with each other. For example, the Atlantic Meridional Overturning

Circulation (AMOC) has slowed down over the past century and may be at a risk of shutdown, with associated severe climate and ocean effects.[41] The prompt detection of such changes and their development is made possible by the data gathered by the Argo floats. By measuring temperature, salinity and oxygen, key variables for these changes, Argo provides insights into how climate change impacts the water and drives for example sea-level rise. This information is in turn used to constrain climate models with vastly more observational data than had previously been possible with single, ship-based measurements. The program was thus presented as an essential subsurface partner to the Jason satellite altimetry program, which had been measuring sea-level height, a key indicator of warming waters, since 1992. Through combined efforts, Argo and Jason would provide comprehensive and integrated knowledge about the ocean–atmosphere interface, including better understanding of the causes, such as temperature changes, behind the rise of global sea level observed by satellite measurements:

> The combination of *Argo* and altimetry will enable a new generation of applications. Global maps of sea level, on time scales of weeks to several years, will be interpreted with full knowledge of the upper ocean stratification. The vertical dependence of the oceanic response to surface forcing will be in view. Global ocean and climate models will be initialized, tested and constrained with a level of information hitherto not available. An adequate sampling network will be in place as a foundation for future studies of climate variability and predictability.[42]

In other words, Argo helps to bring the three-dimensional ocean into climate science, shedding light both on the ocean's role in climate change mitigation and on the impacts of climate change on the ocean environment and its inhabitants. These contributions were recognised and predicted from the start; the Argo proposal notes that if successfully implemented, the new program represented "a near-revolution in ocean measurement," with profound implications for oceanographers as well as for studies of the climate and other Earth systems.[43] The team of authors concluded confidently that readers would find "the initiative, though ambitious, both doable and worth doing" (Figure 7.1).[44]

The prediction proved accurate. The Argo proposal was quickly approved, with institutional backing from both GODAE and CLIVAR. The first floats were deployed already in 1999, only a year after the official proposal and earlier than predicted, and global deployments have been in place since 2004. The goal of 3,000 individual floats was reached in 2007. From a US-based initiative, the program has developed into an international collaboration, with around 30 countries contributing one or more floats to the global array in the early 2020s. The US remains responsible for about half the total number of floats. After two decades of operation, Roemmich, one of the initiators, could state that "Argo's systematic and regular observation of the global subsurface ocean has transformed ocean observing," while leading "the way among ocean observing networks

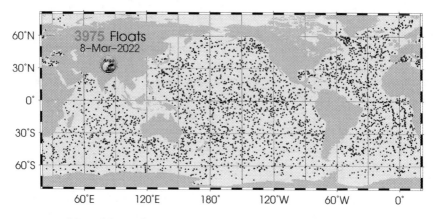

FIGURE 7.1 Map of Argo Floats in operation 2022.

with regard to international cooperation, operations planning, Data Availability, and metadata quality."[45] Keys to the program's success have been identified as the robust and cost-effective technology of the floats, strong consensus on the high value of the program within and beyond the scientific community, and effective partnerships between research teams and commercial suppliers in the continuous development and improvement of float technologies.[46] Argo plays a central role in the Global Ocean Observing System (GOOS) and the Global Climate Observing System (GCOS), as well as the World Climate Research Program (WCRP). In other words, the Argo program is a planetary environing medium, not just for our knowledge of the ocean but also for knowing and observing the climate and the Earth system as a whole.

Argo and the increasing datafication of the marine environment

The environing of the ocean that emerged through post-war and Cold War technologies resulted in scientific understandings fundamentally different from how the marine realm was previously known. Höhler observes that "oceanographic probing and observing the sea in breadth and depth in the second half of the twentieth century provided global overviews which in their geographic and scientific scope increasingly diverged from other established local experiences of the sea."[47] Lehman likewise notes the central importance of the IGY for subsequent developments in oceanographic research and for its role in making what she calls "an Anthropocene ocean" – an ocean that was at the same time better known and further impacted by people, through ventures into the depths, changes to compositions of marine life as well as waters, and extraction of resources. This fundamental change in how the global ocean was observed, sampled and known intensified in the 1990s, as observations and sampling were to a significant extent decoupled from ships. The Argo program played a pivotal role in this development; the global array of autonomous floats was presented as "key to help free the large-scale oceanographic data collection process from the dependency on ships."[48] The Argo proposal explicitly argues for the importance of pursuing and enabling this profound change, predicting that "the oceanographic community is entering a new era where ocean models and data assimilation and ocean state estimation will be the preferred methods for utilizing data."[49]

The Argo program is thus part of a development that has seen the increasing importance of digital data in ocean sciences in the first decades of the 21st century. The networks of sensors made up of Argo floats and other GOOS technologies are "creating a new understanding of the world ocean," as Lehman puts it, that "converts the ocean's properties into flows of information, creating a data double of a dynamic sea."[50] The oceanic network of networks that Argo is part of has been studied by Stefan Helmreich, starting from a different environing medium, the wave buoy. Like the buoy, the Argo floats can be viewed "as a material technology with literary/informational tendrils out into the world, a world stitched together through a media ecology of instruments and social institutions."[51] Through this comprehensive environing media system individual Argo measurements are put together, processed and analysed, and then combined with additional forms of measurements and data to eventually create the "data double" that Lehman refers to (Figure 7.2).

In the environing media of the Argo floats, the actor closest to the floats themselves is the Argo Data Management Team (ADMT), which oversees the flows of data from the physical floats. The original Argo proposal underlines the importance of creating an innovative data management system to make the most of the float recordings, emphasising "the complementary role of the direct and remote observing networks and the role of models and data assimilation in integrating incoming information and producing useful and practical outputs."[52] The ADMT developed a two-step system to achieve this, with one strategy for real time and a second one for delayed-mode data. In the first step, the floats transmit their recordings via satellite to one of several Data Assembly Centres (DACs) around the world, where the data are subjected to automated quality control before being distributed to the Global Telecommunications System (GTS) and then forwarded to two Argo Global DACs (GDACs): one in France and one in the US. This initial process is routinely completed within 24 hours, and primarily serves operational users, such as meteorological agencies who require real-time data for weather forecasting. The second step, performed by the two GDACs, includes thorough quality control and processing to turn the raw data into a user-friendly format. This process produces high-quality data for the scientific community and is usually completed within a year, but may also be revisited at any later date. It was agreed from the start of the Argo program that all data, both raw and processed, "would be publicly available without restriction."[53] This policy has been maintained, making the program "a pioneer in scientific ocean data delivery."[54]

The ocean environing media that the Argo program is a central part of have enacted a large-scale datafication of the marine environment. Höhler describes

FIGURE 7.2 An Argo float is prepared for deployment.

how over the course of the 20th century, "synoptic images created ocean knowledges that began with digits and ultimately resided in digital data sets and the potentials of data recombination."[55] This datafication, as with other forms of digital media transmissions, is not innocent or neutral in its nature. What is included and represented depends on many factors. Lehman has argued for example that "the IGY's oceanography program reveal the ways in which old and new forms of imperialism were knitted together to produce the world ocean as an object of knowledge in a new era of planetary-scale environmental politics,"[56] and moreover that "synoptic geographies entail not just uneven data coverage of the globe but also unequal geopolitical relationships, serving to further scientific expertise in some geographical areas and not others, at the same time creating a notion of the planet as an object of knowledge for all humanity."[57]

Benson has drawn attention to disciplinary dimensions, in the sense that the power and interests of different user groups shape what is prioritised or made technologically possible. In his study, this is reflected in "the differences between global environmental visions of meteorologists and wildlife biologists,"[58] a disciplinary difference that seems present also in the Argo program; the original floats, or Core Argo, record data on temperature, salinity and pressure, that is, geophysical variables central to climate scientists, but do not provide data on biodiversity, for example, which is more difficult to collect. Another limitation of Core Argo is depth; the original floats only descend to 2,000 m beneath the surface, which means that half the ocean remains unaccounted for. While these limitations of the original Argo program are being addressed, through additional programs that measure more variables in more places (including Biogeochemical Argo, Deep Argo and Polar Argo), limitations will always be a factor and no streams of data will ever represent the ocean in its entirety, regardless of claims of a "digital twin" of the ocean.

Governing a datafied ocean

Looking back at Argo's first decade of operation, Roemmich et al. conclude that "Argo has achieved more than anyone imagined it would ten years ago, but the hardest work lies ahead – sustaining the program, broadening its applications and user base, and ensuring that its global observations benefit people in all nations." Plans for the future include substantial expansion in multiple directions: "The objective is to create a fully global, top-to-bottom, dynamically complete, and multidisciplinary Argo Program that will integrate seamlessly with satellite and with other *in situ* elements of the Global Ocean Observing System."[59] There are also plans to further utilise automated machine learning, according to a recent report:

> Looking forward, advances in machine learning algorithms have the potential to provide an important resource to the Argo community by helping to meet the challenge of maintaining the quality of data from more floats and diversified missions as the program continues to expand.[60]

Others have also suggested that machine learning provides an opportunity for quality control and expansion of ocean data, and, by association, for ocean governance.[61]

Increasing the quantity and quality of global ocean observations and knowledge, not least through more and better data, is seen as central to protecting and governing the marine environment. Under the United Nations Convention of the Law of the Sea (UNCLOS), the acquisition of ocean data is directly linked to obligations to share scientific information and knowledge equitably, captured in concepts such as "technology transfer" and "capacity building."[62] The need to share ocean data openly is recognised in best practices for the field, such as the FAIR (findable, accessible, interoperable and reusable) data principles, as well as in UN initiatives to develop ocean science and sustainability, including SDG target 14a to "increase ocean knowledge, develop research capacity and transfer marine technology," and ongoing negotiations for a legally binding instrument to protect and sustainably use marine biodiversity beyond national jurisdiction (BBNJ treaty).

At the same time, it is recognised that current ocean databases are fragmented, siloed between disciplines, actors and regions, which hinders accessibility and usability.[63] A recent study raises concerns around the use of data-driven optimisation algorithms for marine spatial planning and protection specifically, noting that algorithmic approaches can reinforce existing inequities both through the data themselves, where "exclusionary inputs" lead to "exclusionary outputs," due for instance to certain geographical areas or species being more studied than others, and through differing interpretations of data that become reflected but invisible inside complex algorithms: "the values and positionalities of those funding, designing, and implementing algorithms can shape the encoded objectives of these algorithms at the expense of those whose knowledges and experiences are not represented." The same study notes that algorithmic approaches favour standardised scientific data in ways that risk marginalising other, such as traditional or indigenous, knowledges about marine ecosystems.[64]

The current development towards algorithmic rationality through big data analytics that is increasingly permeating the epistemic object of the world ocean has long historical roots reaching back to the early modern era, as we have attempted to show in this chapter. A shift in perception from qualitative to quantitative observations of the environment that began during the late Middle Ages and the Renaissance can still be seen as ongoing today.[65] Through mastery of new scientific techniques for measurement and calculation, new scales of exploitation and domination have been made possible. As we discussed in the beginning of this chapter, this was particularly true for the colonial developments which depended on a new global nautical infrastructure.

The present datafication of ocean science and observations likewise has implications for contemporary marine governance and geopolitics. Lehman contends that the systematic and networked collection, compilation and analysis of observations turn the ocean's flows, just like the flows of data emanating from the activity of contemporary individuals, into isolated and transformed flows of actionable information.[66] As the ocean is rapidly datafied through big data sets that are increasingly open, questions around the use and interpretation of these data, including who has the ability and power to use them towards their chosen ends, are raised. While we can perhaps model the trajectory of a sustainable ocean with the aid of machine learning, the models themselves do not make the political decision-making around marine sustainable development any less fraught than it has been throughout history, and since the second half of the 20th century in particular. More data does not necessarily entail a more protected ocean, as the environing process always depends on human agency.

Notes

1 Stacy Alaimo, "Science Studies and the Blue Humanities," *Configurations* 27, no. 4 (2019): 429.
2 Melody Jue, *Wild Blue Media: Thinking through Seawater* (Durham, NC: Duke University Press, 2020), 3.

3 Helen Rozwadowski, *Vast Expanses: A History of the Oceans* (London: Reaktion, 2019), 9.
4 Stephen C. Riser, Howard J. Freeland, Dean Roemmich, et al., "Fifteen Years of Ocean Observations with the Global Argo Array," *Nature Climate Change* 6 (2016): 145–153.
5 Dean Roemmich, Matthew H. Alford, Hervé Claustre, et al., "On the Future of Argo: A Global Full-Depth, Multi-Disciplinary Array," *Frontiers in Marine Science* 6 (2019), article no. 439.
6 The Argo Science Team, *On the Design and Implementation of Argo: A Global Array of Profiling Floats* (The Hague: International CLIVAR Project Office, 1998); Annie P.S. Wong, Susan E. Wijffels, Stephen C. Riser, et al., "Argo Data 1999–2019: Two Million Temperature-Salinity Profiles and Subsurface Velocity Observations from a Global Array of Profiling Floats," *Frontiers in Marine Science* 7, no. 700 (2020).
7 Bernhard Siegert, "(Not) in Place: The Grid, or Cultural Techniques for Ruling Spaces," *Cultural Techniques: Grids, Filters, Doors and Other Articulations of the Real* (Fordham: Fordham University Press, 2015).
8 Margaret E. Schotte, *The Sailing School: Navigating Science and Skill 1550–1800* (Baltimore, MD: Johns Hopkins University Press, 2019), 17.
9 Rozwadowski, *Vast Expanses*, 10.
10 Ibid., 102.
11 Bernhard Siegert, "Longitude and Simultaneity in Philosophy, Physics, and Empires," *Configurations* 23, no. 2 (2015): 148.
12 Joaquim Alves Gaspar & Henrique Leitao, "What Is a Nautical Chart, Really? Uncovering the Geometry of Early Modern Nautical Charts," *Journal of Cultural Heritage* 29 (2018): 130–136.
13 Rozwadowski, *Vast expanses,* 108.
14 Helen Rozwadowski, *Fathoming the Ocean: The Discovery and Exploration of the Deep Sea* (Cambridge, MA: Harvard University Press, 2008), 14.
15 Rozwadowski, *Vast expanses*, 110.
16 Ibid., 122.
17 Ronald E. Doel, Tanya J. Levin, & Mason K. Marker, "Extending Modern Cartography to the Ocean Depths: Military Patronage, Cold War Priorities, and the Heezen-Tharp Mapping Project, 1952–1959," *Journal of Historical Geography* 32, no. 3 (2006): 605–626.
18 Håkon With Andersen, "A Short Human History of the Ocean Floor," *The Law of the Seabed* (Leiden: Brill Nijhoff, 2020), 61–82.
19 Jessica Lehman, "Making an Anthropocene Ocean: Synoptic Geographies of the International Geophysical Year 1957–1958," *Annals of the American Association of Geographers* 110, no. 3 (2020): 606–622.
20 Eva Lövbrand, Johannes Stripple, & Bo Wiman, "Earth System Governmentality: Reflections on Science in the Anthropocene," *Global Environmental Change* 19, no. 1 (2009): 7–13.
21 John C. Swallow, "A Neutral-Buoyancy Float for Measuring Deep Currents," *Deep Sea Research* 3, no. 1 (1955): 74–81.
22 Lehman, "Making an Anthropocene Ocean," 615; see also Jessica Lehman, "A Sea of Potential: The Politics of Global Ocean Observations," *Political Geography* 55 (2016): 113–123.
23 W. John Gould, "From Swallow Floats to Argo – the Development of Neutrally Buoyant Floats," *Deep-Sea Research II* 52 (2005): 537.
24 Lehman, "Making an Anthropocene Ocean," 615.
25 Jessica Lehman, "Sea Change: The World Ocean Circulation Experiment and the Productive Limits of Ocean Variability," *Science, Technology & Human Values* 46, no. 4 (2021): 839–862.
26 Lehman, "Sea change," 850.

27 Ibid., 840.
28 Sabine Höhler, "Knowledges: Creating the Blue Planet from Modern Oceanography," *A Cultural History of the Sea in the Global Age*, ed. Franziska Torma (London: Bloomsbury Academic, 2021), 21–44.
29 Höhler, "Knowledges."
30 Roemmich et al., "On the Future of Argo," 3.
31 Paul Edwards, *A Vast Machine: Computer Models, Climate Data, and the Politics of Global Warming* (Cambridge, MA: MIT Press, 2010), 88; cf. also Friedrich A. Kittler, *Grammophone, Film, Typewriter* (Berlin: Brinkmann & Bose, 1986), 149.
32 Naomi Oreskes, *Science on a Mission: How Military Funding Shaped What We Do and What We Don't Know about the Ocean* (Chicago and London: Chicago University Press, 2021); see also e.g. John Cloud (ed.). "Earth Sciences in the Cold War," special issue of *Social Studies of Science* 33, no. 5 (2003) and Lino Camprubí & Alexandra Hui, "Testing the Underwater Ear: Hearing, Standardizing, and Classifying Marine Sounds from World War I to the Cold War," *Testing Hearing: The Making of Modern Aurality*, eds. Viktoria Tkaczyk, Mara Mills & Alexandra Hui (New York: Oxford University Press, 2020), 301–326.
33 Bruno Latour, "Why Has Critique Run Out of Steam? From Matters of Fact to Matters of Concern," *Critical Inquiry* 30, no. 2 (2004): 225–248.
34 Etienne Benson, "One Infrastructure, Many Global Visions: The Commercialization and Diversification of Argos, a Satellite-Based Environmental Surveillance System," *Social Studies of Science* 42 (2012): 843–868.
35 The Argo Science Team, *On the Design and Implementation of Argo*, 1–2.
36 Ibid., 8.
37 Ibid., 28.
38 Ibid., ii.
39 Ibid., 27.
40 Ibid., 30.
41 Niklas Boers, "Observation-Based Early-Warning Signals for a Collapse of the Atlantic Meridional Overturning Circulation," *Nature Climate Change* 11 (2021): 680–688.
42 The Argo Science Team, *On the Design and Implementation of Argo*, ii.
43 Ibid., 30.
44 Ibid., i.
45 Roemmich et al., "On the Future of Argo."
46 Ibid.
47 Höhler, "Knowledges."
48 The Argo Science Team, *On the Design and Implementation of Argo*, 2.
49 Ibid., ii.
50 Lehman, "A Sea of Potential," 113.
51 Stefan Helmreich, "Reading a Wave Buoy," *Science, Technology & Human Values* 44, no. 5 (2019): 742.
52 The Argo Science Team, *On the Design and Implementation of Argo*, 4.
53 Dean Roemmich, Gregory C. Johnson, Stephen Riser et al., "The Argo Program: Observing the Global Ocean with Profiling Floats," *Oceanography* 22, no. 2 (2009): 34–43.
54 Wong et al., "Argo Data 1999–2019," 6.
55 Höhler, "Knowledges."
56 Lehman, "Making an Anthropocene Ocean," 606.
57 Ibid., 613.
58 Benson, "One Infrastructure, Many Global Visions," 860–861.
59 Roemmich et al., "On the Future of Argo," 2.
60 The National Oceanographic and Atmospheric Administration, Atlantic Oceanographic and Meteorological Laboratory, "The Argo Program: Two Decades

of Ocean Observations," https://www.aoml.noaa.gov/news/two-decades-argo-program/ (accessed 4 March 2022).
61 E.g. Wong et al., "Argo Data 1999–2019."
62 Harriet Harden-Davies, "Marine Technology Transfer: Towards a Capacity-Building Toolkit for Marine Biodiversity Beyond National Jurisdiction," *Marine Biodiversity of Areas Beyond National Jurisdiction*, eds. Myron H. Nordquist and Ronánn Long (Leiden: Brill Nijhoff, 2021).
63 Annie Brett, Jim Leape, Mark Abbott et al., "Ocean Data Need a Sea Change to Help Navigate the Warming World," *Nature* 582 (2020): 181–183.
64 Cf. Melissa S. Chapman, William K. Oestreich, Timothy H. Frawley, et al., "Promoting Equity in the Use of Algorithms for High-Seas Conservation," *One Earth* 4 (2021): 792.
65 Alfred W. Crosby, *The Measure of Reality: Quantification and Western Society 1250–1600* (Cambridge: Cambridge University Press, 1997).
66 Lehman, "A Sea of Potential," 119.

References

Alaimo, Stacy. "Science Studies and the Blue Humanities." *Configurations* 27, no. 4 (2019): 429–542.
Andersen, Håkon With. "A Short Human History of the Ocean Floor." *The Law of the Seabed*. Leiden: Brill Nijhoff, 2020.
Argo Science Team. *On the Design and Implementation of Argo: A Global Array of Profiling Floats*. The Hague: International CLIVAR Project Office, 1998.
Benson, Etienne. "One Infrastructure, Many Global Visions: The Commercialization and Diversification of Argos, a Satellite-Based Environmental Surveillance System." *Social Studies of Science* 42 (2012): 843–868.
Boers, Niklas. "Observation-Based Early-Warning Signals for a Collapse of the Atlantic Meridional Overturning Circulation." *Nature Climate Change* 11 (2021): 680–688.
Brett, Annie, Jim Leape, Mark Abbott et al. "Ocean Data Need a Sea Change to Help Navigate the Warming World." *Nature* 582 (2020): 181–183.
Camprubí, Lino, & Alexandra Hui. "Testing the Underwater Ear: Hearing, Standardizing, and Classifying Marine Sounds from World War I to the Cold War." *Testing Hearing: The Making of Modern Aurality*, edited by Viktoria Tkaczyk, Mara Mills, & Alexandra Hui, 301–326. New York: Oxford University Press, 2020.
Chapman, Melissa S., William K. Oestreich, Timothy H. Frawley, et al. "Promoting Equity in the Use of Algorithms for High-Seas Conservation." *One Earth* 4 (2021): 790–794.
Cloud, John (ed.). "Earth Sciences in the Cold War." special issue of *Social Studies of Science* 33, no. 5 (2003): 629–633.
Crosby, Alfred W. *The Measure of Reality: Quantification and Western Society 1250–1600*. Cambridge: Cambridge University Press, 1997.
Doel, Ronald E., Tanya J. Levin & Mason K. Marker. "Extending Modern Cartography to the Ocean Depths: Military Patronage, Cold War Priorities, and the Heezen-Tharp Mapping Project, 1952–1959." *Journal of Historical Geography* 32, no. 3 (2006): 605–626.
Edwards, Paul. *A Vast Machine: Computer Models, Climate Data, and the Politics of Global Warming*. Cambridge, MA: MIT Press, 2010.

Gaspar, Joaquim Alves, & Henrique Leitao. "What Is a Nautical Chart, Really? Uncovering the Geometry of Early Modern Nautical Charts." *Journal of Cultural Heritage* 29 (2018): 130–136.

Gould, W. John. "From Swallow Floats to Argo – The Development of Neutrally Buoyant Floats." *Deep Sea Research Part II: Topical Studies in Oceanography* 52 (2005): 529–543.

Harden-Davies, Harriet. "Marine Technology Transfer: Towards a Capacity-Building Toolkit for Marine Biodiversity Beyond National Jurisdiction." *Marine Biodiversity of Areas Beyond National Jurisdiction*, edited by Myron H. Nordquist & Ronánn Long, 231–238. Leiden: Brill Nijhoff, 2021.

Helmreich, Stefan. "Reading a Wave Buoy." *Science, Technology & Human Values* 44, no. 5 (2019): 737–761.

Höhler, Sabine. "Knowledges: Creating the Blue Planet from Modern Oceanography." *A Cultural History of the Sea in the Global Age*, edited by Franziska Torma, 21–44. London: Bloomsbury Academic, 2021.

Jue, Melody. *Wild Blue Media: Thinking through Seawater.* Durham, NC: Duke University Press, 2020.

Kittler, Friedrich A. *Grammophone, Film, Typewriter.* Berlin: Brinkmann & Bose, 1986.

Latour, Bruno. "Why Has Critique Run Out of Steam? From Matters of Fact to Matters of Concern." *Critical Inquiry* 30, no. 2 (2004): 225–248.

Lehman, Jessica. "Sea Change: The World Ocean Circulation Experiment and the Productive Limits of Ocean Variability." *Science, Technology & Human Values* 46, no. 4 (2021): 839–862.

———. "Making an Anthropocene Ocean: Synoptic Geographies of the International Geophysical Year 1957–1958." *Annals of the American Association of Geographers* 110, no. 3 (2020): 606–622.

———. "A Sea of Potential: The Politics of Global Ocean Observations." *Political Geography* 55 (2016): 113–123.

Lövbrand, Eva, Johannes Stripple, & Bo Wiman. "Earth System Governmentality: Reflections on Science in the Anthropocene." *Global Environmental Change* 19, no. 1 (2009): 7–13.

National Oceanographic and Atmospheric Administration (NASA), Atlantic Oceanographic and Meteorological Laboratory. "The Argo Program: Two Decades of Ocean Observations." https://www.aoml.noaa.gov/news/two-decades-argo-program/ (accessed 4 March 2022).

Oreskes, Naomi. *Science on a Mission: How Military Funding Shaped What We Do and What We Don't Know about the Ocean.* Chicago and London: Chicago University Press, 2021.

Riser, Stephen C., Howard J. Freeland, Dean Roemmich, et al. "Fifteen Years of Ocean Observations with the Global Argo Array." *Nature Climate Change* 6 (2016): 145–153.

Roemmich, Dean, Matthew H. Alford, Hervé Claustre, et al. "On the Future of Argo: A Global Full-Depth, Multi-Disciplinary Array." *Frontiers in Marine Science* 6, no. 439 (2019). https://www.frontiersin.org/articles/10.3389/fmars.2019.00439/full

Roemmich, Dean, Gregory C. Johnson, Stephen Riser et al. "The Argo Program: Observing the Global Ocean with Profiling Floats." *Oceanography* 22, no. 2 (2009): 34–43.

Rozwadowski, Helen. *Vast Expanses: A History of the Oceans.* London: Reaktion, 2019.

———. *Fathoming the Ocean: The Discovery and Exploration of the Deep Sea.* Cambridge, MA: Harvard University Press, 2008.

Schotte, Margaret E. *The Sailing School: Navigating Science and Skill 1550–1800.* Baltimore, MD: Johns Hopkins University Press, 2019.

Siegert, Bernhard. "Longitude and Simultaneity in Philosophy, Physics, and Empires." *Configurations* 23, no. 2 (2015): 145–163.

Siegert, Bernhard. "(Not) in Place: The Grid, or Cultural Techniques for Ruling Spaces." *Cultural Techniques: Grids, Filters, Doors and Other Articulations of the Real*, edited by Bernhard Siegert, 97–120. Fordham: Fordham University Press, 2015.

Swallow, John C. "A Neutral-Buoyancy Float for Measuring Deep Currents." *Deep Sea Research* 3, no. 1 (1955): 74–81.

Wong, Annie P.S., Susan E. Wijffels, Stephen C. Riser, et al. "Argo Data 1999–2019: Two Million Temperature-Salinity Profiles and Subsurface Velocity Observations from a Global Array of Profiling Floats." *Frontiers in Marine Science* 7, no. 700 (2020). https://www.frontiersin.org/articles/10.3389/fmars.2020.00700/full

8
ENVIRONING TIME
Mediating climate modeling

Nina Wormbs

Introduction

Is the Anthropocene about the past or the future? Being interested in the temporalities of climate change, I sometimes wonder. The age of humankind should arguably be about both, not only capturing the geological era when humans made a permanent impact on Earth, but also incorporating a future, where we struggle to manage this impact. Often enough, however, I get the impression that the Anthropocene is mostly about the past and where to put the spike in the horizontally organized geological calendar of the Earth, the strata of previous times which display the imprint from earlier flora and fauna, used by scientists to make order in change and create chronologies. Western intellectuals have indeed engaged with the long term since geologists started to question the Biblical description of time,[1] long before the term Anthropocene. When physicists formulated the idea of the Big Bang, time also took center stage. Recent writings that address this extreme long term have reached a rather broad audience.[2] Ironically, or perhaps congenially, this historical interest coincides with our inability to manage climate change. It is as if we find comfort in the fact that we did have a history, even if said change has made our future hazy.

This historic focus is of course legitimate and important. The tension between the age of humans and the extreme long term of the geological gaze holds promise for the intellectual work we are facing as planet-altering creatures. To place ourselves alongside dinosaurs are not only attractive for children in a particular age, but it also affords a more holistic perspective of stunning complexity. If we could envision time and understand change in temporal perspectives of varying scales, much would be gained for humankind. However, the future is also important for us to envision and understand. And there is an ongoing battle for the future, played out by different actors in different genres, resulting in a multitude of possible futures for humanity.[3]

I am interested in this future – or rather these futures – and how time and possible futures are mediated through scientific practices. I suggest that we can regard these practices as *environing technologies*, that is, technologies that create environments. Environment is normally understood as a spatial concept, but I argue that it is also temporal, working with time and change. The chapter will discuss how we can understand these futures brought to us by one of the most prominent organizations in the business, namely the Intergovernmental Panel on Climate Change. There are indeed many ways to talk about the future, but for climate change, *models* have become central. Models are key epistemic tools in climate science and the basis for much of the politics surrounding climate-change action and mitigation.[4] The model results are often mediated through classic *visual techniques* of the natural sciences, such as graphs and diagrams.[5] In this chapter I will look closer at how these visual techniques work and what they might convey regarding the temporalization of climate change. This temporalization fundamentally affects our perception of the planet in the years to come, a perception which is key in the response to climate change and should therefore be of central importance. In the light of their importance, I contend that we have not paid enough attention to these temporalities.

In the following I will first discuss how some of the results from the IPCC assessments are presented visually in the reports, and how we can understand the temporalities in play. I will then present the framework of environing technologies and its possible usefulness, and finally, I will discuss if environing media could be an alternative concept when analyzing the graphs that convey the output from climate-change models.

Modeling and mediating the future

Climate-change models frame the climate issue for humankind and structure our appreciation of what is to come. The futures that these models allow enable an analysis of the temporal dimensions of climate change.[6] The main actor is the Intergovernmental Panel on Climate Change which was created as a sub-organization to the United Nations in 1988. The IPCC releases assessments with some regularity, putting together state-of-the-art knowledge on climate change which will guide the international system in policy decisions. The First Assessment Report was published in 1990, the fifth in 2014.[7]

The IPCC reports have undergone change since the first publication in 1990. At first, they were graphically simple without color and relatively sparse with illustrations other than graphs and tables. In the Second Assessment Report (1995) blue was introduced and in the Third Assessment Report (2001) full color was used, which allowed for more elaborate illustrations and visualizations. There is no clear tendency in the number and type of graphic aids other than that complexity increases over time and that more dimensions are incorporated into a common frame. The publication of the report has increasingly attracted attention of news media and the Summaries for Policy Makers (SPMs) most likely have a much larger readership than the full scientific reports. The images from the SPMs therefore enjoy a greater circulation in the public sphere and are thus a focus of my interest.[8]

Climate change and its consequences are increasingly difficult to grasp. It is not primarily the sheer science of the change that is challenging, which in earnest is not too complicated regarding the basic processes, but the scale of change and the intricate relations between our ordinary lives and the consequences for people on the other side of the globe. Individual and collective emissions in the small scale together and over the long term create an aggregate impact which transcends the planetary boundaries and remains forceful over many years to come.[9]

The mediation of climate change has a long history and is deeply politicized in many parts of the world.[10] In particular, news media has played a central role in conveying the scientific knowledge on climate change, but arguably failed on many arenas as the main message often was one of disunity among scientists when there in fact have been an almost total agreement on the main points for a very long time.[11] Even when true to scientific consensus it has proven difficult for the issue of climate change to take center stage as the crisis it is.

Time in relation to climate-change science has in general attracted less attention in the reflective and critical scholarship on climate change, where uncertainty, inertia, and denial have been thoroughly studied.[12] This is somewhat paradoxical as time is central to change. We know that the climate is changing because we can compare with earlier climates, and our survival depends on our ability to manage the change to come. Still, the temporal dimension is shadowed by sea-level rise, global mean temperatures, and CO_2 concentrations in the atmosphere – all three elusive enough, yet more concrete than time.

The greenhouse effect, and later climate change, was for long portrayed and understood as something that would happen in the distant future. In fact, this view was also held by scientists who based their decisions on target years allowing model results to be noticeable. Central to much early climate-change science was to establish if and how much of the change was anthropogenic and what could be attributed to natural variation, i.e. fluctuations that depend on astronomical, geological, chemical, and other processes that are not connected to human existence. Since climate change is a slow process, the consequences would indeed lie in the future. Thus, when modeling started in the 1960s and 1970s, a certain timeframe was required to get a significant signal. In the First Assessment Report of the IPCC, which was published in 1990, this was framed as a need: "100 years or more are necessary to support study of potential anthropogenic impacts on the climate system".[13] A target year far in the future was hence central.

The choice to model the long term was dependent not only on the needs for a significant signal but also on the tools available. Computational power increased exponentially from the 1960s and onward, i.e. doubling regularly, allowing for a greater number of components and variables to be included in the simulations.

A great challenge early on was the poor spatial resolution, due precisely to computer capacity, which resulted in very crude estimates and averages. Increased spatial resolution contributed to more useful results. Extremely important was to also incorporate more complex processes simulating the climate system. Early models were so-called equilibrium models that calculated how the climate system reacted on a doubling of CO_2 concentration in the atmosphere. Later, so-called transient models would instead work with constantly changing CO_2 concentration that would better reflect the changes in the system.[14]

In the First Assessment Report, the dominant target year of the scenarios building on climate-change models was 2100. In fact, in the following assessments up until the Fifth Assessment Report, published in 2014, the target year of 2100 has been the most common one.[15] There are reports in which also the year 2300 is featuring, like the Third Assessment Report, but in comparison to the number of figures where the x-axis ends on 2100, they are very few.

I propose that putting 2100 as target year for the scenarios has consequences for how we understand the futures humankind is facing. It frames the issue temporarily. The unintended paradox of choosing 2100, a year that would allow a large enough signal, is that it is so distant in the future that none of those who conceived of it will be alive then. This is also true for the politicians and business leaders who make decisions today. Thus, a year that works for science does not work for policy. To some extent, we can regard this as a matter of scale. Anne Pasek has framed this as a tug of war between "scales germane to the problem and scales more appropriate to mobilizing political action".[16] Depending on how we articulate the problem at hand, the mediated message becomes elusive. Let me elaborate further in the next section.

The power of the graph: 2100 as the end of time

Lynda Walsh has taken an interest in the visual rhetoric of climate change and proposes that graphs make an argument that supports a scientific claim.[17] When it comes to modeled change over a chosen timeframe, we must ask what the scientific claim of such a graph consists of. In the graphs in focus here, the particular claims vary, since they deal with different change in temperature, sea-level rise, ppm, etc. What unites them is how far into the future the models run. Thus, the repeated claim is arguably that 2100 is the most important temporal frame of climate change.

James Risbey has criticized this focus and called it a "2100ism", which has created a paradigm for the climate-change issue with severe consequences. Risbey argues that this focus "obscures the connection between impacts beyond 2100 and policy actions in the present".[18] Since impact will continue well into the coming centuries, stopping at 2100 gives us a wrongful picture of the futures at hand and might even lead to an unwillingness to act now. At the same time, Risbey acknowledges that 2100 is convenient as it connects to human timescales.[19] The year 2100 serves some functions well, and other poorly.

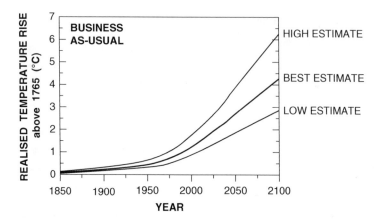

FIGURE 8.1 First Assessment Report, *Policymaker Summary of Working Group I, section 5.1, page 74. IPCC 1990.*

I would argue, however, that even though this target year is far away in the future, it can also be seen as the time *when* climate change happens. Indeed, that is by no means what the graph tells us. However, such a misunderstanding might not be as farfetched as one might think. Let us look at a graph from the First Assessment Report (Figure 8.1).

In the graph from the First Assessment Report, three business-as-usual scenarios are displayed, and we can clearly see that the best estimate will result in a temperature rise above 4 degrees in 2100. The lines leading up to the three resulting temperatures can be used to trace changes earlier in time, such as 2050 for example, but it is difficult and unclear – one would almost have to use a ruler.

In her elaboration on the so-called hockey-stick curve, the temperature change from the year 1400 until the present, Anne Pasek has talked about *charismatic data*.[20] The graph, building on a plethora of sources, displayed very forcefully the abrupt change in average temperatures on the Northern Hemisphere and had a wide circulation far beyond the first publication in *Nature* in 1998 and the following prominent role in both the Third Assessment Report and Al Gore's film "An inconvenient truth". The graph became iconic and managed to convey complicated scientific results in an image that could not be misunderstood.[21]

The examples of Pasek deal with data from the field rather than modeled data. However, *I argue that also modeled data can be charismatic and convey messages beyond the mere figure*. In fact, these graphs often do not make a clear distinction between what is modeled and what is measured. The IPCC reports frequently merge historically measured and re-analyzed data with model projections resulting in graphs that stretch both backward and forward from today. In the First Assessment Report the graph above displayed temperatures from 1850 to 2100 depending on various scenarios.

Building on Walsh and Pasek, I suggest that the target year attracts attention through its position in the graph, where it displays the end of time and what will happen at that point. As mentioned, in the following assessment reports, the visual arguments become more complicated. In the Fifth Assessment Report, color is widely used, and the graphics are elaborate and complex. Graphs are combined with bars and maps and include a geographic overview of the impacts on a continental level. But the bottom line is more often than not the same. Several scenarios are displayed and result in temperature change that is projected up until 2100.

The fact that the target year has stayed the same since the first report in 1990 is striking and remarkable, and furthermore adds to the message that this is what we must deal with. There are obvious pros of maintaining the same target year as comparison becomes easy, but at the same time, keeping the target year means that we approach the end. Side by side and one after another, these reports covey a steady message: the future of humankind is shrinking.

This was not what modelers imagined when choosing 2100 as target year. However, some did recognize that model time could be connected to culture time and thereby different temporalities synchronized, to use a concept by Helge Jordheim.[22] The year 2100 ends a century and in that capacity carries historic meaning. The endings of centuries or even millennia are points in time where stories abound about change being ushered in and about the old giving way to the new. They translate into a human scale of generations and forefathers. It is possible to remember the turn of the century as something told by those before us, or something experienced as a transition by ourselves. The year 2100 indeed frames the climate issue in a temporal context that is possible to grasp for humans.

At the same time, it is noteworthy how seldom this year features in the public discourse on climate change. It totally dominates the assessment reports but only rarely becomes the focus of a daily discussion in the public sphere. Instead, other temporalities have become more functional, other scales more apt. The Sustainable Development Goals, for example, have 2030 as their target and the period 2020–2030 has been declared a "Decade of Action". This is a timeframe easy to overview and allowing for different goals to be broken down.[23] Yet another example is the Paris Agreement, in which the signatories to the Convention strive to keep warming below 2 degrees, and ideally 1.5 degrees. This shifts the focus from scenarios for 2100 to the effects of the absolute and total emissions of greenhouse gases and instead results in a global carbon budget. This in turn translates the climate issue to a so-called stock problem, giving rise to an understanding of time as running out but in a much shorter timeframe than 2100 given the present emission rate. We will soon use up our budget long before 2100 and the end is brought closer.[24] In relation to the Paris Agreement, a 2100-ism has been replaced by a deadline-ism.

Environment, technology and media: What is in a concept?

Let me now move to a discussion of concepts and of environing. A central starting point for this chapter is the claim that environment is a human creation, whereas nature is not. The process of creating environment can be captured by the verb environ, an early modern word describing how land was encirculated and domesticated.[25] Etymologically, the word has siblings in many roman languages. Environment is the result of environing, and the action requires technology. To stake out your territory, enclose the sheep, and screen off the fox, you need the technology of the fence. Human settlement in various forms, farming and agriculture, mobility, and transport – all need technology that shape and structure nature into environments. Over time and with changing scale environing technologies have come to include enormous and complex tools, networks, and artifacts.[26] They include gigantic mines above and below Earth, oceans filled with vessels, wrecks and plastic, a space occupied by satellites and debris. The Anthropocene is the ultimate illustration of the planet as environment. Our alterations have become global and impact not just the entire Earth, but also reach into outer space and the bottom of the sea.

When we assess the environmental impact of technology, terraforming tools are the most common of technologies that environ. These environing technologies *shape* and re-shape our physical world, sometimes turning the planet inside-out as Gabrielle Hecht has put it.[27] They involve devices that allow us to build not just the shaky fence but also the Chinese wall, the dirt road and the autostrada, to cultivate not just the garden but to manage the industrialized agriculture of the 21st century. Indeed, the Anthropocene Garden could be understood as a monumental scaling of the original enclosure of the land around a settlement.[28]

There are, however, also environing technologies that work with conceptualizations and framings. The *shaping* environing technologies mentioned above can be supplemented with environing technologies that *sense* and *write*. These two terms should be understood broadly as collecting and conveying, or with key concepts in the information age: as input and output. Often these different kinds of technologies are connected and work together to form a resulting environment, which is both materially and conceptually different. The Anthropocene is in itself a conceptualization of the Earth, not just the result of shaping practices of the Holocene. As such, it might be just as powerful in helping us understand the human condition in relation to the material world. The word itself does environing work as it allows us to perceive and grasp these alterations. However, even if the shaping dimensions are limited, sensing and writing are often – but not always – part and parcel of the same environing. To be able to write down sustainable development goals, a sensing of the dimensions and the possible targets is a prerequisite. To paint a picture that claims to resemble the archipelago, you must have seen it or had someone tell you about it.

There are many such environing technologies that work primarily with our appreciation and understanding rather than with materially transforming and shaping. These conceptual environing technologies can also be epistemic, economic, existential, and emotional. Ecosystem services, for example, is a conceptualization of the environment that takes economy as baseline, translating the value of species, habitats, and a raspberry thicket on a clear-felled slope to something countable, quantitative, possible to factor into plans and politics. Red lists are not just written estimations of species in danger, but epistemic objects that highlight certain parts of flora and fauna and thereby influence our understanding of biodiversity loss and change. Moreover, they show us global degradation and they can be deeply emotional as well as existential. Many writing environing technologies have the potential to work with our emotions through the different available genres. Film, literature, and art can all speak to us on levels that are not primarily intellectual.

In the previous sections I have focused on certain types of *writing* environing technologies that mediate an understanding of climate change, namely graphs. Is it possible to call these writing environing technologies for environing media? And what would be gained with such a term? To answer that we need to look closer at media and technology and their respective students.

Media and mediation are non-trivial concepts. The saturation of media in the present society has been termed mediatization, to separate it from the more specific term mediation which refers to the process of conveying.[29] That mediation and mediatization demand various technologies and practices of different kinds adds to the complexity of any analysis. Moreover, media are not just mass media, but involve forms of interpersonal and group communication as well as many possible hybrid forms. These forms differ within themselves in turn also because of the technologies involved. Susan Douglas argues that the relation between media and technology has been differently understood by media scholars and theorists on the one hand and historians and sociologists of technology on the other, and she contends that this has been the case for over half a century. Seemingly determinist stances from a global and macro-perspective have been challenged by micro—case studies deeply influenced by a constructivist approach.[30] Ian Hutchby has suggested the term *affordances* which allows technology to enable and limit without arguing that it totally determines the outcome, escaping the detested theory of technological determinism.[31]

The usefulness of a theoretical concept rests on its ability to capture and explicate something that through this concept becomes known in a new way. However, whether it catches on in a discipline or even manages to transcend different fields of knowledge also depends on how it resonates with previous and ongoing scholarly debates and approaches. That affordances have gotten greater traction within history and sociology of technology is much due to the discussion on *what technology does* in the scholarly work of those disciplines. Within the much larger scholarly domains of media and communication studies, *what media does* is similarly central. The concepts *technology* and *media* are in themselves and respectively foci of debates and discussions in the respective fields; or put differently, humanist and social science scholars interested in technology and media have both broad and deep understanding of the central concepts of their interests. The opposite is likely less true.

This could mean that *writing environing technologies* and *environing media* surface as two very different conceptual constructs in certain domains, whereas they are almost exchangeable in others. Depending on what you put into media and technology respectively, and where you place your discussion, the understanding and analytical power might shift. Whereas an extensive and deep discussion of the meaning of technology is limited to a few narrow disciplinary fields, clearly the media concept has recently been altogether challenged by an expansion that transcends earlier understandings even outside of media and communication studies. The scholarship on elemental media by John Durham Peters is a useful example.[32] The coining of the term environing media by Johan Gärdebo and Adam Wickberg builds partly on this broader understanding of the term media. See further the introduction to this volume.

The consequences of the fact that technology and media are contextual might be that an innovative use of media in connection to environing could have greater traction than the corresponding compound writing environing technologies, both because media studies engage more academics and students than do technology studies and because the media concept in itself is already undergoing change. I suggest, however, that writing environing technologies is a broader concept than environing media, even when media is understood in an expansive way. This is because of the reach of the term technology, which can incorporate much of human activity and practice. Still, in certain contexts environing media might do precisely the work needed from a concept, which is to capture and explicate and allow for an understanding of something known in a new way. In the next section I will discuss whether the concept of environing media can be used to analyze how time, futures, and change are conveyed through scientific practices of mediation and how that in turn environs. I will use the term media and mediation in a more traditional and limited way than the recent one discussed above and in the introduction to this volume. My aim is to see if environing media can do a different job than writing environing technologies and if so, what the results might be.

Graphs as environing media?

I have argued that the graphs in the IPCC summary for policy makers frame the climate issue temporally. These graphs in turn build on results from the climate models and scenarios which are central in climate-change science. Can the concept of environing media be usefully employed to understand the work that these practices carry out? As detailed above, conceptual environing technologies work with our understanding of the environment, creating and framing it in a particular way that allows for certain actions and limits other. The examples that have previously been put forward, however, all work with the physical and spatial environment, and even though change is always temporal, time in itself has not been in focus for such an analysis by scholars interested in environing. A key issue is if we would accept time as a dimension that forms environment – in other words, something that with the help of technology can be environed.

If we regard the Anthropocene a term that is a writing environing technology, and we also accept that the Anthropocene is a temporal concept, it will mean that environing could also be temporal. The interest in history that is now growing illustrates this, and puts human activity in perspective, challenging, in fact, what it is to be human. This interest is increasingly matched by parallel interest in the futures of humanity, of which the most spectacular is perhaps the plans of re-settlement on Mars, a plan B nourished both by a specific idea of progress and the understanding that Earth one day will have to be abandoned. These plans also work with timeframes that are distant and often unprecise, albeit much shorter than those for history. In both cases, time structures the understandings and possibilities of humanity, central to environing. Thus, I would suggest that environment is not just spatial but also temporal and that there are technologies that also work temporally, environing human existence, past and future. This is just as important as any physical environing.[33]

Climate models are complex technologies with encompassing input, intricate computational labor, and advanced output, which can be thought of as conceptual environing technologies. The models and scenarios themselves do not mediate or transform in any straightforward way; this is done by visual representations of the results from models and scenarios. In the form of graphs, temporalities that are of interest for human action in the Anthropocene are displayed. The graphs *mediate* the numerical results of the model runs and the scenario work and could therefore be regarded as *environing media* rather than environing technologies. This would be in line with a more general understanding of the visual as media in climate-change communication. This would also be true for the bucket, which transforms the stock problem to a flow problem, and mediates the proposal that time is running out. One could argue that the entire IPCC reports are environing technologies as they indeed frame the climate issue. The temporal environing, however, is specifically achieved by the visual mediation.

I suggest that the term environing media can be used to capture the temporal work that the IPCC graphs do. The term might furthermore be more attractive than environing technology since the mediation is a key function of the graph, a particular visual media technology. Environing media in this case underlines that there is ongoing translational work done by the graph, which is not conveyed by the term writing environing technology. Even though it is possible to further detail the technologies involved by introducing the word communication, to stack terms in that way is less attractive. Using the term environing media makes the process more specific and precise.

Conclusion

I have argued that climate-change models have become central contemporary environing technologies since models are key epistemic tools in climate science and the basis for much of the politics surrounding climate-change action and mitigation. Environing technology creates what we understand as environment through processes of both material alterations and cognitive framings. The results of the models are conveyed visually, and these graphs can be regarded as environing media, which is more precise and brings the translational aspect of these graphs to the fore.

The key point in assessing climate-change temporality is to also incorporate the future in environing and to suggest that the fourth dimension of time is linked to the geographical and ideological dimensions put forward in previous scholarship. The focus has been not on how models incorporate certain Earth-system components and exclude others but rather on the temporalities climate-change models span and create. The models themselves and their input, together with the general tools of modeling, have shifting affordances in environing our future Earth.

The target year of 2100 is a paradox as it forcefully frames the climate issue temporarily, allowing for a big enough signal to show change, but at the same time being of a scale that does not easily translate into action. I suggested initially that our growing interest in history now, when our future seems to vanish, was congenial. Perhaps the paradox of the target year is congenial too, and in line with the wickedness of the climate problem itself.

Acknowledgment

The author would like to thank the editors and Sverker Sörlin and Erik Ljungberg for insightful comments on earlier versions.

Notes

1 Martin J. S. Rudwick, *Worlds Before Adam: The Reconstruction of Geohistory in the Age of Reform* (Chicago: University of Chicago Press, 2008).
2 I am here thinking of Yuval Noah Harari, *Sapiens: A Brief History of Humankind* (London: Harvill Secker, 2014) or David Christian, *Origin Story: A Big History of Everything* (London: Allen Lane, 2018, but also Stephen Hawking, *A Brief History of Time: From the Big Bang to Black Holes* (London: Bantam Press, 1988).
3 Jenny Andersson & Eglė Rindzevičiūtė, eds., *The Struggle for the Long-Term in Transnational Science and Politics: Forging the Future* (New York: Routledge, Taylor & Francis Group, 2015). In this context see also for example Birgit Schneider, "The Future Face of the Earth: The Visual Semantics of the Future in the Climate Change Imagery of the IPCC," *Cultures of Prediction in Atmospheric and Climate Science: Epistemic and Cultural Shifts in Computer-Based Modelling and Simulation*, ed. Matthias. Heymann, Gabriele Gramelsberger, & Martin Mahony (New York: Routledge, 2017), 231–51, and Nina Wormbs, ed., *Competing Arctic Futures: Historical and Contemporary Perspectives* (Cham: Palgrave Macmillan, 2018) for a discussion on futures.
4 Paul N. Edwards, "Representing the Global Atmosphere: Computer Models, Data, and Knowledge about Climate Change," *Changing the Atmosphere: Expert Knowledge and Environmental Governance*, eds. Clark A. Miller & Paul N Edwards (Cambridge, MA: MIT Press, 2001); Mikaela Sundberg, Parameterizations as Boundary Objects on the Climate Arena," *Social Studies of Science* 37, no. 3 (1 June 2007): 473–88; https://doi.org/10.1177/0306312706075330; Martin Mahony & Mike Hulme, "Model Migrations: Mobility and Boundary Crossings in Regional Climate Prediction," *Transactions of the Institute of British Geographers* 37, no. 2 (2012): 197–211.

5 Cf. Birgit Schneider & Thomas Nocke, *Image Politics of Climate Change: Visualizations, Imaginations, Documentations* (Bielefeld: Transcript, 2014). See also a discussion on cultural techniques by the editors in this volume's introduction.
6 The empirical material for this argument overlaps with the one used in a longer book chapter, Nina Wormbs, "Model Time and Target Year: On the End of Time in IPCC Futures," *Times of History, Times of Nature: Temporalization and the Limits of Modern Knowledge*, eds. Anders Ekström & Staffan Bergwik (New York: Berghahn Books, 2022), 284–307. There I argue that we need to pay attention to what I call "model time" in the temporalities of models and their relation to our understanding of climate change, whereas I here focus on these models as environing technology.
7 They are all open access and can be found at the IPCC web: ipcc.ch. The IPCC also publishes a lot of reports and material that are not the regular assessment reports. The 2018 report on the 1.5-degree target is such an example. I do not use that material in this chapter but focus solely on the assessment reports. Different parts of the sixth report are being published as I prepare this manuscript and are not part of my empirical material.
8 Also, others judge the summaries for policy makers to have a higher circulation. See for example Lynda Walsh, *Scientists as Prophets: A Rhetorical Genealogy* (New York: Oxford University Press, 2013).
9 For a discussion on the Planetary Boundaries framework see the contribution by Sverker Sörlin, this volume.
10 See for example Mike Hulme, *Why We Disagree about Climate Change: Understanding Controversy, Inaction and Opportunity* (Cambridge: Cambridge University Press, 2009).
11 Miyase Christensen, Annika E. Nilsson, & Nina Wormbs, eds., *Media and the Politics of Arctic Climate Change: When the Ice Breaks*, 1st ed. (New York: Palgrave Macmillan, 2013); Naomi Oreskes, "The Scientific Consensus on Climate Change," *Science* 306, no. 5702 (2 December 2004): 1686.
12 See key publications like Kirsten Hastrup & Martin Skrydstrup, eds., *The Social Life of Climate Change Models : Anticipating Nature* (London: Routledge, 2013) and Matthias Heymann, Gabriele Gramelsberger, & Martin Mahony, eds., *Cultures of Prediction in Atmospheric and Climate Science: Epistemic and Cultural Shifts in Computer-Based Modelling and Simulation* (New York: Routledge, 2017). See also Shinichiro Asayama et al., "Why Setting a Climate Deadline Is Dangerous," *Nature Climate Change* 9, no. 8 (1 August 2019): 570–572, https://doi.org/10.1038/s41558-019-0543-4 who argues that it is easier to relate time to human experience, than mean temperatures and other climate metrics. There are indeed historians dealing with climate change who have taken an interest in time. See for example Dipesh Chakrabarty, "The Climate of History: Four Theses," *Critical Inquiry* 35, no. 2 (2009): 197–222.
13 IPCC First Assessment Report Overview and Policymaker Summaries and 1992 IPCC Supplement, 11.
14 Edwards, *A Vast Machine*; Spencer R. Weart, *The Discovery of Global Warming* (Cambridge, MA: Harvard University Press, 2008). See also the contribution by Christoph Rosol, this volume.
15 This builds on my analysis of the summaries for policy makers of all five reports.
16 Anne Pasek, "Mediating Climate, Mediating Scale," *Humanities* 8, no. 4 (2019), DOI: 10.3390/h8040159.
17 Lynda Walsh, "The Visual Rhetoric of Climate Change," *WIREs Climate Change* 6, no. 4 (1 July 2015): 361–368, https://doi.org/10.1002/wcc.342, page 362.
18 James S. Risbey, "The New Climate Discourse: Alarmist or Alarming?" *Global Environmental Change* 18, no. 1 (1 February 2008): 26–37, https://doi.org/10.1016/j.gloenvcha.2007.06.003. Quote page 33.
19 Risbey, 33.
20 Pasek.

21 Pasek. The acquired position also meant that climate skeptics chose to attack it.
22 Helge Jordheim, "Introduction: Multiple Times and the Work of Synchronization," *History and Theory* 53, no. 4 (1 December 2014): 498–518, https://doi.org/10.1111/hith.10728. For an elaboration see Wormbs (2022).
23 Apparently, 15 years is a timeframe that is most suitable for humans to overview. See Sabine Pahl et al., "Perceptions of Time in Relation to Climate Change," *WIREs Climate Change* 5, no. 3 (1 May 2014): 375–388, https://doi.org/10.1002/wcc.272.
24 Bård Lahn, "A History of the Global Carbon Budget," *WIREs Climate Change* 11, no. 3 (1 May 2020): e636, https://doi.org/10.1002/wcc.636. It has been criticized by, for example, Asayama et al.
25 Sverker Sörlin & Paul Warde, eds., *Nature's End: History and the Environment* (Houndmills, Basingstoke: Palgrave Macmillan, 2009); Sverker Sörlin, "Environment," *Companion to Environmental Studies*, eds. Noel Castree, Mike Hulme, & James D. Proctor (New York: Routledge, 2018).
26 The concept environing technology was first coined by Sverker Sörlin in 2011 and subsequently discussed at the Division of History at KTH, Royal Institute of Technology over several years. Key publications discussing the term are Sverker Sörlin & Nina Wormbs, "Environing Technologies: A Theory of Making Environment," *History and Technology* 34, no. 2 (3 April 2018): 101–125, https://doi.org/10.1080/07341512.2018.1548066; Johan Gärdebo, *Environing Technology: Swedish Satellite Remote Sensing in the Making of Environment 1969–2001* (Stockholm: KTH Royal Institute of Technology, 2019); Sabine Höhler & Nina Wormbs, "Remote Sensing : Digital Data at a Distance," *Methodological Challenges in Nature-Culture and Environmental History Research*, ed. Stephanie Rutherford Jocelyn Thorpe L. Anders Sandberg (London, New York: Routledge, 2017), 272–283.
27 Gabrielle Hecht, "Inside-Out Earth," manuscript in review, and session "The Anthropocene as a provocation to the history of technology – a performative debate" at the annual meeting with the Society for the history of technology, Milan, October 26th, 2019.
28 Nina Wormbs, & Johan Gärdebo, "The Distant Gardener: Remote Sensing of the Planetary Potager," *Gardens and Human Agency in the Anthropocene*, eds. Maria Paula Diogo et al. (London: Routledge, 2019), 124–142.
29 Stig Hjarvard, "The Mediatization of Society: A Theory of the Media as Agents of Social and Cultural Change," *Nordicom Review* 29 (2008): 105–134.
30 Susan J. Douglas, "Some Thoughts on the Question 'How Do New Things Happen?'" *Technology and Culture* 51, no. 2 (2010): 293–304.
31 Ian Hutchby, "Technologies, Texts and Affordances," *Sociology* 35, no. 2 (2001): 441–456. Technology as a concept is also elusive and an object of debate. For a recent reflection see John Agar, "What Is Technology?" *Annals of Science*, Palgrave studies in the history of science and technology, 77, no. 3 (2020): 377–382. On a more general level, Thomas Misa has suggested that looking at a meso-level for analysis can avoid black boxing while at the same time allow for enough but not too much case-specific detail. Thomas J. Misa, "Retrieving Sociotechnical Change from Technological Determinism," *Does Technology Drive History? The Dilemma of Technological Determinism*, eds. Merritt Roe Smith & Leo Marx, vol. 1994 (Cambridge, MA: MIT Press, n.d.), 101–114.
32 John Durham Peters, *The Marvelous Clouds: Toward a Philosophy of Elemental Media* (Chicago: The University of Chicago Press, 2015) and this volume.
33 For a discussion on environment as a temporal category see also Sverker Sörlin, "Environmental Times: Synchronizing Human-Earth Temporalities from Annales to Anthropocene, 1920s–2020s," *Times of History, Times of Nature: Temporalization and the Limits of Modern Knowledge*, eds. Anders Ekström & Staffan Bergwik (New York: Berghahn Books, 2022), 64–101.

References

Agar, John. "What Is Technology?" *Annals of Science*, Palgrave studies in the history of science and technology, 77, no. 3 (2020): 377–82.

Andersson, Jenny, & Eglė Rindzevičiūtė (eds.). *The Struggle for the Long-Term in Transnational Science and Politics: Forging the Future*. New York: Routledge, Taylor & Francis Group, 2015.

Asayama, Shinichiro, Rob Bellamy, Oliver Geden, Warren Pearce, & Mike Hulme. "Why Setting a Climate Deadline Is Dangerous." *Nature Climate Change* 9, no. 8 (1 August 2019): 570–572. https://doi.org/10.1038/s41558-019-0543-4.

Chakrabarty, Dipesh. "The Climate of History: Four Theses." *Critical Inquiry* 35, no. 2 (2009): 197–222. https://doi.org/10.1086/596640.

Christensen, Miyase, Annika E. Nilsson, & Nina Wormbs (eds.). *Media and the Politics of Arctic Climate Change: When the Ice Breaks*. 1st ed. New York: Palgrave Macmillan, 2013.

Christian, David. *Origin Story: A Big History of Everything*. London: Allen Lane, 2018.

Douglas, Susan J. "Some Thoughts on the Question "How Do New Things Happen?"" *Technology and Culture* 51, no. 2 (2010): 293–304.

Edwards, Paul N. *A Vast Machine: Computer Models, Climate Data, and the Politics of Global Warming*. Cambridge, MA: MIT Press, 2010.

Edwards, Paul N. "Representing the Global Atmosphere: Computer Models, Data, and Knowledge about Climate Change." *Changing the Atmosphere: Expert Knowledge and Environmental Governance*, edited by Clark A. Miller & Paul N Edwards. Cambridge, MA: MIT Press, 2001.

Gärdebo, Johan. *Environing Technology: Swedish Satellite Remote Sensing in the Making of Environment 1969–2001*. Stockholm: KTH Royal Institute of Technology, 2019.

Harari, Yuval Noah. *Sapiens: A Brief History of Humankind*. London: Harvill Secker, 2014.

Hastrup, Kirsten, & Martin Skrydstrup (eds.). *The Social Life of Climate Change Models: Anticipating Nature*. London: Routledge, 2013.

Hawking, Stephen. *A Brief History of Time: From the Big Bang to Black Holes*. London: Bantam Press, 1988.

Hecht, Gabrielle. "Inside-Out Earth." manuscript in review.

Heymann, Matthias, Gabriele Gramelsberger, & Martin Mahony (eds.). *Cultures of Prediction in Atmospheric and Climate Science: Epistemic and Cultural Shifts in Computer-Based Modelling and Simulation*. New York: Routledge, 2017.

Hjarvard, Stig. "The Mediatization of Society: A Theory of the Media as Agents of Social and Cultural Change." *Nordicom Review* 29 (2008): 105–134.

Höhler, Sabine, & Nina Wormbs. "Remote Sensing: Digital Data at a Distance." *Methodological Challenges in Nature-Culture and Environmental History Research*, edited by Stephanie Rutherford Jocelyn Thorpe L. Anders Sandberg, 272–283. London, New York: Routledge, 2017.

Hulme, Mike. *Why We Disagree about Climate Change: Understanding Controversy, Inaction and Opportunity*. Cambridge. Cambridge University Press, 2009.

Hutchby, Ian. "Technologies, Texts and Affordances." *Sociology* 35, no. 2 (2001): 441–456.

Jordheim, Helge. "Introduction: Multiple Times and the Work of Synchronization." *History and Theory* 53, no. 4 (1 December 2014): 498–518. https://doi.org/10.1111/hith.10728.

Lahn, Bård. "A History of the Global Carbon Budget." *WIREs Climate Change* 11, no. 3 (1 May 2020): e636. https://doi.org/10.1002/wcc.636.

Mahony, Martin, & Mike Hulme. "Model Migrations: Mobility and Boundary Crossings in Regional Climate Prediction." *Transactions of the Institute of British Geographers* 37, no. 2 (2012): 197–211.

Misa, Thomas J. "Retrieving Sociotechnical Change from Technological Determinism." *Does Technology Drive History? The Dilemma of Technological Determinism*, edited by Merritt Roe Smith & Leo Marx, 101–114. Cambridge, MA: MIT Press, 1994.

Oreskes, Naomi. "The Scientific Consensus on Climate Change." *Science* 306, no. 5702 (2 December 2004): 1686. https://doi.org/10.1126/science.1103618.

Pahl, Sabine, Stephen Sheppard, Christine Boomsma, & Christopher Groves. "Perceptions of Time in Relation to Climate Change." *WIREs Climate Change* 5, no. 3 (1 May 2014): 375–388. https://doi.org/10.1002/wcc.272.

Pasek, Anne. "Mediating Climate, Mediating Scale." *Humanities* 8, no. 4 (2019). https://doi.org/doi:10.3390/h8040159.

Peters, John Durham. *The Marvelous Clouds: Toward a Philosophy of Elemental Media*. Chicago: University of Chicago Press, 2015.

Risbey, James S. "The New Climate Discourse: Alarmist or Alarming?" *Global Environmental Change* 18, no. 1 (1 February 2008): 26–37. https://doi.org/10.1016/j.gloenvcha.2007.06.003.

Rudwick, Martin J. S. *Worlds Before Adam: The Reconstruction of Geohistory in the Age of Reform*. Chicago: University of Chicago Press, 2008.

Schneider, Birgit. "The Future Face of the Earth: The Visual Semantics of the Future in the Climate Change Imagery of the IPCC." *Cultures of Prediction in Atmospheric and Climate Science, Epistemic and Cultural Shifts in Computer-Based Modelling and Simulation*, edited by Matthias Heymann, Gabriele Gramelsberger, and Martin Mahony, 231–251. New York: Routledge, 2017.

Schneider, Birgit, & Thomas Nocke. *Image Politics of Climate Change: Visualizations, Imaginations, Documentations*. Bielefeld: Transcript, 2014.

Sörlin, Sverker. "Environmental Times: Synchronizing Human-Earth Temporalities from Annales to Anthropocene, 1920s–2020s." *Times of History, Times of Nature: Temporalization and the Limits of Modern Knowledge*, edited by Anders Ekström & Staffan Bergwik, 64–101. New York: Berghahn Books, 2022.

———. "Environment." *Companion to Environmental Studies*, edited by Noel Castree, Mike Hulme, & James D. Proctor. New York: Routledge, 2018.

Sörlin, Sverker, & Paul Warde (eds.). *Nature's End: History and the Environment*. Houndmills, Basingstoke: Palgrave Macmillan, 2009.

Sörlin, Sverker, & Nina Wormbs. "Environing Technologies: A Theory of Making Environment." *History and Technology* 34, no. 2 (3 April 2018): 101–125. https://doi.org/10.1080/07341512.2018.1548066.

Sundberg, Mikaela. "Parameterizations as Boundary Objects on the Climate Arena." *Social Studies of Science* 37, no. 3 (1 June 2007): 473–488. https://doi.org/10.1177/0306312706075330.

Walsh, Lynda. "The Visual Rhetoric of Climate Change." *WIREs Climate Change* 6, no. 4 (1 July 2015): 361–368. https://doi.org/10.1002/wcc.342.

———. *Scientists as Prophets: A Rhetorical Genealogy*. New York: Oxford University Press, 2013.

Weart, Spencer R. *The Discovery of Global Warming*. Cambridge, MA: Harvard University Press, 2008.

Wormbs, Nina. "Model Time and Target Year: On the End of Time in IPCC Futures." *Times of History, Times of Nature: Temporalization and the Limits of Modern Knowledge*, edited by Anders Ekström & Staffan Bergwik, 284–307. New York: Berghahn Books, 2022.

Wormbs, Nina (ed.). *Competing Arctic Futures: Historical and Contemporary Perspectives*. Cham: Palgrave Macmillan, 2018.

Wormbs, Nina, & Johan Gärdebo. "The Distant Gardener: Remote Sensing of the Planetary Potager." *Gardens and Human Agency in the Anthropocene*, edited by Maria Paula Diogo, Ana Simões, Ana Duarte Rodrigues, & Davide Scarso, 124–142. London: Routledge, 2019.

9
TIMING THE OCEAN FLOOR

Environing media and the Swedish Deep-Sea Expedition (1947–1948)

Erik Isberg

Introduction

In 1953, the scientific journal *Deep-Sea Research* published its first ever issue. The journal was going to be solely dedicated to the deep-sea floor, an environment so remote and inaccessible that it had up until this point not been the subject of systematic scientific research, much less its own scientific journal. But in the 1940s, C.D. Ovey, the Secretary of the recently formed Joint Commission on Oceanography, explained in his foreword to the first issue, things had changed. He cited the increased international collaboration – much of it coordinated by the Swedish oceanographer Hans Pettersson and UNESCO's founder Julian Huxley – and new technologies for sensing and sampling the deep-sea floor. One technology, according to Ovey, was of particular importance: the piston corer, a deep-sea core drill invented by Börje Kullenberg, Pettersson's colleague at the Institute of Oceanography in Gothenburg.[1] With these developments, Ovey continued, deep-sea research could "produce important and far-reaching results, which might well revolutionize many of the theories concerning the history and development of our planet".[2]

Ten years earlier, in 1943, Pettersson and Kullenberg were interviewed by Swedish Radio. They advertised their plans to conduct a circumnavigation of the Earth, the first by Swedish oceanographers, and motivated their ambitious plans by pointing to Kullenberg's piston corer.[3] With this instrument, Pettersson and Kullenberg could take samples of the deep-sea floor that reached several meters down into the seabed. Previous attempts at sampling the deep-sea floor had remained on a surface level, and by reaching further down, Pettersson and Kullenberg explained, much longer geochronologies of the deep-sea floor could be made visible. The deep-sea floor had not only been a spatially distant geography, but also lacking any temporal qualities. It was a space without a history or

DOI: 10.4324/9781003282891-12

a future. Drilling down through the seabed, Pettersson and Kullenberg hoped, could change the picture.

In this chapter, I will focus on the years between the radio show and the first publication of *Deep-Sea research* and the subsequent rise of paleoceanography as a new scientific discipline. The emergence of the piston corer in the 1940s enabled temporally oriented mediations of the deep-sea floor, as the long cores provided both a stratigraphic view of the deep-sea floor and the opportunity to use isotope dating on the organic remains found in the cores. Deep-sea core drilling was a new way of sensing the oceans and the cores themselves an environing medium through which the deep-sea floor could be translated into data.[4] After being tested in a small scale along the Swedish coasts, the piston corer was used on the already mentioned Swedish Deep-Sea Expedition (1947–1948) and deep-sea cores were extracted from locations across the world.[5] In the years following the expedition, connections were drawn between field work in the deep ocean on the one hand, and isotope dating technologies and computer modeling on the other. The cores that had been extracted during the expedition caught the interest of scientists beyond the domain of oceanography and the materials from the deep-sea floor became interwoven with the intellectual framework of isotope dating. Despite the seemingly clear chronology the stratigraphy in the cores render visible, I will argue that different mediations of time from the cores depended on factors beyond the cores themselves. As they left the limited Swedish oceanographic context and became enrolled to the larger geophysical project of producing a coherent planetary system, they came to realize new temporal ontologies and became a particular form of environing media.

The invention of the piston corer and the establishment of deep-sea core drilling as a scientific practice were not isolated events, but part of the making of what Jessica Lehman has called the "Anthropocene ocean".[6] In the 1950s, and particularly during the International Geophysical Year 1957–1958, she argues, the world ocean came together as a coherent, interconnected object of knowledge. The planetary-scale view of the IGY relied on a synoptic approach, coordinated data practices distributed across different geographies, which could be scaled up to encompass the entire planet. Deep-sea core drilling followed this pattern while simultaneously doing more than just connect geographies: the cores effectively synchronized multiple timescales into coherent planetary-scale temporalizations.[7] They rendered the deep-sea floor a proxy of planetary processes, rather than just being a study object in itself.[8] As Ovey put it in his foreword: the journal *Deep-Sea Research* was not only basic research about the deep-sea floor, as the aim should be to working toward "piercing together the many problems which arise in this domain, concerning the geological and climatological history of the Earth".[9]

As the planet is, as Dipesh Chakrabarty put it, appearing as an "emergent humanist category" in an era of human geological agency, the history of conceptualizing and mediating planetary-scale environmental knowledge surfaces as an increasingly pressing object of inquiry.[10] Recent scholarship has identified the years after World War II, and the IGY in particular, as formative for the understanding of the planet as an interconnected scientific and environmental object.[11] The very notion of "the environment" itself is also a product of these years, and in particular the year 1948 has been identified as a threshold moment for environmental ideas gaining global circulation.[12] Even though this process can appear as primarily spatial, interconnecting smaller geographies to produce a planetary-scale view, it was also fundamentally concerned with time.[13] Deep-sea cores – and the *Albatross* expedition – can therefore be situated not only in the history of ocean sciences, but in the larger history of making, mediating and temporalizing planetary-scale environmental knowledge.

Deep-sea cores as environing media

Given its inaccessibility, knowledge about the deep-sea floor always had to be mediated in some form. As Jacob Darwin Hamblin points out, the interior of the ocean cannot be seen with the naked eye, it "must be made comprehensible by some intervening technology – instruments, maps, equations. To borrow a term from James Scott, it must be made 'legible'"[14] In the early 19th century, when scientific exploration of the deep-sea floor was just beginning, rudimentary attempts of sounding and dredging provided glimpses of the world beneath the water surface. Financial interests in laying telegraph cables across the Atlantic necessitated some knowledge about the depths of the ocean and the demand for more detailed navigational tools also opened up commercial possibilities in mapping the ocean depths.[15] During the second half of the 19th century, the methods grew increasingly elaborate: steam-powered winches, wires rather than ropes and mechanic sinkers all made the deep-sea floor technologically more accessible. Oceanography began to come together as a coherent scientific endeavor, worthy of public and private funding, and thereby also extended the spatial dimension of commercialism and imperialism from the terrestrial to the aquatic.[16]

The deep-sea floor was increasingly mediated as samples and soundings could be translated into maps, charts and diagrams. An increased number of scientific instruments, in particular acoustic sounding technologies, further enabled the deep-sea floor to emerge as a discrete scientific object.[17] When the German *Meteor* expedition set sail in 1925, a multi-dimensional set of instruments were part of the inventory (deep-sea thermometers, current meters, water samplers, closing nets, bottom samplers and coring tubes) and contributed to a three-dimensional, dynamic perception of the ocean as well as the beginning of systematic mapping of the deep-sea floor.[18] In 1942, the publication of Harald Sverdrup, Martin W. Johnson and Richard H. Fleming's seminal *The Oceans: Their Physics, Chemistry, and General Biology* consolidated the multi-dimensional view of the ocean and brought together a wide set of technologies and practices into a coherent methodology for studying the oceans. "Since 1900", they wrote "great advances have been made within all of the marine sciences, and the contacts between the special fields have become more and more intimate".[19]

Environing media and the Swedish deep-sea expedition (1947–1948) **153**

It was in this setting Kullenberg's piston corer made its first appearance (Figure 9.1).[20] In many ways, it was a product of its time: as it could provide quantifiable results across geographical boundaries, it fitted nicely with the perception of the ocean as interconnected and dynamic. But it also produced a peculiar research object: the deep-sea core. The cores themselves were scientific objects in their own right, and were not just studied *in situ* at sea, but could be brought back, circulated, subjected to radiocarbon dating methods and function as proxies for the climatological and geological history of the entire planet.

In other words, the cores were part of producing a new kind of oceanic environmental knowledge, which more firmly placed oceanography in the domain of "artificial geophysics" and a bourgeoning understanding of the planet – the oceans included – as an interconnected system.[21] They functioned as environing media, drawing together the planetary processes made legible in the sedimentation and the cultural and scientific turn toward the global and planetary scale.[22] "A crucial dimension of environing media is that different media produce different epistemologies", Adam Wickberg and Johan Gärdebo write in their introduction to this volume, and thereby highlight the possibilities of approaching the deep-sea cores as realizing particular epistemologies at specific moments in time, rather than providing unmediated access to the Earth's past.[23]

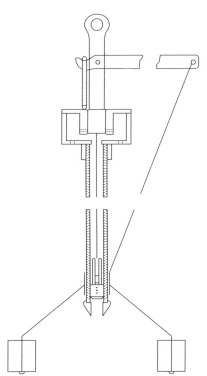

FIGURE 9.1 A sketch of the piston corer as it was presented in 1944.

Deep-sea cores, as well as other paleoclimate archives, appear as a particular form of environing media, since they are oriented toward time rather than space. Mark Carey and Alessandro Antonello have argued that the production of time and temporality have, despite its centrality to the conceptualization of environments on different scales, often been taken for granted as naturally given and remained outside the scope of much historical research.[24] Further, Tim Ingold, in his theorizations about the relationship between time and materiality, writes that we should understand materials as being "not in time, but the stuff of time itself".[25] Deep-sea cores do, almost self-evidently, fit Ingold's description of time being deeply interwoven with the materials in which it appear. But, looking at the historical evolution of deep-sea cores and the environmental data they have been translated into, Ingold's assertion only takes us halfway. In order for the cores to materialize in the first place, human intervention is needed (in the form of Kullenberg's piston corer), and in order for the time to become legible, a vast set of scientific practices and translations are necessary. Additionally, the interpretive framework, as we shall see in the upcoming sections, relies on broader political and social contexts.

Understanding deep-sea cores as environing media can provide a sensitivity to the processual nature of drilling and interpreting the deep-sea cores as well as situate them in a broader historical narrative of a shifting human-Earth relationship. In the rest of this chapter, I will follow the preparations, execution and aftermath of the *Albatross* expedition and, in particular, consider how the deep-sea floor was mediated as the piston corer emerged as the condition for knowing these hitherto unknown areas of the planet.

Hans Pettersson and the formation of Swedish deep-sea research

When Hans Pettersson sat down in the Gothenburg radio studio and declared his plans for a circumnavigation of the Earth, he was already a leading figure in oceanography, both in Sweden and internationally. He had not reached his prominent position accidentally. He was consciously raised by his father, Otto Pettersson, who was Sweden's first professor of oceanography, to inherit his scientific project and began working as an assistant at his research station Bornö during the summer vacations as a schoolboy.[26] He went on to do an undergraduate degree at Uppsala University and a PhD at the University College in Stockholm, with his father's friend Svante Arrhenius as his supervisor.[27] Arrhenius work on what he called "cosmic physics" – an early predecessor to geophysics, which also included cosmology and astrophysics – sparked Hans Pettersson's interest in the interactions of the ocean and the atmosphere and how they could be studied through the lens of atomic physics and radioactivity.[28] After his PhD, and a stint as his father's research assistant, Hans tried to break away from his father's influence and chart out a research trajectory of his own by starting a position at the Radium Institute in Vienna in 1921. He remained in Vienna until 1928, having published extensively and tried, but failed, to run his own research group in nuclear physics. He reluctantly returned to Gothenburg and his father's patronage to take a position in oceanography at the University of Gothenburg. Staffan Bergwik argues that Hans Pettersson, despite his attempts to distance himself from his father, inherited the entrepreneurial style of fundraising and institution building from Otto, while simultaneously staking out his own research program at the intersection of oceanography and nuclear physics.[29]

The *Albatross* expedition appears as a crystallization of Hans Pettersson's ability to, like his father, successfully acquire funds and materials from the local corporate and political elites in Gothenburg while simultaneously bringing recent developments in atomic physics to oceanographic research. The particular focus of the expedition was to extract deep-sea cores from the deep-sea floor, and Pettersson was especially interested in how radioactive substances in the cores could be studied in order to create longer geochronologies than had hitherto been possible. Even though the theoretical framework of the expedition was novel, the institutional context was not: the *Albatross* expedition was, as Peder Roberts puts it, "emblematic of the pre-1939 age" by relying on local civic patronage and having an almost entirely Swedish crew (and a Swedish ship).[30] Hans Pettersson himself was also fond of the idea of a circumnavigatory expedition around the world, and often alluded to the *Challenger* expedition and other adventurous predecessors when talking about the *Albatross*.[31] As scientists in adjacent fields – Hans Ahlmann in glaciology is one contemporary Swedish example – tried to distance themselves from the idea of the adventurous explorer in favor of a more modern and scientific persona, Pettersson consciously built his expedition upon the route of the *Challenger* expedition.[32]

Pettersson can perhaps be situated at the threshold between a nationalist and heroic narrative of exploration and an international and modernist ideal of global collaboration and large-scale research projects. An example of this is visible in Hans Pettersson's contacts with Julian Huxley and his interest in global-scale surveying of the deep-sea floor. Pettersson was invited, in 1946, a few months before the *Albatross* were to depart from Gothenburg, as one of the speakers at UNESCO's inaugural conference in Paris. Other speakers at the event included intellectual celebrities like Jean-Paul Sartre and A. J. Ayer, and the program concerned a wide range of philosophical, scientific and political topics. Pettersson's lecture, entitled "The Submarine Underworld", argued for the global reach of deep-sea core studies, rather than merely being of interest to other ocean scientists. As Pettersson put it: "In those catalogues of the deep, hidden under tens of thousands of meters of water, we may expect to find evidence of the great tectonic, volcanic and climatic catastrophes which this planet as undergone".[33] He also noted how he had been able to see volcanic ashes in deep-sea cores from the Mediterranean and that these ashes could be traced back to the eruption of Pompeii 79 A.D., thereby connecting deep-sea sediments with the history of Western civilization.[34] The submarine underworld was, in other words, part of the one global world that UNESCO sought to realize.[35]

At the same time, Pettersson was also keen to emphasize how the upcoming *Albatross* expedition was a distinctly Swedish, or even Gothenburg, operation.

"I sincerely hope that this Swedish expedition, which for the most part will be using methods from Sweden, will induce other expeditions to explore the unknown depths of the sea-bed", Pettersson put it toward the end of his lecture. He simultaneously praised the international collaborative efforts while still operating within an older scientific structure based on local patronage and heroic expeditions.

A similar tension between the national and the planetary scale is visible in the development of the piston corer itself. In the first publications outlining the construction and utility of the piston corer, Börje Kullenberg and his co-author, geologist Erik Fromm, connected the corer to a national project of making Swedish geochronology and "connecting the Swedish glacial timescale to historical time".[36] The corer was placed in a longer Swedish tradition of geochronological research, stemming from the geologist Gerard de Geer and a nationally oriented research program from the late 19th and early 20th centuries.[37] Kullenberg and Fromm used the corer in Ångermanälven, in northern Sweden, in an effort to both prove the utility of the new instrument and contribute to the national natural history of Sweden. Fromm later continued working on Swedish quaternary geology and became the state geologist in 1952.[38] With the *Albatross* expedition however, the cores, stemming from the very same corer that had been used in Ångermanälven, were rather conceived of as part of a global mission to construct coherent geohistorical knowledge. This tension between national and planetary would continue as the expedition came to an end in 1948, as competing modes of engaging with deep-sea cores and new scientific infrastructures emerged in the 1950s.

The gold rush that never was: *Albatross* and its return to Gothenburg

After years of preparation, the *Albatross* left the harbor of Gothenburg on July 4, 1947. The route was planned by Pettersson and based on both scientific and historical reasons: Pettersson picked drilling locations in part based on where the *Challenger* had gone seven decades before.[39] During the fifteen-month voyage, the main activity was to sample the deep-sea floor for sediments, but the expedition members also conducted studies in ocean optics, marine biology and hydrochemistry. Some studies were conducted onboard the ship, even though a key incentive was to gather deep-sea sediments to bring back to Gothenburg, which in turn could be subjected to different forms of analysis. The work onboard was labor intensive and physically demanding, and the tough conditions in combination with the strong personalities in the crew strained relationships among the scientists (Figure 9.2).[40]

As the expedition returned to the harbor in Gothenburg, relationships between Pettersson and Kullenberg as well as other crew members were fraught and the reception back at home was smaller and less bombastic than expected. Pettersson's approach and ability to narrate dramatic descriptions of his work had been an asset in his fundraising for the expedition, but it could also sometimes cause him to miscalculate the interest in his work. As the expedition was coming

FIGURE 9.2 Deep-sea cores recovered during the Swedish Deep-Sea Expedition 1947–1948.

to an end, and the *Albatross* was crammed with deep-sea cores and other samples, Hans Pettersson expected a "gold rush" of international scientists wanting to use the material.[41] Instead, the opposite happened, as the scope of the material was so vast it was hard to find someone with enough resources to take on the entirety of the samples.[42]

The cores from the expedition were dispersed to individual scientists who took on a few samples at the time. Gustaf Arrhenius, a young geochemist who was part of the crew onboard, used his father Olof's estate Kagghamra outside Stockholm, which had its own laboratory facilities because of Olof Arrhenius interest in biochemistry, to conduct his analysis on some of the cores. An early publication that came out of Arrhenius work in Kagghamra can be seen as an emblematic example of how the deep-sea cores altered the way the deep-sea floor was made legible. Appearing in *Tellus*, a Stockholm-based journal in geophysics founded in 1949, the article was co-written by Arrhenius, the physical chemist and inventor of the C14 radiocarbon dating method W. F. Libby and the computer scientist Göran Kjellberg from Matematikmaskinnämnden (The Swedish Board for Computing).[43] The long cores that the piston corer had enabled, in combination with the new dating technologies spearheaded by Libby and his group in Chicago, made the work to make the cores legible increasingly data intensive. BARK, a computer developed domestically in Sweden as a part of the increased military interest in computing technologies, offered Arrhenius and Libby the computational power needed to analyze the deep-sea cores.[44]

In the *Tellus* article, they relied on just one deep-sea core, number 61B. The core was, through the article, enrolled to a larger scientific infrastructure, which connected the material contents of the core, the labor onboard the *Albatross*, isotope dating technologies and the rise of computers as tools for data intensive calculations. That this individual core traveled to Kagghamra with Arrhenius and then later, in quantified form, to Libby in Chicago and BARK in Stockholm, in order to become a publishable dataset in a scientific journal points toward the infrastructure needed to produce timescales out of the deep-sea floor. The environing capacity of the deep-sea cores, and their ability to provide a mediated temporalization of the ocean floor, depended on the intertwined relationship between manual data gathering and computing capacity.

Even though Arrhenius and Libby could work with Kjellberg and Matematikmaskinnämnden for this particular publication, the Swedish lack of resources for processing the *Albatross* cores posed a problem. Hans Pettersson outlined a review of different available methods in a 1949 article and concluded that: "The different approaches to the chronology of the deep-sea deposits reviewed above will be tried out during the working up of the great material, 1640 meters of deep-sea cores, collected by the Swedish Deep-sea Expedition".[45] However, the practical feasibility of doing this work in Sweden was not evident. It demanded a different kind of research infrastructure than the one needed to conduct the expedition, and different competencies as well.

At the same time in the United States, deep-sea core drilling was becoming part of the postwar project to map and control oceanic spaces. Maurice Ewing at the Lamont-Doherty Geological Observatory in New York and Roger Revelle at Scripps Institution of Oceanography in La Jolla, California, were two major players in American oceanography who saw the possibilities in deep-sea core drilling. In particular, they found the piston corer to be a necessary technology in order for future deep-sea drillings to be a worthwhile endeavor. Rather than showing interest in the actual cores from the *Albatross*, the U.S. American oceanographers rather sought to import the technologies that had made them possible, in order to conduct their own studies with their own equipment and facilities. Ewing constructed his own piston corer, inspired by the Swedish version, and began gathering deep-sea cores in 1947 for his "library" of deep-sea cores at Lamont-Doherty.[46] For Pettersson in Gothenburg, these kinds of resources were not available. Pettersson could not establish a "library" of deep-sea cores and the global scale enterprise of the *Albatross*, with its funding structure based on local patronage, made it difficult to repeat in order to gather more cores. In comparison, Ewing was able to utilize different global-scale American naval expeditions to drill for cores, thereby quickly surpassing the work of the *Albatross*.[47]

In the winter of 1954, Hans Pettersson, together with his wife Dagmar, decided to travel to two leading research institutions in his field: the Scripps

Institution of Oceanography in La Jolla, California, and the Institute for Nuclear Studies at the University of Chicago. Six years had passed since the *Albatross* arrived in Gothenburg after its expedition, and Pettersson only had two more years left in his position before his retirement. The main reason for the trip was for Pettersson to maintain his international network and find new collaborators, as the interest in deep-sea samples had grown considerably in the last decade. Gustaf Arrhenius, whose work with deep-sea cores in Kagghamra had catapulted him to a position at Scripps, served as a host.[48]

The postwar research landscape that met Pettersson in the United States was significantly different than his own environment in Gothenburg, but also compared to how oceanography had been conducted in the United States just two decades before. World War II had brought the Navy and oceanographic research closer together and after the war oceanography became a beneficiary of the dramatic influx of funding into the geosciences.[49] Pettersson arrived in La Jolla during a decisive shift, in which oceanography was relocating its most central research from Northern Europe to the United States. For Pettersson, this shift was felt on a personal level too: during the 1950s, several members from the *Albatross* relocated to the United States, and the temporally oriented deep-sea research Pettersson had spearheaded in Gothenburg found a new home in the United States. The new generation of deep-sea core scientists differed from Pettersson in their research approach: they were part of larger research institutions, spent more time in the lab than at sea and could utilize the massive funding opportunities that the Cold War mobilization in the geosciences made possible.

In Chicago, Pettersson encountered another research institution that was typical of its time and, much like Scripps, a quintessential product of World War II and its aftermath. Harold Urey and W. F. Libby at the institute had both worked with the development of nuclear weapons in the Manhattan Project during the war and afterward created a research environment that brought together different strands of research into radioisotopes and radioactivity.[50] Cesare Emiliani, who is often hailed as the "founder of paleoceanography", had received his PhD in at the Department of Geology at the University of Chicago in 1950, and combined his training in geology and geochemistry with an interest in deep-sea research and long-term changes in the oceans.[51] He was keen on meeting with Pettersson and, after Pettersson had failed to convince Urey about the prospects of his upcoming research plans, Pettersson was happy to be invited to dinner with the Emilianis.[52]

The two would later stay in touch and Pettersson helped Emiliani establish his own laboratory at the Institute of Marine Science at the University of Miami in 1957. Emiliani's Miami laboratory would become a leading research environment for geochemical and paleoceanographic studies of deep-sea sediments, effectively combining the empirical work of Pettersson and Kullenberg with the temporally oriented and interdisciplinary approach to isotope dating from the Institute of Nuclear Studies in Chicago. In the 1950s, Emiliani drew from the work on isotope analysis from Chicago, which, together with the cores from the *Albatross*, established a new, historically oriented ocean research program.[53]

Once back in Sweden again, Pettersson continued to work with his cores, but the moment for Swedish deep-sea core research had passed. Fritz Koczy, a close friend of Pettersson and a member of the *Albatross* expedition, was hired to run Emiliani's lab in Miami.[54] More Swedes would join the Miami research environment, making it, in Kozcy's words: "…the strongest geochemical group in marine science in the world and the largest Swedish laboratory in the United States".[55] As the International Geophysical Year began in 1957, the Oceanographic Institute in Gothenburg was left outside. The leading researchers had either retired or moved to the United States and the research ship *Skagerak* had broken down. Börje Kullenberg, who replaced Pettersson as director of the institute in 1956, tried to defend himself against bad press about the demise of Swedish deep-sea research and argued that while Sweden was falling out of global collaborations, research to be conducted in the Baltic Sea in collaboration with Finland was valuable for the future of the institute too.[56]

Conclusion

In this chapter, my aim has been to show how the rise of deep-sea core drilling transformed the deep-sea floor as a scientific object. By understanding deep-sea cores as environing media, which can realize different epistemologies and environments at different moments in time, they can be situated in a longer history of making planetary-scale environmental knowledge. From the early attempts of using the piston corer in Ångermanälven in the early 1940s to the mobilization around paleoceanographic studies on a global scale in the mid-1950s, the deep-sea cores expanded their temporal, geographical and epistemological scope from the national to the planetary. With the rise of integrative geophysics as well as global political institutions such as UNESCO, the deep-sea cores played a role in bringing the ocean into the growing interest in the planetary scale. As Pettersson's lecture at UNESCO's inaugural conference shows, the connection between the cores and the global had to be made explicit in particular settings in order to take hold. Conceiving of the cores as environing media enables us to historicize how a remote environment such as the ocean floor can become legible in particular ways and realize different political and scientific conceptualizations at different points in time. Rather than the stable and ahistorical popular description of deep-sea cores as "natural archives", the notion of environing media opens up the possibility to study them as processual, existing at the intersection of the material ocean floor, data gathering practices, computational capabilities and broader ideological projects.

Another key point I have sought to make with this chapter is the centrality of time in the construction of environments. Deep-sea cores environed a temporally oriented understanding of both the oceans and the planet itself, thereby underpinning the scientific developments in the late 20th century which would result in the Anthropocene concept. Creating planetary-scale environmental knowledge is, in other words, about time as much as it is about space. The media of environmental times – deep-sea cores being one prominent example – can be studied as historical phenomena in themselves and point to a heterogeneous history of negotiating, mediating and synchronizing time in order to produce environmental knowledge. As the present deliberations on the planetary and the Anthropocene continue, tracing the environing media of planetary timescales can bring the often abstract discourse on Anthropocene temporalities back to the ground.

Notes

1 C. D. Ovey, "Foreword," *Deep-Sea Research* 1 (1953): 1–2.
2 Ovey, 1.
3 Manuscript for radio show 10/4, 1943, with Julius Rabe, head of radio programming Swedish Radio Gothenburg, Carl Skottsberg, professor of botany, Orvar Nybelin, professor of marine biology, Hans Pettersson, professor of oceanography, and Börje Kullenberg, associate professor of oceanography. Börje Kullenberg Papers, University Library of Gothenburg, vol. 1, folder 1, pp. 1–8.
4 There had been previous attempts at drilling through the deep-sea floor. The German *Meteor* expedition (1925–1927) brought home some sediment samples and the American oceanographer C. S. Piggot made some attempts at systematic deep-sea core drilling in the 1930s. But the cores were still small, some less than 1 m, and on average 243 m, which can be compared with the piston corer's 20 m cores. C. S. Piggot, "Foreword", United States Department of Interior Professional Paper 196-A, *Geology and Biology of North-Atlantic Deep-Sea Cores between Newfoundland and Ireland* (Washington, D.C.: United States Government Printing Office, 1940). Rosol, Christoph. "Hauling Data. Anthropocene Analogues, Paleoceanography and Missing Paradigm Shifts." *Historical Social Research/Historische Sozialforschung* 40, no. 2 (152) (2015): 37–66. http://www.jstor.org/stable/24583163.
5 Hans Pettersson, *Med Albatross över havsdjupen* (Stockholm: Albert Bonniers Förlag, 1950).
6 Jessica Lehman, "Making an Anthropocene Ocean: Synoptic Geographies of the International Geophysical Year (1957–1958)," *Annals of the American Association of Geographers* 110, no. 3 (2020): 606–622.
7 Helge Jordheim, "Introduction: Multiple Times and the Work of Synchronization," *History and Theory* 53 (2014): 498–518.
8 In comparison to instrumental records, which are direct measurements of for example temperature, proxy records are materials from the Earth's past which can reveal information about the composition of former climatic conditions. The proxies (the word itself stems from a legal term in Early Modern English which refers to a person who has the authority to speak on someone else's behalf) can vary in kind: ice, sediments from the deep-sea floor and lakes, tree rings, corals, sea shells and plant fossils are some of the most commonly used proxy archives.
9 Ovey, 2.
10 Dipesh Chakrabarty, "The Planet: An Emergent Humanist Category," *Critical Inquiry* 46, no. 1 (2019): 1–31.
11 Benjamin W. Goossen, "A Benchmark for the Environment: Big Science and 'Artificial' Geophysics in the Global 1950s," *Global Intellectual History* 15, no. 1 (2020): 149–168; Christy Collis & Klaus Dodds, "Assault on the Unknown: The Historical and Political Geographies of the International Geophysical Year," *Journal of Historical Geography* 34 (2008): 555–567; Lehman, "Making an Anthropocene Ocean."
12 Rosol, in this volume; Paul Warde, Libby Robin, & Sverker Sörlin, *The Environment: A History of the Idea* (Baltimore, MD: Johns Hopkins University Press, 2018).
13 Sverker Sörlin & Erik Isberg, "Synchronizing Earthly Timescales: Ice, Pollen, and the Making of Proto-Anthropocene Knowledge in the North-Atlantic Region," *Annals of the American Association of Geographers* 111, no. 3 (2021): 717–728.

14 Jacob Darwin Hamblin, "Seeing the Oceans in Shadow of Bergen Values," *Isis* 105, no. 2 (2014): 357. See also James Scott, *Seeing Like a State: How Certain Schemes to Improve the Human Condition Have Failed* (New Haven, CT: Yale University Press, 1998). Hamblin, as well as Vera Schwach and Deborah day have argued that a particular way of knowing the oceans, which emphasized mathematical approaches and standardized models, stemmed from the "Bergen school" of meteorology and geophysics. See Vera Schwach, "The Sea around Norway: Science, Resource Management, and Environmental Concerns 1860–1970," *Environmental History* 18, no. 1 (2012): 101–110 and Deborah Day, "Bergen West: Or how Four Scandinavian Geophysicists Found a Home in the New World," *Historisch-Meereskundliches Jahrbuch* 6 (1999): 69–82.

15 Helen M. Rozwadowski, *Fathoming the Ocean: The Discovery and Exploration of the Deep Sea* (Cambridge, MA: The Belknapp Press of Harvard University Press, 2005), 77–78.

16 Sabine Höhler, "Creating the Blue Planet from Modern Oceanography," *A Cultural History of the Sea in the Global Age*, ed. Franziska Torma (London: Bloomsbury Academic, 2021), 28.

17 Sabine Höhler, "Depth Records and Ocean Volumes: Ocean Profiling by Sounding Technology, 1850–1930," *History and Technology*, 18, no. 2 (2002): 119–154.

18 Höhler, "Creating the Blue Planet", 31.

19 Harald Sverdrup, Martin W. Johnson, & Richard H. Fleming, *The Oceans: Their Physics, Chemistry, and General Biology* (New York: Prentice Hall Inc., 1942), 1.

20 Börje Kullenberg & Erik Fromm, "Nya försök att upphämta långa sedimentprofiler från havsbotten", *Geologiska Föreningen i Stockholm Förhandlingar* 66, no. 3 (1944): 501–510.

21 Goossen, "A Benchmark for the Environment."

22 Wickberg & Gärdebo, in this volume; "Where Humans and the Planetary Conflate: An Introduction to Environing Media," *Humanities* 9, no. 3 (2020): 1–12. Joyce E. Chaplin makes a useful distinction between global and planetary: "The global is social", Joyce E. Chaplin writes, "as it implies the social relations that extend over the globe. The planetary, however, is physical, implying the physical planet itself." I deliberately use both "global" and "planetary" here, as the cultural interests in the global, visible in for example the founding of UNESCO, and the planetary, visible in the IGY, both intersected with the rise of deep-sea core drilling. Joyce E. Chaplin, *Round about the Earth. Circumnavigation from Magellan to Orbit* (New York: Simon & Schuster, 2012), 11.

23 Wickberg & Gärdebo, in this volume, 16.

24 Mark Carey & Alessandro Antonello, "Ice Cores and the Temporalities of the Global Environment," *Environmental Humanities* 9, no. 2 (2017): 186–187.

25 Tim Ingold, "Toward an Ecology of Materials," *Annual Review of Anthropology* 41 (2012): 427–442.

26 For an overview of the history of Swedish oceanography, see Urban Wråkberg, "Om djuphavets gåtor och ett fiskeri på vetenskaplig grund: historiska perspektiv på oceanografin i Sverige," *Oceanerna* (Lund: Svenska Sällskapet för Antropologi och Geografi, 1991).

27 Staffan Bergwik, "Father, Son, and the Entrepreneurial Spirit: Otto Pettersson, Hans Pettersson and the Early Twentieth Century Inheritance of Oceanography," *Domesticity in the Making of Modern Science*, eds. Staffan Bergwik, Don Optiz, & Brigitte van Tiggelen (London: Palgrave Macmillan, 2015), 199.

28 Gustaf Arrhenius, Karin Caldwell, & Svante Wold, *A Tribute to the Memory of Svante Arrhenius: A Scientist Ahead of His Time* (Stockholm: Royal Swedish Academy of Engineering Sciences, 2008), 32–33.

29 Bergwik, "Father, Son, and the Entrepreneurial Spirit," 206–207.

30 Peder Roberts, "Traditions, Networks and Deep-Sea Expeditions After 1945," *Expeditions as Experiments: Practicing Observation and Documentation*, edited by Ulrike Spring & Marianna Klemun (London: Palgrave Macmillan, 2016), 216.

31 Roberts, "Traditions" 217. See also Hans Pettersson, *Med Albatross över havsdjupen* (Stockholm: Albert Bonniers Förlag, 1950).
32 Sverker Sörlin, "The Anxieties of a Science Diplomat: Field Co-production of Climate Knowledge and the Rise and Fall of Hans Ahlmann's 'Polar Warming'," *Osiris* 26, no. 1 (2011): 66–88.
33 Hans Pettersson, "The Submarine Underworld," *Reflection on Our Age: Lectures Delivered at the Opening Session of UNESCO at the Sorbonne University of Paris*, edited by David Hardman (London: Allan Wingate, 1949), 202.
34 Pettersson, "The Submarine Underworld", 206–207.
35 Glenda Sluga, "UNESCO and the (One) World of Julian Huxley", *Journal of World History* 21, no. 3 (2010): 393–418.
36 Kullenberg & Fromm, "Nya forsook," 503.
37 For an overview of Gerard de Geer's career, see Staffan Bergwik, "A Fractured Position in a Stable Partnership: Ebba Hult, Gerard de Geer, and Early Twentieth Century Swedish Geology," *Science in Context* 27, no. 3 (2014): 423–451. Christer Nordlund has written about Swedish geology and ice age research in *Det upphöjda landet: Vetenskapen, landhöjningsfrågan och kartläggningen av Sveriges förflutna 1860–1930* (Umeå: Kungl. Skytteanska Samfundet, 2001).
38 "Fromm, Erik," *Svensk Biografisk Handbok* (1993) http://runeberg.org/vemardet/1993/0355.html
39 In his recollection of the expedition, Gustav Arrhenius expressed his skepticism of the approach, claiming that Pettersson was "emotional rather than scientific" in his way of conducting research. Gustaf Arrhenius, "Den svenska djuphavsexpeditionen med Albatross – ett retrospektiv," *Oceanerna*, edited by Anna Karin Johansson & Sören Floderus (Lund: Svenska Sällskapet för Antropologi och Geografi, 1991), 22.
40 An example of this is visible in a letter Hans Pettersson wrote to Börje Kullenberg in 1948, during the expedition, which he handed over to Kullenberg as he did not believe they would be able to have a face-to-face conversation because of their "hot-tempered nature". The letter conveys that Kullenberg had expressed that he regretted joining the expedition because of Pettersson's "poor planning" and Pettersson felt that Kullenberg, despite his talents, was the most difficult colleague he "had ever tried to collaborate with". Hans Pettersson, Letter to Börje Kullenberg, 1948, unknown date, Hans Pettersson papers, GUL, vol. 7.
41 Arrhenius, "Den svenska djuphavsexpeditionen med Albatross," 20.
42 Ibid., 21.
43 Gustaf Arrhenius, Göran Kjellberg, & W. F. Libby, "Age Determination of Pacific Chalk Ooze by Radiocarbon and Titanium Content," *Tellus* 3, no. 4 (1951): 222–229. *Tellus* is in itself an interesting example of how different forms of field science became increasingly interwoven under the "geophysics" label in the late 1940s and early 1950s. The first issue of *Tellus*, for example, featured articles by Hans Pettersson, Hans Ahlmann and Carl-Gustaf Rossby.
44 For early Swedish computer history, see Per Lundin, *Computers in Swedish Society: Documenting Early Use and Trends* (New York: Springer, 2012).
45 Hans Pettersson, "The Geochronology of the Deep Ocean Bed," *Tellus* 1, no. 1 (1949): 5.
46 Laurence Lipsett (ed.). *Lamont Doherty-Earth Observatory: Twelve Perspectives of the First Fifty Years, 1949–1999* (New York: Lamont-Doherty Earth Observatory of the Columbia University, 1999). The Lamont-Doherty Core Repository is still in use today and is the largest deep sea core archive in the world. See https://www.ldeo.columbia.edu/core-repository (accessed 18 November 2021).
47 For an overview of how Ewing and the postwar American oceanographers approached global space, see Naomi Oreskes, *Science on a Mission: How Military Funding Shaped What We Do and Don't Know about the Ocean* (Chicago: Chicago University Press, 2021).
48 Hans Pettersson, *Diary Entry*, February 1, 1954, GUL, Hans Pettersson papers, vol. 3. Arrhenius had a fraught relationship with Pettersson, who disliked his "careerism" and

recent relocation to Scripps. "Behind the affable surface, GA is still doctrinaire [...] This will not be a pleasant collaboration", Pettersson wrote in his diary the first day at Scripps.
49 Jacob Darwin Hamblin, *Oceanographers and the Cold War: Disciples of Marine Science* (Seattle: University of Washington Press, 2005), 11–12.
50 John F. Marra, *Hot Carbon: Carbon-14 and a Revolution in Science* (New York: Columbia University Press, 2019), 54–56.
51 William W. Hay & Eloise Zakevich, "Cesare Emiliani (1922–1995): The Founder of Paleoceanography," *International Microbiology* 2 (1999): 52–54.
52 Hans Pettersson, *Diary Entry*, 21 April 1954, GUL, Hans Pettersson papers, vol. 3. Pettersson recalls his pitch to Urey in a diary entry from April 11 and noted that Urey "seemed to like it at first, but then lost interest."
53 E.g., Cesare Emiliani, "Pleistocene Temperatures," *The Journal of Geology* 63, no. 6 (1955): 538–578; Cesare Emiliani, "Depth Habitats of Some Species of Pelagic Foraminifera as Indicated by Oxygen Isotope Ratios," *American Journal of Science* 252 (1954): 149–158; Cesare Emiliani, "Temperature of Pacific Bottom Waters and Polar Superficial Waters during the Tertiary," *Science* 119 (1954): 853–855 and Cesare Emiliani, "Temperature and Age Analysis of Deep Sea Cores," *Science* 125 (1957): 383–385.
54 Pettersson recommended Emiliani to hire Kozcy, see Interview of Cesare Emiliani and Donald R. Moore by Jean Yehle on 29 March 1990, Niels Bohr Library & Archives, American Institute of Physics, https://www.aip.org/history-programs/niels-bohr-library/oral-histories/32405
55 Fritz Kozcy, *Letter to Hans Pettersson*, 21 January 1963, Hans Pettersson papers, GUL, vol. 3.
56 Börje Kullenberg, Letter to the editor at *Nautisk Tidskrift*, 7 December 1956, Börje Kullenberg papers, vol. 4.

References

Archival material
Gothenburg University Library Archives
    Hans Pettersson papers, vols. 3, 7, 8, 9, 10
    Börje Kullenberg papers, vols. 1, 10, 14.

Published material
Adler, Anthony. *Neptune's Laboratory: Fantasy, Fear and Science at Sea*. Cambridge, MA: Harvard University Press, 2019.
Arrhenius, Gustaf. "Den svenska djuphavsexpeditionen med Albatross – ett retrospektiv." *Oceanerna*, edited by Anna Karin Johansson & Sören Floderus, 8–34. Lund: Svenska Sällskapet för Antropologi och Geografi, 1991.
Arrhenius, Gustaf, Karin Caldwell, & Svante Wold. *A Tribute to the Memory of Svante Arrhenius: A Scientist Ahead of His Time*. Stockholm: Royal Swedish Academy of Engineering Sciences, 2008.
Arrhenius, Gustaf, Göran Kjellberg, & W. F. Libby. "Age Determination of Pacific Chalk Ooze by Radiocarbon and Titanium Content." *Tellus* 3, no. 4 (1951): 222–229.
Bergwik, Staffan. "Father, Son, and the Entrepreneurial Spirit: Otto Pettersson, Hans Pettersson and the Early Twentieth Century Inheritance of Oceanography." *Domesticity in the Making of Modern Science*, edited by Staffan Bergwik, Don Optiz, & Brigitte van Tiggelen, 192–214. London: Palgrave Macmillan, 2015.
———. "A Fractured Position in a Stable Partnership: Ebba Hult, Gerard de Geer, and Early Twentieth Century Swedish Geology." *Science in Context* 27, no. 3 (2014): 423–451.

Carey, Mark, & Alessandro Antonello. "Ice Cores and the Temporalities of the Global Environment." *Environmental Humanities* 9, no. 2 (2017): 186–187.

Chakrabarty, Dipesh. "The Planet: An Emergent Humanist Category." *Critical Inquiry* 46, no. 1 (2019): 1–31.

Chaplin, Joyce E. *Round about the Earth. Circumnavigation from Magellan to Orbit.* New York: Simon & Schuster, 2012.

Collis, Christy, & Klaus Dodds. "Assault on the Unknown: The Historical and Political Geographies of the International Geophysical Year." *Journal of Historical Geography* 34, (2008): 555–567.

Day, Deborah. "Bergen West: Or How Four Scandinavian Geophysicists Found a Home in the New World." *Historisch-Meereskundliches Jahrbuch* 6 (1999): 69–82.

Emiliani, Cesare. "Temperature and Age Analysis of Deep Sea Cores." *Science* 125 (1957): 383–385.

———. "Pleistocene Temperatures." *The Journal of Geology* 63, no. 6 (1955): 538–578.

———. "Temperature of Pacific Bottom Waters and Polar Superficial Waters During the Tertiary." *Science* 119 (1954): 853–855.

———. "Depth Habitats of Some Species of Pelagic Foraminifera as Indicated by Oxygen Isotope Ratios." *American Journal of Science* 252 (1954): 149–158.

Goossen, Benjamin W. "A Benchmark for the Environment: Big Science and 'Artificial' Geophysics in the Global 1950s." *Global Intellectual History* 15, no. 1 (2020): 149–168.

Hamblin, Jacob Darwin. "Seeing the Oceans in Shadow of Bergen Values." *Isis* 105, no. 2 (2014): 352-363.

———. *Oceanographers and the Cold War: Disciples of Marine Science.* Seattle: University of Washington Press, 2005.

Hay, William W., & Eloise Zakevich. "Cesare Emiliani (1922–1995): The Founder of Paleoceanography." *International Microbiology* 2 (1999): 52–54.

Höhler, Sabine. "Creating the Blue Planet from Modern Oceanography." *A Cultural History of the Sea in the Global Age*, edited by Franziska Torma, 21–44. London: Bloomsbury Academic, 2021.

———. "Depth Records and Ocean Volumes: Ocean Profiling by Sounding Technology, 1850–1930." *History and Technology* 18, no. 2 (2002): 119–154.

Ingold, Tim. "Toward an Ecology of Materials." *Annual Review of Anthropology* 41 (2012): 427–442.

Jordheim, Helge. "Introduction: Multiple Times and the Work of Synchronization." *History and Theory* 53 (2014): 498–518.

Kullenberg, Börje, & Erik Fromm. "Nya försök att upphämta långa sedimentprofiler från havsbotten." *Geologiska Föreningen i Stockholm Förhandlingar* 66, no. 3 (1944): 501–510.

Lehman, Jessica. "Making an Anthropocene Ocean: Synoptic Geographies of the International Geophysical Year (1957–1958)." *Annals of the American Association of Geographers* 110, no. 3 (2020): 606–622.

Lipsett, Laurence (ed.). *Lamont Doherty-Earth Observatory: Twelve Perspectives of the First Fifty Years, 1949–1999.* New York: Lamont-Doherty Earth Observatory of the Columbia University, 1999. https://www.ldeo.columbia.edu/core-repository (accessed 18 November 2021).

Lundin, Per. *Computers in Swedish Society: Documenting Early Use and Trends.* New York: Springer, 2012.

Marra, John F. *Hot Carbon: Carbon-14 and a Revolution in Science.* New York: Columbia University Press, 2019.

Nordlund, Christer. *Det upphöjda landet: Vetenskapen, landhöjningsfrågan och kartläggningen av Sveriges förflutna 1860–1930.* Umeå: Kungl. Skytteanska Samfundet, 2001.

Oreskes, Naomi. *Science on a Mission: How Military Funding Shaped What We Do and Don't Know About the Ocean*. Chicago: Chicago University Press, 2021.
Ovey, C. D. "Foreword." *Deep-Sea Research* 1 (1953): 1–2.
Pettersson, Hans. "The Geochronology of the Deep Ocean Bed." *Tellus* 1, no. 1 (1949): 1-5.
Pettersson, Hans. "The Submarine Underworld." *Reflection on Our Age: Lectures Delivered at the Opening Session of UNESCO at the Sorbonne University of Paris*, edited by David Hardman, 198–211. London: Allan Wingate, 1949.
Pettersson, Hans. *Med Albatross över havsdjupen*. Stockholm: Albert Bonniers Förlag, 1950.
Piggot, C. S. "Foreword," United States Department of Interior Professional Paper 196-A, *Geology and Biology of North-Atlantic Deep-Sea Cores between Newfoundland and Ireland*. Washington, D.C.: United States Government Printing Office, 1940: XI–XIII.
Roberts, Peder. "Traditions, Networks and Deep-Sea Expeditions after 1945." *Expeditions as Experiments: Practicing Observation and Documentation*, edited by Ulrike Spring & Marianna Klemun. London: Palgrave Macmillan, 2016: 213–234.
Rosol, Christoph. "Hauling Data. Anthropocene Analogues, Paleoceanography and Missing Paradigm Shifts." *Historical Social Research / Historische Sozialforschung* 40, no. 2 (152) (2015): 37–66. http://www.jstor.org/stable/24583163.
Rozwadowski, Helen M. *Fathoming the Ocean: The Discovery and Exploration of the Deep Sea*. Cambridge, MA: The Belknapp Press of Harvard University Press, 2005.
Schwach, Vera. "The Sea around Norway: Science, Resource Management, and Environmental Concerns 1860–1970." *Environmental History* 18, no. 1 (2012): 101–110.
Scott, James. *Seeing Like a State: How Certain Schemes to Improve the Human Condition Have Failed*. New Haven, CT: Yale University Press, 1998.
Sluga, Glenda. "UNESCO and the (One) World of Julian Huxley." *Journal of World History* 21, no. 3 (2010): 393–418.
Sörlin, Sverker. "The Anxieties of a Science Diplomat: Field Co-production of Climate Knowledge and the Rise and Fall of Hans Ahlmann's 'Polar Warming'." *Osiris* 26, no. 1 (2011): 66–88.
Sörlin, Sverker, & Erik Isberg. "Synchronizing Earthly Timescales: Ice, Pollen, and the Making of Proto-Anthropocene Knowledge in the North-Atlantic Region." *Annals of the American Association of Geographers* 111, no. 3 (2021): 717–728.
Svensk Biografisk Handbok. "Fromm, Erik." 1993. http://runeberg.org/vemardet/1993/0355.html
Sverdrup, Harald, Martin W. Johnson, & Richard H. Fleming. *The Oceans: Their Physics, Chemistry, and General Biology*. New York: Prentice Hall Inc., 1942.
Warde, Paul, Libby Robin, & Sverker Sörlin. *The Environment: A History of the Idea*. Baltimore, MD: Johns Hopkins University Press, 2018.
Wickberg & Gärdebo, in this volume; "Where Humans and the Planetary Conflate: An Introduction to Environing Media." *Humanities* 9, no. 3 (2020): 1–12.
Wråkberg, Urban. "Om djuphavets gåtor och ett fiskeri på vetenskaplig grund: historiska perspektiv på oceanografin i Sverige." *Oceanerna*, edited by Anna Karin Johansson & Sören Floderus. Lund: Svenska Sällskapet för Antropologi och Geografi, 1991.
Yehle, Jean. *Interview of Cesare Emiliani and Donald R. Moore*. 29 March 1990, Niels Bohr Library & Archives, American Institute of Physics, https://www.aip.org/history-programs/niels-bohr-library/oral-histories/32405.

10

AFTERWORD: CATCH THE VAPORS

Getting steamrolled by environing media

Bernard Dionysius Geoghegan

For centuries, *medium* presupposed *environing*. Media did not necessarily produce environments, mind you. Nor was a medium necessarily environmental or elemental (in John Durham Peters's sense of the term).[1] Both of those formulations concern our present moment, and its rubrics for marking the relationality of medium and environing. Extant records suggest that speakers of Old English had somewhat different presuppositions about how, exactly, media and environing belonged to one another. Their medial environing stemmed from a different manner of doing and dwelling, marked by regimes of vocational, economical, and geographical production distinct from ours. To put the matter in concise and sweeping terms, in medieval and early modern England, *medium* and *environment* encompassed a communicative chain sustained by lively mortals, spirits, images, texts, homes, fields, plants, beasts of burden, blessings, tax assessments, and much more. Their in-mixing precluded thinking one term entirely separate from the others.

One of the earliest written records of *medium* in English, a 1573 inquiry addressed to the Mayor of London, sketches elements populating then-current cosmologies of communications.[2] In the midst of a longer inquiry bearing on bakers, brewers, and barley, the letter inquires of the mayor,

> What mediam have you made of the price of the severall sorte of the said corne & what assise have you sett to the bakers & brewers in that behalf howe doth the Assise that nowe is in the moneth of marche vary from that which was in decembre or January[?][3]

For all the academic talk of biopolitics in the last few decades, and the necessity of thinking life with governmental calculation, this passage reminds us it wasn't

DOI: 10.4324/9781003282891-13

always so challenging to think these terms together, as of a whole cloth. In this passage, we find a robust vernacular relationality among living bodies, signs, and surroundings, in which the character and agency of medium involves ongoing and open-ended environing. It is not that "mediam" (presumably a mathematical averaging of prices, in this context) refers to environing, but rather that medium, environs, signs, territory, farming, and collective life constellate as elements of a common matter of concern. The semio-technical processing of community, the calculus by which government recasts agricultural labor and goods, calendrical cycles, and professions, form part of a collective, environmental becoming.

What happened, in the intervening centuries, that so sundered media from the environment? One factor seems to be that 19th and 20th century communication engineering recast irreducibly phenomenal dimensions such as *near*, *far*, *earth*, and *air* as bare mathematical functions like *time*, *space*, and *resistance*.[4] In this light, the much vaunted "annihilation of time and space" announced by Karl Marx concedes too much ground to what it purports to contest. That is, the very phrasing *annihilation of time and space* glosses over the fact that the scientific conceptions of a deworlded *time* and *space* do the conquering and annihilation. They are terminological vessels for a homogeneous scientism, emptied out of substantive difference, that expropriate a material and lively expanse of trees, rocks, clouds, roots, labor, first nations, winds, critters, and mountains.[5]

While I have not undertaken a systematic analysis of telecommunications advertising, it strikes me that across the 20th century, in the United States at least, these ads register the retreat of environments from popular thinking about communications. A 1930 advertisement for the Bell Telephone System (Figure 10.1) announces its firm's goal "to clear all barriers for the human voice," which includes the installation of "underground cables" and "service to ships at sea."[6] In the latter half of the 20th century, AT&T advertising focuses more narrowly on personal intimacy across environmentally undifferentiated time and space. A 1986 advertisement (Figure 10.2) for AT&T reads, "Flirt with her again. Call the U.K.," superimposed over a man and woman with graying hair, pensioners perhaps.[7] Accompanying text tells the reader "even though so much has happened since you left London, since you left her side, you still carry a torch for her. Why not give her a call and tell her?...[I]t costs less than you'd think to stay close." Whatever this is, it is not the annihilation of time and space. It is, on the contrary, an annihilation of environments—places appear, but surroundings have almost no role whatsoever in the spatial calculus.[8] Environments have been replaced by communications that count only as time (cost per minute) and space (long-distance zones). The communicative triumph of time and space, as measures that count, steamrolled land, sea, and human ingenuity. When it came to communications, surrounding elements no longer merited acknowledgment.[9]

And yet, even as thinking on media and the environment seemed to part ways, they persisted as mutual points of reference, determining their reciprocal intelligibility of one another. For example, the 1960s and 1970s renewal of interest

Afterword: Catch the vapors **169**

FIGURE 10.1 "To clear all barriers for the human voice." American Telephone and Telegraph Company, 1931, *Popular Science*, February 1931, p. 17.

in ecology took place under the sign of cybernetics (e.g., Bateson, Lovelock, and Margulis), and its conception of nature as a quasi-informatic system.[10] Indeed, as Giulia Rispoli shows in the present volume, cybernetics figured centrally in 20th century scientists' definition of the "biosphere" as a "system" integral to the planet Earth. Despite the foundational role informatic reasoning played in making environments politically and scientifically visible, environmental activism of the period often imagined the environment and technology as distinct

FIGURE 10.2 "Flirt with her again. Call the U.K." AT&T, *New York Magazine*, January 12, vol. 20, no. 2, 1987, p. 115.

domains, with the former in want of defense from the latter. Everyday artifacts like the West German children's board game, *Ecolopoly: A Game of the Cybernetic Environment* (1980, 1984), revealed this entangling of environmental and technological reasoning (Figure 10.3).[11] It is as if the collapse of a reliable distinction between nature and technology affected by the Great Acceleration (see Rosol, this volume) brought these two domains into nostalgic, possibly ironic, conceptual relief. Another exemplary artifact from the environmental consciousness of that period, Canadian-American folk singer Joni Mitchell's 1970 song "Big Yellow Taxi," acknowledges as much. Reflecting on a trip to Hawaii, Mitchell sang

> They took all the trees, put 'em in a tree museum, and they charged all the people a dollar and a half just to see 'em. Don't it always seem to go, that you don't know what you've got till it's gone.[12]

Her words, as much as farming or governmental texts from half a millennium earlier, witness the deep relationality of media and environing. The difference, in

Afterword: Catch the vapors **171**

FIGURE 10.3 Ökolopoly: Ein kybernetisches Umweltspiel von Frederic Vester, *Ravensburger, 1984 [1980]*.

the intervening centuries, is largely a matter of inflection: by the 1970s, the force of technical enclosure and systematization, even for critics of such measures, figured centrally in commentaries on media, technology, and the environment. It was unavoidable. The relationality among media and environment proved striated, fractured, piecemeal, and coercive, even for those who wished to privilege one term over the other.

Recognizing these historical precedents, wherein "medium" and "environment" intermingled, sharpens the shock appropriate to encountering the present volume's survey of "environing media." To consider how media environ is, also, to acknowledge their unsettled grounds today. The terrible affront of environing media lay in the fact that, much as it joins philosopher Bruno Latour in challenging what he termed "the modern constitution," that divides the world into subjects and objects, culture and nature, environing media offer no return to nonmodern relationality.[13] Whatever inroads Latour has made in arguing we have never been modern, it remains the case that we cannot experience our environments in a nonmodern fashion. Today's environing and elemental media attest to the scars wrought on our surroundings by centuries of programmatic insistence on separating bodies from their surroundings. The chapters in the present volume reflect on their belated and piecemeal recomposition in the wake of the great and terrible disruption wrought by planetary technics of the past few centuries. Christoph Rosol's talk of the technosphere,

John Durham Peters and Adam Wickberg's meditations on the cultural techniques of the Aztecs and Conquistadores, and Nina Wormbs's climate change models, like the other contributions to this volume, attest, in varied manners, to the great and terrible shattering of environments made possible by modernity. The furious trade these chapters find at work among media and the environment follows routes carved out by our colonial, imperial, scientific, and commercial traffic, whose ways and thoroughfares persist as deep fissures on the face of the present.

If the environing media of today does have something of a nonmodern quality, it is less the extant medievalism of *A Midsummer's Night's Dream* (ca. 1595), a misty realm peopled by fairies, than the industrial ferocity of Richard Wagner's *Der Ring des Nibelungen* (1848–1874, 1876). As musicologist Gundula Kreuzer brilliantly recounts, the early staging of Wagner's operatic cycle wielded vast locomotive boilers in manufacturing a quintessentially environing medium, fog-enshrouded landscapes, in this case of imagined German and Scandinavian mythology.[14] As Kreuzer explains, this use of industrial steam apparatuses had conflicting dramaturgical effects. It fulfilled Wagner's dream of an exhibition that, in his words, took place "in some beautiful solitude, far away from the fumes and industrial stench of our urban civilization."[15] However, it also brought the chief instrument of that civilization—steam power—into the center of this mythic, nonmodern scene. In the wake of industrialization, the nonmodern, when it appears, does so through the systematically brutal manners availed by modernity.

Indeed, much as we might like to imagine environing media as a return to nature—the Black Forest clearings, for example, enamored by Heidegger—the brute, elemental force of the steamroller offers a more relevant image for the paths clearing our way to thought. As Wagner's contemporary Karl Marx famously put it, in the wake capitalist industry, "alles Ständische und Stehende verdampft."[16] The usual translation, "All that is solid melts into air," might suggest fantastical flight.[17] The original German phrasing indicates a more elemental and environmental violence, by which industrial power "steams away all the familiar estates and orders," i.e., steam engines vaporize religious, aristocratic, and national orders.[18] Or, rendered in the freest of translations, under industrialization, "outstanding estates and standing orders get steamrolled," clearing the way for humankind to see, "with unclouded eyes, their reciprocal relations" [ihre gegenseitigen Beziehungen mit nüchternen Augen anzusehen]. For Wagner as for Marx, there is a distinctly theatrical quality to how the elements confront us with the conditions of modern existence. A terrible clearing away figures in our belated encounter with the surroundings that play host to the spectacular revelation of our actual state of affairs. In this sense, the nonmodernism of Wagner's spectacle anticipates what critic Walter Benjamin would later attribute to the industrial mechanisms responsible for Hollywood's wonders: "Self-alienation has reached the point where it can experience its own annihilation as a supreme aesthetic pleasure."[19] So yes, environing media are back. The force of the Earth is on display—wielding and wielded—by technical media. And these wonders should be nothing less than terrifying.

Notes

I thank Sean DiLeonardi for support editing this text. The title is a homage to Biz Markie's "Vapors," and its elemental sense for environmental vibing. I also thank Adam Wickberg and Johan Gärdebo for their editorial contributions, including organizing this volume, inviting me to participate, and supporting my writing.

1 On elemental media, see John Durham Peters, *The Marvelous Clouds: Toward a Philosophy of Elemental Media* (Chicago: University of Chicago Press, 2015).
2 For more on communicative cosmologies, see Bernard Dionysius Geoghegan, "Architectures of Information: A Comparison of Wiener's and Shannon's Theories of Information," *Computer Architectures: Constructing the Common Ground*, eds. Theodora Vardouli & Olga Touloumi (London: Routledge, 2019), 135–159. On cosmology, science, and technology, more broadly, see John Tresch, "Cosmologies Materialized: History of Science and History of Ideas," *Rethinking Modern European Intellectual History*, eds. Darrin McMahon & Samuel Moyn (New York: Oxford University Press, 2014), 153–172.
3 Unsigned text reprinted as "Appendix J: 'A Special Direction for Divers Trades,'" *The Evolution of the English Corn Market from the Twelfth to the Eighteenth Century* (Cambridge, MA: Harvard University Press, 1915), 450.
4 For a seminal critique on the tendency to undervalue phenomenal and thingly relations, see Martin Heidegger, "The Origin of the Work of Art," *Basic Writings*, ed. David Farrell Krell (San Francisco, CA: Harper, 1977), 151–152.
5 On the critique of empty, homogeneous time, see Walter Benjamin, "On the Concept of History," trans. Harry Zohn, eds. Howard Eiland & Michael W. Jennings, *Walter Benjamin: Selected Writings, Volume 4, 1938–1940* (Cambridge: Belknap Press, 2003), 389–400. For more on the media technical fashioning of such a temporality, see Mary Ann Doane, The *Emergence of Cinematic Time: Modernity, Contingency, the Archive* (Cambridge: Harvard University Press, 2002); and Noam M. Elcott, *Artificial Darkness: An Obscure History of Modern Art and Media* (Chicago: University of Chicago Press, 2016).
6 American Telephone & Telegraph Company, "To Clear All Barriers for the Human Voice," *Popular Science,* February 1931, 17.
7 American Telephone & Telegraph Company, "Flirt with Her Again. Call the U.K.," *New York Magazine* 20, no. 2 (January 12, 1987): 115.
8 For more on the techno-scientific mastery of environments, see Christina Wessely, "Watery Milieus: Marine Biology, Aquariums, and the Limits of Ecological Knowledge circa 1900," trans. by Nathan Stobaugh, *Grey Room* 75 (2019): 36–59; Florian Sprenger, *Epistemologien des Umgebens: Zur Geschichte, Ökologie und Biopolitik künstlicher Environments* (Bielefeld: Transcript, 2019) and Etienne S. Benson, *Surroundings: A History of Environments and Environmentalisms* (Chicago: University of Chicago Press, 2020).
9 For more on the peculiar manners in which media dissimulate their environmentality, see Lisa Parks, "Around the Antenna Tree: The Politics of Infrastructural Visibility," *Flow,* May 6, 2009, http://www.flowjournal.org/2009/03/around-the-antenna-tree-the-politics-of-infrastructural-visibilitylisa-parks-uc-santa-barbara/. For more on the vast media infrastructures that disappear in their environmental embedding, erasing signs of their own mediation, see Nicole Starosielski, *The Undersea Network* (Durham, NC: Duke University Press Books, 2015).

10 Gregory Bateson, *Steps to an Ecology of Mind* (New York: Ballantine Books, 1972); James Lovelock, *Gaia: A New Look at Life on Earth* (Oxford: Oxford University Press, 2000 [1979]); and Lynn Margulis, "Symbiosis and Evolution," *Scientific American* 225, no. 2 (1971): 48–61. For secondary literature on these themes, see Bruce Clarke & Mark B. N. Hansen, eds., *Emergence and Embodiment: New Essays on Second-Order Systems Theory* (Durham, NC: Duke University Press, 2009); and Fred Turner, "The Politics of the Whole Circa 1968—and Now," *The Whole Earth: California and the Disappearance of the Outside,* eds. Diedrich Diedrichsen & Anselm Franke (Berlin: Sternberg Press, 2013), 38–43.

11 For more on this board game, see Werner Ulrich, "Can Nature Teach Us Good Research Practice? A Critical Look at Frederic Vester's Bio-Cybernetic Systems Approach," *Journal of Research Practice* 1, no. 1 (2005): 1–10; and David Kuchenbuch, "Ökolopoly: Spielen, Wissen und Politik um 1980." Edited by Nils Güttler, Margarete Pratschke, and Max Stadler. *Nach Feierabend: Zürcher Jahrbuch für Wissensgeschichte* 12 (2016): 145–159.

12 Joni Mitchell, *Big Yellow Taxi,* 1970, Siquomb Publishing Corporation, https://jonimitchell.com/music/song.cfm?id=13.

13 Bruno Latour, *We Have Never Been Modern,* trans. Catherine Porter (Cambridge: Harvard University Press, 1993), 29.

14 On fog as a medium, see Yuriko Furuhata, *Climatic Media: Transpacific Experiments in Atmospheric Control* (Durham, NC: Duke University Press, 2022).

15 The words are Wagner's, but the analysis and framing of the words is Kreuzer's. Gundula Kreuzer, "Wagner-Dampf: Steam in Der Ring Des Nibelungen and Operatic Production," *The Opera Quarterly* 27, no. 2 (2011): 196.

16 Karl Marx & Friedrich Engels, "Manifest der Kommunistischen Partei," *The German Text Archive,* 1848, https://www.deutschestextarchiv.de/book/view/marx_manifestws_1848?p=5.

17 Karl Marx & Friedrich Engels, *Manifesto of the Communist Party,* trans. William Reeves (Utrecht: Open Source Socialist Publishing, 2008), 10.

18 For more on translating this passage, see Jonathan Sperber, *Karl Marx: A Nineteenth-Century Life* (New York: Liverwright Publishing Corporation, 2013), 155; and Richard J. Evans, "Marx v. The Rest," *London Review of Books* 35, no. 20 (May 23, 2013). See also the discussion of this passage in McKenzie Wark, "The Vectoralist Class," *E-Flux* 65 (May 2015), https://www.e-flux.com/journal/65/336347/the-vectoralist-class/

19 Walter Benjamin, "The Work of Art in the Age of Its Technological Reproducibility," trans. Michael W. Jennings, *Grey Room* 39 (Spring 2010): 36.

References

American Telephone & Telegraph Company. "To Clear All Barriers for the Human Voice." *Popular Science* (February 1931): 17.

Appendix J. "A Special Direction for Divers Trades." *The Evolution of the English Corn Market from the Twelfth to the Eighteenth Century.* Cambridge, MA: Harvard University Press, 1915.

AT&T. "Flirt with Her Again. Call the U.K." *New York Magazine* 20, no. 2 (January 12, 1987): 115.

Bateson, Gregory. *Steps to an Ecology of Mind.* New York: Ballantine Books, 1972.

Benjamin, Walter. "On the Concept of History." *Walter Benjamin: Selected Writings, Volume 4, 1938–1940,* translated by Harry Zohn, edited by Howard Eiland & Michael W. Jennings, 389–400. Cambridge: Belknap Press, 2003.

Benjamin, Walter. "The Work of Art in the Age of Its Technological Reproducibility." Translated by Michael W. Jennings, *Grey Room* 39 (Spring 2010): 11–37.

Benson, Etienne S. *Surroundings: A History of Environments and Environmentalisms.* Chicago, IL: University of Chicago Press, 2020.
Clarke, Bruce, & Mark B. N. Hansen (eds.). *Emergence and Embodiment: New Essays on Second-Order Systems Theory.* Durham, NC: Duke University Press, 2009.
Doane, Mary Ann. *The Emergence of Cinematic Time: Modernity, Contingency, the Archive.* Cambridge: Harvard University Press, 2002.
Durham, John Peters. *Marvelous Clouds: Toward a Philosophy of Elemental Media.* Chicago: University of Chicago Press, 2015.
Elcott, Noam M. *Artificial Darkness: An Obscure History of Modern Art and Media.* Chicago: University of Chicago Press, 2016.
Evans, Richard J. "Marx v. The Rest." *London Review of Books* 35, no. 20 (May 23, 2013).
Furuhata, Yuriko. *Climatic Media: Transpacific Experiments in Atmospheric Control.* Durham, NC: Duke University Press, 2022.
Geoghegan, Bernard Dionysius. "Architectures of Information: A Comparison of Wiener's and Shannon's Theories of Information." *Computer Architectures: Constructing the Common Ground*, edited by Theodora Vardouli & Olga Touloumi, 135–159. London: Routledge, 2019.
Heidegger, Martin. "The Origin of the Work of Art." *Basic Writings*, ed. David Farrell Krell. San Francisco, CA: Harper, 1977.
Kreuzer, Gundula. "Wagner-Dampf: Steam in Der Ring Des Nibelungen and Operatic Production." *The Opera Quarterly* 27, no. 2 (2011): 196.
Kuchenbuch, David. "Ökolopoly: Spielen, Wissen und Politik um 1980." Edited by Nils Güttler, Margarete Pratschke, and Max Stadler. *Nach Feierabend: Zürcher Jahrbuch für Wissensgeschichte* 12 (2016): 145–159.
Latour, Bruno. *We Have Never Been Modern.* Translated by Catherine Porter. Cambridge: Harvard University Press, 1993.
Lovelock, James. *Gaia: A New Look at Life on Earth.* Oxford: Oxford University Press, 2000 [1979].
Margulis, Lynn. "Symbiosis and Evolution." *Scientific American* 225, no. 2 (1971): 48–61.
Marx, Karl, & Friedrich Engels. *Manifesto of the Communist Party.* Translated by William Reeves. Utrecht: Open Source Socialist Publishing, 2008.
———. "Manifest der kommunistischen Partei." The German Text Archive, 1848, https://www.deutschestextarchiv.de/book/view/marx_manifestws_1848?p=5.
Mitchell, Joni. *Big Yellow Taxi.* Siquomb Publishing Corp, 1970. https://jonimitchell.com/music/song.cfm?id=13.
Parks, Lisa. "Around the Antenna Tree: The Politics of Infrastructural Visibility." *Flow* (May 6, 2009). http://www.flowjournal.org/2009/03/around-the-antenna-tree-the-politics-of-infrastructural-visibilitylisa-parks-uc-santa-barbara/.
Sperber, Jonathan. *Karl Marx: A Nineteenth-Century Life.* New York: Liverwright Publishing Corporation, 2013.
Sprenger, Florian, *Epistemologien des Umgebens: Zur Geschichte, Ökologie und Biopolitik künstlicher Environments.* Bielefeld: Transcript, 2019.
Starosielski, Nicole. *The Undersea Network.* Durham, NC: Duke University Press Books, 2015.
Tresch, John. "Cosmologies Materialized: History of Science and History of Ideas." *Rethinking Modern European Intellectual History*, edited by Darrin McMahon & Samuel Moyn, 153–172. New York: Oxford University Press, 2014.

Turner, Fred. "The Politics of the Whole Circa 1968—and Now." *The Whole Earth: California and the Disappearance of the Outside*, edited by Diedrich Diedrichsen & Anselm Franke, 38–43. Berlin: Sternberg Press, 2013.

Ulrich, Werner. "Can Nature Teach Us Good Research Practice? A Critical Look at Frederic Vester's Bio-Cybernetic Systems Approach." *Journal of Research Practice* 1, no. 1 (2005): 1–10.

Wark, McKenzie. "The Vectoralist Class." *E-Flux* 65 (May 2015), https://www.e-flux.com/journal/65/336347/the-vectoralist-class/.

Wessely, Christina. "Watery Milieus: Marine Biology, Aquariums, and the Limits of Ecological Knowledge circa 1900," trans. by Nathan Stobaugh, *Grey Room* 75 (2019): 36–59.

INDEX

Note: *Italic* page numbers refer to figures.

ADMT *see* Argo Data Management Team (ADMT)
affordances 4, 9, 37, 141, 144
Ahlmann, Hans 154
air 9, 96, 105; as *circumfusum* 102; disappearance of 105–108; as elemental medium 96–98, 100, 101, 103; as environing medium 97, 98, 100, 103, 106; hazardous matters in 101; pollution 103–106; sensing 102
airborne disease 95, 108
Airs, Waters, Places (Hippocrates) 39, 44, 99
Alaimo, Stacy 114
Albatross expedition 80, 82–83, 152–160, *157*
Al Gore 138
Allied Forces Central Europe 81
"αβγ-paper" 90n31
annihilation 168, 172
Anthropocene 2, 8, 9, 35, 37, 42, 43, 54, 57, 67, 84, 90n23, 97, 108, 134, 140, 142–143
"Anthropocene ocean" 124, 151
Anthropocene Working Group 85
Anthropos 2, 62
Antonello, Alessandro 153
Apollo missions 56, 63
Arbuthnot, John 101; "The effects of Air on Human Bodies" 100
Argo Data Management Team (ADMT) 125

Argo floats program 6, 7, 125
Argo program 114, 116, 120, 121–124, *124*; and marine environment datafication 124–127, *126*
Argo Steering Team (AST) 121, 122
Arnhem Expedition 83
Arrhenius, Gustaf 157, 159, 163n39, 163n48
Arrhenius, Olof 157
Arrhenius, Svante 154, 158
AST *see* Argo Steering Team (AST)
Atlantic Meridional Overturning Circulation (AMOC) 122–123
AT&T advertising 168, 170
autopoietic system 61, 62, 66
Avery, Oswald 79
Ayer, A. J. 155
Aztec calendar 23
Aztec empire 5–6
Aztec media 22–25, *25*
Aztec temples 23

BARK 158
Barthes, Roland 38; *Mythologies* 37
bathymetric maps 118
bathythermograph 119
Bean, Louis: *How to Predict Elections* 88–89n5
Bell Telephone System advertisement 168, *169*
Benjamin, Walter 172
Benson, Etienne 121, 126

Bergwik, Staffan 154
Bernard, Claude 62
Bezos, Jeff 17
big-bang nucleo-synthesis 90n31
biodiversity beyond national jurisdiction (BBNJ treaty) 127
biological communities interdependency 55
biosphere 54–56, 60, 62, 66, 67; biological communities interdependency 55; as cosmic medium 57–61; definitions of 55, 169; and Earth functioning 57–58; Earth system and 8, 54–57; as a thermodynamic system 59; visions of 63
Borlaug, Norman 79
Bretherton, Francis 63
Bretherton diagram 63, *65*

Cabanis, Pierre-Jean-Georges 103
cadastral mapping 3
Canadian fur trade 16
Cannon, Walter 62
Carey, James 27, 28
Carey, Mark 153
Casa de la Contratación 19
Chakrabarty, Dipesh 151; "The Planet: An Emergent Humanist Category" 151
Challenger expedition 118, 154, 156
Chargaff, Erwin 80
Charles II, King 103
Chase, Martha 80
"circular causal system" 61
circumfusa 102, 103, 105, 106
civilization: emissions of modern 103; media in 5, 16, 17; *see also* Western civilization
climate: and Earth system 85–86, 123, 124; in geographical sense 99
climate change 9, 108; graph power in 137–139, 142–143; mediation of 136; models 7, 135–137, 143, 144, 172; public discourse on 139; state-of-the-art knowledge on 135; temporalization of 135; visual rhetoric of 137
climate-change science 136, 142
climate prediction models 122
climate science 41, 48n28
Climate Variability and Predictability (CLIVAR) 121, 123
Cohen, Jeffrey Jerome 96
Collingwood, R. G. 38, 41; *The Idea of History* 37
colonialism 2, 86, 116
constructivist approach 141
contagion 95, 107
continents 116–118

Corbin, Alain 102
Core Argo 126
Cortés, Hernan 20, 23, 28
cosmic medium: biosphere as 57–61
cosmic physics 154
Council of the Indies 18, 19, 26
COVID-19 9, 95, 107, 108
Crick, Francis 80
"critical zone," Earth 46n3, 58
cultural techniques 3–4, 21, 22, 26, 87, 98, 105, 172
"cultures of prediction" 3
cybernetics 60–63, 66, 169
Cybernetics: Or Control and Communication in the Animal and the Machine (Wiener) 75
cybernetic-styled global systems ecology 86

Darwin's theory of evolution 60
Data Assembly Centres (DACs) 125
data-driven optimisation algorithms: for marine spatial planning 128
datafied ocean 127–128
"Decade of Action" 139
deep ocean 7, 114, 151
deep-sea cores 7, 160; drilling 151, 158, 160, 161n4; as environing media 152–153; "library" of 158; as "natural archives" 7, 160; time *vs.* materiality in 153
deep-sea floor 83, 150–152, 154–158, 160, 161n8
Deep-Sea Research 150, 151
deep-sea sediments 155, 156, 159
del Castillo, Bernal Diaz 20; *Historia verdadera* 20–21
Deloraine, Maurice 75, 76
DeLoughrey, Elizabeth 63, 64
Der Ring des Nibelungen (Wagner) 172
Des Voeux, Henry A. 104
Diaz, Bernal 23
Dickens, Charles 104
digital: computer 18; media 15, 26; technologies 8, 84, 86–87
digitalization 86
DiLeonardi, Sean 173
disease transmission 107, 110n22
Dokuchaev, Vasily V. 55, 56
Domesday Boke (book of reckoning) 18
Douglas, Susan 141
Duckert, Lowell 96

Earth: atmosphere of 6; circumnavigation of 150, 154; "critical zone" 46n3, 58; scaled-down visualization 64; as techno-ecological system 54, 56
Earth Observing System (EOS) 63

Earth system 61–67, *65*, 85–86; biosphere and 8, 54–57; climate and 85–86, 123, 124; environing media infrastructure and 41; human-impacted 87; mediation process of 7, 115; monitoring 86; nine dimensions of 35; socioeconomic activities and effects on 84
Earth System Science (ESS) 38, 41, 42, 54, 61, 64, 66
Ecopoly: A Game of the Cybernetic Environment (board game) 170, 174n11
ecomedia studies 4
ecosystems 41, 60–62, 66; services 140
"The effects of Air on Human Bodies" (Arbuthnot) 100
Electronic Numerical Integrator and Computer (ENIAC) 76
elemental media/medium 5, 6, 16; air as 96–98, 100, 101, 103
elements: and environments 96–98, 105
Emiliani, Cesare 81, 159, 160
environing media/environing medium 1–9, 45, 97, 115, 143; air as 97, 98, 100, 103, 106; of Argo floats 125; biosphere and 55, 57, 66; in cybernetics 54; deep-sea cores as 152–153, 160; Earth system and 41; environing technologies for 141–142; graphs as 142–143; and human-Earth relationship 40–42; infrastructures 40–42, 48n26; ocean 117, 118, 125; survey of 171, 172; tragic and global 25–26
environing process 1, 2, 5, 44–45, 55; epistemic effect of 6; physical changes in 44; practices of 3; as relational agency 38–40; technologies in 44, 46
environing technologies 37, 41, 59, 135, 140, 143, 146n26; shaping process 140
environment 2, 3, 37–39, 43–46, 140, 152; human-Earth relationship and 37–38, 44–46; influences of 39; media for 45; as medium 97; and nature 37–39, 45; related to human action 39; survival equipment for 40–41
environmental control: exigencies of 61
environmental epistemologies 2, 4–6, 8, 115, 120
environmental historiography 43, 45
Environmental History and Environmental Archaeology 38
environmental humanities 5, 9, 42, 43
environmental medicine 102, 107
environmental object 115
"epistemic evolution" 59–60
equilibrium models 137
ESS *see* Earth System Science (ESS)

Evelyn, John 104; *Fumifugium* 98, 103
Ewing, Maurice 158

"Fat Man" bomb 83
Ferdinando I de Medici 22
Fifth Assessment Report (2014), IPCC 137, 139
First Assessment Report (1990), IPCC 135–138
Fleming, Richard H.: *The Oceans: Their Physics, Chemistry, and General Biology* 152
Florentine Codex 22
Föhn, Alpine 100
Forrestal, James 78
Forrester, Jay 88n4
Fressoz, Jean-Baptiste 103, 106
Freymann, Enrique 88
Friedman, Herbert 63
Fromm, Erik 155
Fumifugium (Evelyn) 98, 103

Gabrys, Jennifer: *Program Earth* 58
Gaia 6, 62–64, 66–67, 70n54
Gallie, W. B. 35
Gallo, Rubén: *Mexican Modernity* 16
Gärdebo, Johan 6, 109n1, 142, 153
Gates, Bill 17
GATT *see* General Agreement on Tariffs and Trade (GATT)
Geer, Gerard de 155
General Agreement on Tariffs and Trade (GATT) 77, 86
geo-anthropology 42–43, 49n36
Geoghegan, Bernard 4
geographical explorations 56
German media theory 3–5
Global DACs (GDACs) 125
global environment 1, 2, 5, 6, 36, 57, 62, 65, 81, 82, 84, 108, 126; *directions* and *rates of change* 36
Global Ocean Data Assimilation Experiment (GODAE) 121, 123
Global Ocean Observing System (GOOS) 124, 125, 127
Global South 35
GODAE *see* Global Ocean Data Assimilation Experiment (GODAE)
Goldmark, Peter Carl 90n37
Golinski, Jan 100
GOOS *see* Global Ocean Observing System (GOOS)
graphs: as environing media 142–143
Great Acceleration 38, 40, 43, 84, 86, 170
Great Britain: pollution in 105
Great Dying in the Americas 25, 26

The Great Synchronization 3; geo-anthropology 42–43
"Green Revolution" 79
Grevsmühl, Sebastian 64
Grinevald, Jacques 58
Guide to Health (Lynch) 101

Haff, Peter 7, 56
Hallé, Jean Noël 102
Hamblin, Jacob Darwin 152
Harrison, John 117
Havana Charter (1948) 76–77, 88–89n5
Hayes, Joy: *Radio Nation* 16
Hecht, Gabrielle 140
Heezen, Bruce 118
Heidegger, Martin 5, 172
Helmreich, Stefan 125
The Herenigde Nasionale Party, South Africa (1948) 78–79
Hernández, Francisco 21, 22
Hershey, Alfred 80
Hippocrates 97, 99, 101, 102; *Airs, Waters, Places* 39, 44, 99; *Epidemics* I 98
Hippocratic tradition 99–101, 107
historia naturalis 37
Historia verdadera (del Castillo) 20–21
Höhler, Sabine 120, 124, 125
Holocene 85, 140
homeostasis 66
homogeneous scientism 168
Horn, Eva 9
Hotel Commodore 75, 76, 79, 87, 90n34
House of Trade, Seville 116
Howard, Luke 104
How to Predict Elections (Bean) 88–89n5
"human barometer" 100, 107
human-Earth relationship 1, 3, 7, 35, 55, 153; environing as relational agency 38–40; environing media infrastructures 40–42; and environment 37–38, 44–46; geo-anthropology 42–43; operational logic 36
human-reconfigured biosphere 64, 66
humans 37; role in environment care 106–107; transformation of 38, 39
Hutchby, Ian 141
Hutchinson, George Evelyn 60–62, 66
Huxley, Julian 150, 155
hygiene 102, 106, 108

The Idea of History (Collingwood) 37
IGBP *see* International Geosphere-Biosphere Programme (IGBP)
IGY *see* International Geophysical Year (IGY)

"An inconvenient truth" (Film) 138
industrialization 86, 172
industrial steam apparatuses 172
informatic reasoning 169
information science 61
Ingold, Tim 153
Innis, Harold Adams 16–19, 23–25, 28; research on staples circulation 16–18
Institute of Radio Engineers (I.R.E.) 75
integrated planetary environmental system 118
Intergovernmental Panel on Climate Change (IPCC) 9, 135, 138, 142, 143, 145n7
international environmental governance 41–42
International Geophysical Year (IGY) 40, 82, 118, 119, 124, 126, 151, 152, 160; planetary-scale view of 151
International Geosphere-Biosphere Programme (IGBP) 63, 64, 66
International Institute of Applied Systems Analysis (IIASA) 65
International Standard Industrial Classification of All Economic Activities 87
International Union for the Conservation of Nature and Natural Resources (IUCN) 81
International Union for the Protection of Nature (IUPN) (1948) 81
IPCC *see* Intergovernmental Panel on Climate Change (IPCC)
I.R.E. *see* Institute of Radio Engineers (I.R.E.)
Isberg, Erik 7
IUPN *see* International Union for the Protection of Nature (IUPN)

Janković, Vladimir 102
Jason satellite mission 120, 123
Jenner, Mark 103
Jennings, Brewster 78
Jet Propulsion Laboratories 6
Johann Gottlieb, Herder 43
Johnson, Martin W.: *The Oceans: Their Physics, Chemistry, and General Biology* 152
Jordheim, Helge 139
Jue, Melody: *Wild Blue Media* 114

Kendrew, John 63
Kirkuk-Haifa oil pipeline (1948) 77–78
Kittler, Friedrich 5, 27
Kjellberg, Göran 157

Index

Koch, Robert 107
Koczy, Fritz 160
Kreuzer, Gundula 172
Kullenberg, Börje 150, 151, 153, 155, 156, 160, 163n40

The Lamont-Doherty Core Repository 158, 163n46
Lamont Geological Observatory 118
Latin America: colonial heterotopia in 19
Latour, Bruno 46n3, 171
Lehman, Jessica 119–121, 124–126, 128, 151
Lenin Academy of Agricultural Sciences (1948) 79
Lenton, Tim 46n3
Levi, Hilde 81
Libby, W. F. 157–159
Libby, Willard 81
Lidström, Susanna 6
life sciences 56
Limits to Growth report 35
living organisms 57–59, 62, 101
Locher, Fabien 106
London: air pollution 103–104; "smog" 104
longitude determination 117
Lovelock, James 6, 9, 60, 62, 63, 66
Lysenko, Trofim Denisovich 79, 80

Macauley, David 96
machine computing 40
McLuhan, Marshall 16
Macy conferences 61
Malone, Thomas 63
Man and Nature (Marsh) 44
Manhattan Project 76
Man's Role in Changing the Face of the Earth (conference) 38
mapping program 118
maps: notions of space and territory 28
Margulis, Lynn 62
marine chronometer 117
marine environment: datafication of 124–127, *126*
Markie, Biz 173
Marsh, George Perkins: *Man and Nature* 44
Marshall Plan 78
The Marvelous Clouds (Peters) 5
Marx, Karl 168, 172
Masco, Joseph 64
mass media 3, 141
"A Mathematical Theory of Communication" 75–76
Maury, Matthew Fontaine 117

media 2, 3; in civilizations 17; description of 15; of documentation 22; for environment 45; in histories 16–18; political and ethical task of 17; and technology 141, 142; theory 4, 5, 15, 17
medial environing 167
mediated ocean 114–116
mediation 58, 141, 142; of climate change 136; process of Earth system 7, 115
mediatization 141
message dissemination 5
Meteor expedition 152, 161n4
meteorological medicine 100, 105, 107
Mexican Agricultural Program of the Rockefeller Foundation 79
Mexican Modernity (Gallo) 16
Mexico: environing media in 16, 26–28; media history of 26, 27
miasma 100–103, 105–107
microbial life 62
microelectronics 86
"milieu" 2, 58, 62, 97
militarism 64
mineralogy 59
Misa, Thomas 146n31
Mitchell, Joni 170
Mitman, Greg 61
MIT Radiation Laboratory 76
model time: climate change 139, 145n6
"modern constitution" 171
modern meteorology 107
molecular biology: descendant techniques of 82
molecular genetics 79–80
"molecular mobilization" 86
monitoring systems 3
monopoly of knowledge 17, 23
Müller, Paul Hermann 89n11
Munns, David 61
Mythologies (Barthes) 37

NASA *see* National Aeronautics and Space Administration (NASA)
NASA Earth System Sciences Committee 63
National Aeronautics and Space Administration (NASA) 55, 63, 64, 120
National Convention of the Institute of Radio Engineers (I.R.E.) (1948) 75
naturalness 38
natural resource inventories 3
natural spheres 84, 87
nature: awareness of 38; environment and 37–39, 45; history from 37; as quasi-informatic system 169

Nature 35, 138
Neumann, John von 75, 76, 83, 86
news media 3, 136
New Spain: conquest of 20; environing media in 25–26; indigenous cartography in 24; natural history of 22; natural resources of 21; paper-making techniques in 24
Nineteen Eighty-Four (Orwell) 83
noosphere 59, 60
North Atlantic basin 117; seafloor map of 118
nuclear colonialism 83
nuclear weapons: development of 87, 159; production of 83; testing 83, 90n23

ocean: circulation 119–120; datafication of 127–128; environing media 117, 118, 125; interior of 152; knowledge 6, 115, 116, 118, 126, 127; mapping 118; media history 6–7; multi-dimensional view of 152; role in climate change mitigation 123; variability 120
oceanography 80, 85, 116–117, 121, 152, 153, 159
The Oceans: Their Physics, Chemistry, and General Biology (Sverdrup and Johnson) 166
Odum, Eugene 60–62
Oedipus Rex (Sophocles) 101
O'Gorman, Edmundo 28
oil glut 78
On Psychology (Spencer) 39
ontological concepts 4
operational logic 36
operational space 36
Operation Sandstone: nuclear tests of 83
orbiting satellites 3
Organization for European Economic Cooperation (OEEC/OECD) 78
Organization of the Petroleum Exporting Countries (OPEC) 78
Orwell, George: *Nineteen Eighty-Four* 83
Osborne, Fairfield: *Our Plundered Planet* 81
Our Plundered Planet (Osborne) 81
Ovando, Juan de 19, 21, 22
Ovey, C.D. 150

P-ALACE floats *see* Profiling Autonomous Lagrangian Circulation floats (P-ALACE floats)
paleoceanography 7, 151
Paris Agreement 139
Pasek, Anne 137, 138

Passage des Digitalen (Siegert) 18
Passagiere und Papiere (Siegert) 19
Pasteur, Louis 107
Patten, Bernard C. 61
Paz, Octavio 27, 28
pedosphere 55
Peters, John Durham 6, 96, 97, 142, 172; *The Marvelous Clouds* 5
Pettersson, Hans 150, 151, 156–160, 163n39, 163n40, 163n48; "The Submarine Underworld" 155; and Swedish deep-sea research 154–155, *155*
Pettersson, Otto 154
Philip II (king of Spain) 18, 21, 22
physiographic map 118
Piggot, C. S. 161n4
piston corer 80, 150, 151, 153, *155*, 158
piston cores 7
"The Planet: An Emergent Humanist Category" (Chakrabarty) 151
planetary *see individual entries*
planetary boundaries 35, 36; "safe operating space" of 37
"Planetary Boundaries Framework" 35
planetary digital infrastructure 15
planetary-scale environmental knowledge 7, 126, 151, 152, 160
Pliny the elder 37
pollution 103–108
"productive limits" 120, 121
Profiling Autonomous Lagrangian Circulation floats (P-ALACE floats) 119, 120
Program Earth (Gabrys) 58
pulse-code modulation 76

Rabi, Isidor Isaac 75, 76
radiation 58
radiocarbon dating method 81
Radio Nation (Hayes) 16
RAND corporation 81
reciprocal environment 39
Relaciones geográficas de indias 21
remote-sensing 64, 76
Renn, Jürgen 59, 109n1
Revelle, Roger 158
Rio "Earth" Summit of 1992 42
Risbey, James 137
Rispoli, Giulia 8, 169
Road to Survival (Vogt) 81
Roberts, Peder 154
Robinson, Benjamin 109n1
Roemmich, Dean 121, 123, 127
Rosol, Christoph 7, 8, 171

Rozwadowski, Helen 114, 116

Sahagún, Bernardino de 22
Sartre, Jean-Paul 155
satellite oceanography 120
satellites 6, 41, 56, 87, 119, 121, 125; technologies 64, 66
scaled-down visualization 64
Schneider, Birgit 64
Scott, James C. 40, 152
Second Assessment Report (1995), IPCC 135
self-alienation 172
self-organizing rhythmic systems 75
self-reflection 55
sensing environing technologies 140
Sequera, Rodrigo de 22
Seville: House of Trade in 19, 116
Shannon, Claude Elwood 75, 76, 80
shaping process: environing technologies 140
Siegert, Bernhard 18–20, 25, 27, 28; *Passage des Digitalen* 18; *Passagiere und Papiere* 19
Simondon, Gilbert 58
Sirocco 100
societal transformations 43
soil's biosphere 55
Sophocles 101
Sörlin, Sverker 3, 59, 97, 146
space biased media 15–18, 24–26
Spaceship Earth 56
Spanish cultural techniques 21
Spanish empire: "inquisition" in 18; maps in 28; simulation of 19
Spanish media 20–22
spatial revolution 116
Spencer, Herbert: *On Psychology* 39
SPMs *see* Summaries for Policy Makers (SPMs)
Stalin, Josef 79, 89n11
Stifter, Adalbert 102, 108
stock problem 139
"The Submarine Underworld" (Pettersson) 155
Suess, Eduard 57
Summaries for Policy Makers (SPMs) 136
Sustainable Development Goals 139
Sustainable Development of the Biosphere 65
Sverdrup, Harald: *The Oceans: Their Physics, Chemistry, and General Biology* 152
Swallow, John 119
Swedish Albatross research (1948) 80–81
Swedish Deep-Sea Expedition (1947–1948) 151, 158

Swedish deep-sea research 154–155, *155*
system-oriented sciences 41
Szerszynski, Bronislaw 97

Taylor, Peter J. 61
techno-ecological system 54, 56
technological autopoiesis 87, 90n32
technological force 60
"technological optimism" 62
technology(ies): affordances 141; in environing 44, 46; environmental impact of 140; and media 141, 142; *see also* environing technologies
techno-medial regime 8
technoscientific fragments 84
technosphere 7, 56, 60, 61, 171–172; crystallization of 84–88
telecommunications advertising 168
Tellus 157, 158, 163n43
temporalization: of climate change 135, 143, 144
Teozacoalco map 24, *25*
terraforming tools 140
Tharp, Marie 118
Third Assessment Report (2001), IPCC 135
Thomas, Martin 89n21
time: Biblical description of 134; in climate-change science 136; and possible futures 135
time biased media 15–17, 24–26
TOGA *see* Tropical Ocean Global Atmosphere program (TOGA)
TOPEX/Poseidon satellite 120, 121
"topocentric approach" 103
transatlantic telegraph cables 117
transient models 137
Tropical Ocean Global Atmosphere program (TOGA, 1985–1994) 119, 121
Truman, Harry 88n5
Trump, Donald 90n34
"2100ism" 137–139, *138*, 144

UNESCO 160
United Nations conference on "the human environment" 42
United Nations Convention of the Law of the Sea (UNCLOS) 127
United States: deep-sea core drilling 158; experiment in creating culture 27; oceanography in 159
urban air 101–102
urban climate 105
Urdaneta, Andrés de 21

Urey, Harold C. 80, 81, 159

Vanderbilt, Cornelius 90n34
Velasco, López de 21, 24
Vernadsky, Vladimir 54, 57–61, 66, 67
Vespucci, Amerigo 19
visual techniques: of natural sciences 135
Vogt, William: *Road to Survival* 81

Wagner, Richard 172, 174n15
Walsh, Lynda 64, 137, 138
Watson, James 80
WCRP *see* World Climate Research Program (WCRP)
Weaver, Warren 79–80
Western civilization 9, 59, 155
Wickberg, Adam 5, 6, 109n1, 142, 153, 172
Wiener, Norbert 61, 88n2; *Cybernetics: Or Control and Communication in the Animal and the Machine* 75

Wild Blue Media (Jue) 114
winds 98–100, 105; deleterious influences of 99–100
WOCE *see* World Ocean Circulation Experiment (WOCE)
work, strands of 42
World Climate Research Program (WCRP) 119, 121, 124
world ocean 6, 115, 116, 125, 126, 128, 151
World Ocean Circulation Experiment (WOCE, 1990–2002) 119–121
Wormbs, Nina 8–9, 59, 172
Worster, Donald 42
writing environing technologies 140–143

xerography technology 90n28
X-ray crystallography 80

zooming tool 64

Printed in the United States
by Baker & Taylor Publisher Services